Volume IV
The Foundations of Ethics
and Its Relationship
to Science

Knowing and Valuing

The Search for Common Roots

Edited by
H. Tristram Engelhardt, Jr.
and Daniel Callahan

THE HASTINGS CENTER
Institute of Society, Ethics and the Life Sciences

Institute of Society, Ethics and the Life Sciences
360 Broadway
Hastings-on-Hudson, New York 10706

Library of Congress Cataloging in Publication Data
Main entry under title:

Knowing and valuing.

(The Foundations of ethics and its relationship to science; v. 4)
Includes index.
1. Science and ethics—Addresses, essays, lectures. I. Engelhardt, Hugo Tristram, 1941-   II. Callahan, Daniel J., 1930 III. Series: Foundations of ethics and its relationship to science; v. 4.
BJ57.K58   170   79-23838
ISBN 0-916558-04-5

Printed in the United States of America

Contents

78388

Contributors

RICHARD D. ALEXANDER is Professor of Biology in the Division of Biological Sciences and Curator of Insects in the Museum of Zoology of the University of Michigan. Since 1971 he has published about fifteen articles on the significance of evolutionary biology for human understanding of humans, and a book, *Darwinism and Human Affairs*.

TOM L. BEAUCHAMP, Ph.D., Professor of Philosophy and Senior Research Scholar at the Kennedy Institute, Center for Bioethics, Georgetown University, is the author of *Principles of Biomedical Ethics* (with James F. Childress) and *Hume and the Problem of Causation* (with Alexander Rosenberg). He has also written many articles, and edited a number of philosophical and ethical works.

DANIEL CALLAHAN is Director of the Institute of Society, Ethics and the Life Sciences, The Hastings Center. He received his B.A. at Yale and his Ph.D. in Philosophy at Harvard. He is the author, most recently, of *The Tyranny of Survival* and *Abortion: Law, Choice and Morality*. He is a member of the Institute of Medicine, National Academy of Sciences.

ERIC J. CASSELL, M.D., is Clinical Professor of Public Health at Cornell University Medical College and a Diplomate of Internal Medicine in private practice. For the past several years Dr. Cassell has been doing research and writing on the underlying bases of medical practice and the relationship between doctors, patients, and disease. He is the author of *The Healer's Art*.

GERALD DWORKIN is Professor of Philosophy at the University of Illinois at Chicago Circle. He has written numerous articles in moral, political, and legal philosophy. He is Associate Editor of *Ethics*.

H. TRISTRAM ENGELHARDT, JR., Ph.D., M.D., is Rosemary Kennedy Professor of the Philosophy of Medicine, Kennedy Institute, Center for Bioethics, Georgetown University. He is the author of *Mind-Body: A Categorial Relation* and coeditor of *Evaluation and Explanation in the Biomedical Sciences*, and *Philosophical Dimensions of the Neuro-Medical Sciences*.

LOREN GRAHAM is Professor of the History of Science, Program on Science, at the Massachusetts Institute of Technology. His publications include *The Soviet Academy of Sciences and the Communist Party* (1967) and *Science and Philosophy in the Soviet Union* (1972). He has been a member of the Institute for Advanced Study and has held Guggenheim and Rockefeller Foundation fellowships. He is currently writing a book on the relationship of science to sociopolitical values.

RONALD GREEN is Associate Professor, Department of Religion, Dartmouth College. He received his Ph.D. from Harvard University, and his special field is ethics and the philosophy of religion. He is the author of *Population Growth and Justice*, and he is a member of the Editorial Board of *The Journal of Religious Ethics*.

JAMES M. GUSTAFSON is University Professor of Theological Ethics in the Divinity School of the University of Chicago.

HANS JONAS, Ph.D., D.H.L.h.c., D.L.L.,h.c., D. theol. h.c., is Alvin Johnson Professor of Philosophy Emeritus at the New School for Social Research in New York. He is the author, most recently, of *Philosophical Essays: From Ancient Creed to Technological Man*. He is a Fellow of the American Academy of Arts and Sciences.

ALASDAIR MACINTYRE is University Professor of Philosophy and Political Science at Boston University. He is the author of *A Short History of Ethics* and *Against the Self-Images of the Age: Essays in Ideology and Philosophy*.

PAUL RAMSEY is Harrington Spear Paine Professor of Religion, Princeton University, and author of *The Patient as Person* and *Ethics at the Edges of Life: Medical and Legal Intersections*.

GUNTHER S. STENT is Professor of Molecular Biology at the University of California, Berkeley. His current scientific research interest is the function and development of the nervous system. He is the author of *The Coming of the Golden Age* (1969), *Paradoxes of Progress* (1978), *Molecular Genetics* (2nd ed., 1978), and the editor of *Morality as a Biological Phenomenon* (1978).

STEPHEN TOULMIN is a member of the Committee on Social Thought at the University of Chicago. He has written extensively about philosophical and historical aspects of science, as well as about ethics and practical reasoning. He is at present completing a large-scale work on *Human Understanding*.

Preface

The Hastings Center was established in 1969 to examine the newly emergent ethical problems of medicine, biology, and the life sciences. Although the term was not then common, we were in fact proposing to study questions of "applied ethics" in the biomedical and behavioral sciences. "Applied ethics" was by no means a fashionable subject at that time. On the contrary, many in the field of moral philosophy would then have thought it inappropriate. The basic job of the moral philosopher, many held, is to develop the foundations of ethics and to examine the conditions under which moral arguments can be said to be justified. It was not seen as the job of the philosopher to attack, much less solve, practical moral dilemmas. For those outside the fields of philosophy or religion, the whole domain of ethics, theoretical or applied, was at best poorly understood, and at worst simply dismissed altogether.

Nonetheless, the issues the Center proposed to study could not be evaded—the care of dying patients, the development of genetic technologies, the use of psychosurgery to modify aggressive behavior, experimentation on human subjects. They were obviously important problems, and just as obviously, they directly posed moral questions. From the first we recognized that if we were to be of any service, we would have to take on such problems in all of their concreteness and complexity and, so far as we could, try to find some solutions to them. Naturally, they were and still remain subjects of hot dispute and sharply divided opinions.

Yet, despite the arguments and the disputes, it has often turned out to be easier to find rough agreement on solutions to questions of applied ethics than we or anyone else might have expected. Why is that? The most plausible reason is that people often disagree less about useful practical steps that can be taken than they do about the underlying principles that might justify those steps. Most persons, for instance, would agree with the moral position that potentially harmful research should not be carried out on human subjects without their informed consent. Yet that is a moral position that can be defended on a variety of very different theoretical grounds; and many who agree with the general moral principle could and would differ on its appropriate theoretical grounding. The principle of truth-telling, as another example, would commend itself to most persons; but there are many contradictory theories available to justify truth-telling.

That is by no means to suggest that all problems of applied ethics can be solved, or all practical moral dilemmas resolved. It is only to say that they are frequently easier to deal with than theoretical problems in ethics. Some persons are disinterested in the more theoretical problems; for them it is enough if workable and immediate solutions, however rough, can be found. For others, there can be no solid practical solutions unless they rest upon firm theoretical foundations. In our own case, we came to believe that while theoretical issues can on occasion be put aside, they must eventually be confronted. That much at least our own work in applied ethics made clear. For that reason, beginning in 1974, The Hastings Center established a special research group on "The Foundations of Ethics and Its Relationship to Science."

That title is a cumbersome one, but at least signals the domain of our interest. Our project was concerned not only with the foundations of ethics from a philosophical and theological perspective, but was also directed toward the impact of science on conceptions of the foundations of ethics (and vice versa). The project was far-ranging, and included participants from a number of different disciplines. During the course of its four years, some issues were approached again and again, while others were explored intensively only during one of the four years. It was, for The Hastings Center, an important and rich project, and it had two significant benefits. The first was that it helped us to clarify considerably some fundamental problems in ethics and in the relationship between science and ethics. The second was that it illuminated some of the reasons why practical solutions cannot be found to many problems in applied ethics (or at least not yet found).

This is the fourth and final volume of the series "The Foundations of Ethics and Its Relationship to Science." It is never easy to judge the merit or success of a series of this kind—though we do note that the first two volumes in the series have now been exhausted and are out of print, and there are not many copies of the third volume left. Whatever their value for others, however, the series of conferences, debates, and discussions out of which the four volumes grew were highly valuable to us personally and to the ongoing work of The Hastings Center.

The conclusion of an extended and demanding project is an appropriate occasion for acknowledgments. A grant from the National Endowment for the Humanities made possible the project as a whole, and we are grateful for its assistance. But the Endowment is not simply one more government agency. It is the one federal agency that makes possible serious and sustained work in the humanities; and that is critical to the intellectual life of our society. Nor is the Endowment a collection of nameless and faceless bureaucrats. On the contrary, it is difficult to think of any group in the country more dedicated to the humanities or more willing to give their time and attention to their important public duties. In our case, it was a distinct privilege to work with Dr. Richard Hedrich, Coordinator of the Endowment's Program of Science, Technology and Human Values. He watched our project every step of the way, giving us encouragement when needed and yet, at other times, pressing us to do better work. Those interested in learning how most effectively to wield the carrot and the stick should turn to Dr. Hedrich for tutoring. They will also discover not only a dedicated public servant, but also a person who does not count time, professional or personal, in working toward the best possible outcome of programs supported by the Endowment.

Over the years, we were also privileged to have the editorial services of Elizabeth Bartelme. She knows how the English language should be used, and she knows how to cope diplomatically with sensitive authors. Carol Levine, Managing Editor of the *Hastings Center Report*, gave us the advantage of her high editorial skills also, and, with Nancy deKoven, shepherded us through the printing and production process. Finally, we would like to thank all of those who contributed their time, and their papers, to the project. They worked very hard for us, they took the project seriously, and they contributed immeasurably to what was a long, rich, and complex discussion.

H. Tristram Engelhardt, Jr.
Daniel Callahan

Introduction

Knowing and Valuing: Looking for Common Roots

H. Tristram Engelhardt, Jr.

Cuándo conversan las raíces?

. . .

Es tan poco lo que sabemos
y tanto lo que presumimos
y tan lentamente aprendemos,
que preguntamos, y morimos.

Pablo Neruda[1]

The human capacity to puzzle is exceeded only by the niggardliness of reality in giving answers. Attempts to discover the good and the true are not only fraught with controversies and major revisions of purpose, but the endeavors are often, if not usually, painfully separated from each other. One is confronted with a seeming lack of basic interrelations between the two roots of human reasoning: knowing and valuing. Or at least one is confronted with what at times appears to be the absence of a theoretical basis for such interrelationships. Nevertheless, one is often pressed to seek such a basis. For example, disputes about value questions bearing on the sciences and technology lead to background questions concerning the foundations of ethics and its relationship to the sciences, in that those disputes appear in part to be disputes about facts and in part disputes about value. Such

1

controversies do not appear to fall within neat disciplinary boundaries, and yet they appear to be important for the disciplines of ethics and of the theory of knowledge. Thus it is that the more than four years of analyses, which produced the volumes in this series, arose. Concerns with bioethics and science policy occasioned ever more basic questions addressed to the nature of ethics and its relations to and with the sciences. This led to the formation of the research group that produced this volume and the three volumes preceding it and to their focus upon the foundations of ethics and its relations to the sciences.

The twin intellectual passions, to know the fabric of this world and to know the goods of human life, direct the core of our culture's search for meaning. One wishes to establish the regularities of occurrences in the world and to find useful and enlightening models to account for those regularities. One wants as well to discover or determine what the goods are that should motivate human conduct, what the duties are that should constrain it, and what general accounts show the rationality of such goods and duties. Science and ethics are two collages of practices, which these intellectual passions sustain. Science offers a systematic attempt to evaluate and integrate empirical knowledge claims about the world. Ethics as a philosophical endeavor offers a systematic attempt to evaluate and integrate moral claims about the world and human conduct. Yet, in that one addresses facts and the other addresses values, there appears to be an unbridgeable gap between these two cardinal human endeavors. The gap is between what simply is and what ought to be, between systematic understandings of what *is* the case and what *should* be the case. Thus a puzzle arises concerning the unity or integratibility of the enterprises of explaining reality and those of normatively judging reality. In what ways do facts and values, as well as the systematic study of facts and the systematic study of values, bear upon each other? More particularly, what are the foundations of ethics and how do they relate to the sciences?

When we as a culture saw reality firmly anchored in the will of a Creator God, it was clear that all that was, was one, true, good, and beautiful. The order of knowing and the order of valuing could be supposed to have a deep harmony. However, in our post-Christian age, belief in such harmony has faltered. There is no longer in the West a generally acknowledged view of the Deity as the anchor of the orders of knowing and of valuing. Nor is there a generally embraced understanding of how such an anchoring could undergird both science and ethics. And, though there is in fact a worldwide community of scientists, there is no common acceptance of a metaphysical foundation for science and ethics. And though there is great common understanding regarding the methods and purposes of science, that appears to be far from the case with respect to ethics. In fact, the positivistic views of ethics, and of values generally, which accompanied the success of science in the nineteenth and the first half of the twentieth centuries, have supported the notion that ethics is ephemeral and of less substance than science. However, the ever-increasing success of science and the ever more pervasive character of the technologies it has spawned, have forced us to hope that we can, despite the evidence, take ethics seriously. If science and technology are to be to some purpose, the purpose must be discoverable or at least in some coherent fashion inventable. If the dangers of unchecked technology are to be avoided, then there must be notions of the proper uses of the sciences and technologies. There must be ideas of what should, in what circumstances, count as dangers. In short, though one might hope that science could be developed free from distorting values, one must still hope that a value context can be disclosed for science.

On the other hand, ethical theory cannot be developed without a regard for the data that science has and is accumulating concerning the nature of the world and the nature of the human condition. Though ethics in the abstract may hope to generate rules for rational beings as such, all concrete moral rules will need to reflect an awareness of the human condition and its peculiarities. That is, science can influence ethics by changing our understanding of the facts relevant to ethical choices. Such facts are likely to include information about the nature of the world, along with information concerning the causal roots of moral proclivities. That particular ethics have a causal context should be apparent to anyone who has reflected on the differences between the degrees of relevance of sexual mores for prepubertal versus postpubertal humans. The human goods, values, and interests which direct the concreteness of moral concerns are caused and evolved, as well as chosen, and are therefore open to being illuminated, at least in part, by scientific data. In giving accounts and justifications of social structures it may, then, be very helpful to appreciate how we as human beings are caused to have special moral interests.

As a result, science can influence ethics, both as a systematic account of moral probity and as a set of mores, by providing explanations of the causal basis of various moral and immoral sentiments. Such influence can arise out of a better understanding of the causes of those sentiments as well as from a special interpretation of the genesis of such sentiments. Scientific accounts of moral sentiments have led to attempts to revise the general appreciation of the significance of morality, as the history of psychoanalysis and of behaviorism shows. Such accounts have at times been taken to suggest which moral claims make sense and why, given causal or scientific theories of the genesis of such claims.[2] Explanations of moral sentiments can, then, be influential, even when they are not true. As an example, explanatory approaches to ethics such as sociobiology have become important for contemporary reflections on and in ethics, and that importance obtains even if they should not remain successful explanations.[3] They have a cultural force. Many of the issues on these points are discussed in the interchange in this volume between Richard Alexander and Paul Ramsey, in their considerations of the relevance of sociobiological information to ethics.

The issues raised in that interchange do not, however, bear on the foundations of ethics itself. They indicate, instead, how science can affect the content of ethics as well as how ethics can and should constrain dangerous scientific research. The latter points are discussed, for example, by John Ladd,[4] Marc Lappé,[5] and Edmund Pellegrino[6] in the first volume of this series, where social and ethical responsibilities regarding science are considered. In such discussions ethics stands on the outside looking in. The focus of ethics, in such circumstances, is on the use of human subjects in research, the risks to human populations and to the environment owing to possibly intrinsically dangerous research (e.g., recombinant DNA research); the possible immoral applications of technologies (e.g., the development of nuclear fusion and fission and its use in an unjust war); and the socially disruptive potentials of possible knowledge (e.g., racial basis of differences in I.Q.). Each such genre of considerations involves a possible ground for the constraint of scientific freedom, where the freedom involved is that of using humans, developing technologies, or gaining knowledge. In these cases, ethics and values are not integral to the endeavors of science, but are raised or encountered as extrascientific restrictions.

The analyses and discussions of these four years have often involved moving beyond the consideration of ethical issues *in sensu stricto* to the consideration of the role of nonmoral values in the sciences. Here, for example, belong the analyses of the different senses of physical excellence involved in judgments about the nature of health and disease.[7] Further, as in Gunther Stent's article in this volume, there have been examinations of the basic similarities of problem and of character in ethics and science. After all, one would expect that science and ethics as major rational endeavors would share characteristics in common. Insofar as ethics is the means of intersubjective negotiation of moral intuitions without recourse to force, but instead by mutual reason-giving, and insofar as science is the means of intersubjective negotiation of empirical claims, not by force, but by reason and observational tests of empirical propositions, there should, between science and ethics, be similarities of interests in coherence, in the avoidance of anomalies, in justificatory scope, and in the use of explanatory metaphors. Thus, as Stephen Toulmin showed in the first volume, *Science, Ethics and Medicine*, the notion of organic unity was borrowed and reborrowed between the biological sciences and the ethical assessment of political and social dynamics.[8]

The interrelations of science and ethics are, as a consequence, many-leveled and complex. They range from the external to the internal, from the causal to the logical. The relations are multiform, because ethics and the sciences are not simple practices. They are complex endeavors embedded in various social institutions. As a result, ethical considerations have exerted, and should exert, influences in numerous ways upon the understanding of science, and the converse. In addition, religious and theological perspectives have, at least in the past, dramatically influenced ethical reflections as well as the conduct of science. Because of this heterogeneity of issues, the four years of study in this project on the foundations of ethics and its relationship to science have developed out of numerous approaches, including analyses drawn from philosophy, history, medicine, the sciences, literature, and religious studies. The interdisciplinary viewpoint which this has enabled has led to reexamining the ways in which ethical attitudes, practices, and theories have been strongly influenced by the general culture and by intellectual viewpoints, the latter including prevailing scientific and theological understandings of reality. This has in turn supported the conviction that the nexus of ethics and science is neither simply logical nor causal. In that the causal connections are often initiated by practices of logical or rational interpretation (i.e., the interpretations become cultural forces in history), which practices themselves interpret the causal connections (i.e., science and ethics can and do study and interpret their own mutual influences), studies which view only the causal or logical interrelationships of science and ethics would be onesided. They would fail to indicate the richness of the matrix binding ethics and sciences. In particular, they would be blind to the fact that the assessment of causes always presupposes conceptual frameworks, which are themselves under causal influence. This project has, therefore, been pursued as an interdisciplinary analysis of the foundations of ethics, and of the interrelationships of ethics and science, because those interrelations are not amenable to adequate study by any one discipline.

This interdisciplinary commitment led to a complex address of the interplay of science and ethics. Over the four years of these volumes, the participants in the discussions which produced the series have pursued: (1) sustained and systematic interdisciplinary research concerning the foundations of ethics; (2) research concerning the ways in which the sciences presuppose value-judgments as well as influence value-theory; (3) research concerning the interdisciplinary nature of these issues, as well as (4) examination of the ways in which these interdisciplinary issues require interdisciplinary approaches. This involved three major topical focuses: (1) the foundations of ethics; (2) the relationship of religious attitudes to the perceived significance of ethics and science; and (3) the bearing of social and psychological views of man and nature on the understanding of ethics and science. In short, the four research goals were clustered around three subject areas, the first being tantamount to one of the major research goals. The results of each year's research were developed into a volume.

The research papers making up these volumes are the final result of two major revisions done under the guidance of the interdisciplinary discussions of the research group, after the original presentation of the paper to the group. As a consequence, each paper has been forged in a common fire of interdisciplinary analysis and critique; and each volume has emerged from an ongoing endeavor to understand better the foundations of ethics, and its relationship to the sciences.

In the first volume, *Science, Ethics and Medicine*, the focus was upon the interplay of evaluation and explanation in biomedicine.[9] The analyses addressed the role of hidden value-judgments in medical explanations[10] and the importance of ethics for the proper conduct of biomedicine and the sciences generally. This included a detailed exploration of these interactions in the history of medicine[11] as well as an analysis of the foundations of ethics.[12] The result was the beginning of a sketch of (1) the borrowing of concepts from ethics by the sciences and from science by ethics; (2) the web of conceptual independencies between science and ethics; (3) the role of value-judgments in the sciences; and (4) the place of ethics and science as two cultural enterprises each often sharing a similar historical and conceptual context. In short, the first year of analysis of the interplay of science and ethics showed both to be situated in a complex nexus of value-judgments including explanatory interests, where knowing and valuing are often, if not usually, interwoven.

Knowledge, Value and Belief continued these analyses with a focus on the roles of religion and science in the foundations of ethics.[13] This led to exploring the ways in which concrete arguments in science and ethics are context bound, and to suggesting that much of normal ethics is not a quandary or crisis ethics.[14] This led as well to examining essential tensions among moral values.[15] This also involved exploring the biopsychological undergirding of ethics via the considerations of what Gunther Stent termed a structuralist ethics,[16] and to examining the ways in which the course of evolution could have implications for ethics.[17] The result was a much better appreciation of the contextual nature of ethical and scientific claims and accounts. In this regard, even religious foundations of ultimate motives for ethical activity were seen to be surd unless placed within a particular historical context—at least insofar as they could be offered as reasons for actions.[18] In short, the historical character of science and ethics was adumbrated.

These themes were then further developed in *Morals, Science and Sociality*, which addressed the psychological and cultural contexts that frame scientific and ethical views.[19] Here the intellectual milieus of Soviet Russia and Germany in the 1920s were compared as case examples in order to study the relationship between different political viewpoints and the developments of scientific orthodoxies. In this case, the focus was upon the establishment on the one hand of a neo-Lamarckian and on the other hand of a neo-Darwinian view of genetics and of eugenics.[20] The general goal of this analysis was to display how ethical and political views interacted in the growth of particular views of science. In that volume the relationships between different moral psychological ideals of scientists and views of science,[21] the development of psychoanalysis,[22] the relevance of sociobiology for ethical theory,[23] and different views of the foundations of ethics were also examined.[24] The result was, as Alasdair MacIntyre put it, a moral account of objectivity in science, an account that shows objectivity in both science and ethics to turn on regulative ideals that develop and function in particular historical and cultural contexts.

> The scientific community is one among the moral communities of mankind and its unity is unintelligible apart from the commitment to realism. Thus the continuities in the history of that community are primarily continuities in its regulative ideals . . . the building of a representation of nature is, in the modern world, a task analogous to the building of a cathedral in the medieval world or to the founding and construction of a city in the ancient world, tasks which might also turn out to be interminable.
>
> To be objective, then, is to understand oneself as part of a community and one's work as part of a project and part of a history. The authority of this history and this project derives from the goods internal to the practice. Objectivity is a moral concept

before it is a methodological concept, and the activities of natural science turn out to be a species of moral activity. It is therefore less surprising than it seemed at first that the history of the philosophy of science should replicate the history of moral philosophy.[25]

As Gerald Dworkin demonstrated in his essay in the third volume, objectivity in ethical analysis shows a similar binding to historical and social contexts.[26] Objectivity becomes then, one should note, explicable only by reference to a historical context. It is because of this contextual character that adequate accounts of ethics and science must be mixed and complex, not simple, straightforward, or unidisciplinary. As a consequence, the first three volumes portray both logical and causal elements of the social construction of morals and science in order to reveal the concrete interconnections and similarities between these two major human enterprises.

The last year of these investigations drew upon the focuses of the first three years of examinations: medicine, religion, and cultural forces. The goal was to bring together, in as much detail as possible, the understandings that had been gleaned concerning the nature of ethics, the interplay between science and ethics, and the interdisciplinary character of the investigations of that interplay. In this final year, it became ever clearer that science and ethics share common problems and common roots. In each we approach reality as if we could decipher from it an ingredient meaning beyond that which we as knowers and doers bring to it. In both knowing and valuing reality we presuppose order or impose order. A minimum level of coherence is a necessary condition for the possibility of blame and praise and for talk about moral goods, as it is for the domain of scientific explanation and control of reality. Thus, insofar as we knowers and valuers construct meaning, we should expect to find meanings common to the domains of evaluation and explanation. Both domains should reflect human purposes. Both evaluation and explanation are done by the same reasoning creatures. Or put less subjectively, insofar as reality accords with *our* basic patterns of knowing and doing, we should expect to find, and will undoubtedly find, similarities between the foundations of ethics and the foundations of the sciences. In short, systematically acting, conducting ourselves as moral agents, shares much in common with deporting ourselves as systematic knowers, and the converse.

As a result, science and projects of evaluation overlap through borrowing ideas and borrowing methods. As Stephen Toulmin in his essay, "How Can We Reconnect the Sciences With the Foundations of Ethics?" notes, "[1] the basic concepts of the sciences range along a spectrum from the effectively 'value free' to the irretrievably 'value laden'; [2] the goals of the scientific enterprise range along a spectrum from a purely abstract interest in theoretical speculations to a direct concern with human good and ill; [3] the professional responsibilities of the scientific community range along a spectrum from a strictly internal and intellectual to the most public and practical; . . ." (Toulmin, p. 47) This point is made in an even more radical fashion by Gunther Stent in his study, "Science and Morality as Paradoxical Aspects of Reason," in which he argues that both science and morality show complementary, nonrational elements. In fact, as he indicates, the examination of ethics and of science over the last four years may have disclosed irresolvable inconsistencies or paradoxes in the foundations of each. One may thus be forced to accept the view that the various dimensions of human life are complementary, though their unity is not stateable in a systematic and immediately consistent fashion. However, it does seem clear that science can suggest various empirical lineaments within which ethics or morality in any concrete sense must function. Concrete views of ethics and of human values generally presuppose accounts of human nature and the nature of reality. They should thus, for example, be influenced by the deliverances of evolutionary biology insofar as those concrete views of ethics will be able to guide action in particular circumstances and situations. Therefore, the fact that enterprises such as sociobiology can have force for moral decisions increases our obligation to inspect their validity with care. This is the point of the second year of Richard Alexander's exploration of the significance of sociobiology. In his study, "Evolution, Social Behavior, and Ethics," he forwards an account of how biological inclinations predispose humans to accept certain social structures and how these inclinations must be taken into account in any full-blown theory of morals.

On the other hand, as the essay "Doctoring the Complaint, Treating the Illness, Helping the Patient: Some of the Works of Hygeia and Panacea" in this volume shows, the intrusions of values into science are also, at least in many instances, very significant. In knowing the world, we often impose categories and classify elements of reality with respect to those elements satisfying or failing to satisfy goals we have in mind. This is particularly the case in medicine where the goals of evaluation and explanation intertwine in the concepts of health and disease. At least in such cases, in the process of knowing the world, we often evaluate it. As a result, science can be as dependent upon evaluations as ethics is dependent upon scientific data. Moreover, one should realize that many concepts, not simply those in medicine, have normative as well as descriptive dimensions, a point that the results of the four years of discussions have repeatedly emphasized. The concept of fitness is but one other example.

As in the past volumes in this series a central problem in understanding the foundations of ethics and its relation to science has been the problem of understanding the nature and scope of reason. In fact, while attempting to find greater unity in reason, the investigations have disclosed not only unities but fragmentations. Reason fragments into domains and projects that may in part be incommensurable. Views of morality and of scientific truth are embedded in particular historical and cultural contexts as the papers of Burrell and Hauerwas and of Graham have shown.[27] Such possible fragmentation raises the prospect of an uncontrollable incommensurability—a point signaled by historians of science, such as Ludwik Fleck in his *Entstehung und Entwicklung einer wissenschaftlichen Tatsache*[28] and Thomas Kuhn in *The Structure of Scientific Revolutions*.[29] If we are bound within particular styles of thought and thought collectives so that, as Fleck put it, a fact must be experienced in the style of its community of thinkers, and tend to be in line with the interests of that community, then science runs the risk of losing its traditional commitment to explaining reality. The force of these observations would seem to be at least equally strong for ethics. Objectivity, in fact, runs the risk of being fragmented into many somewhat discontinuous domains of reason, with disparate views of reality and of values.

These issues are addressed in this volume by the studies of Alasdair MacIntyre, Gerald Dworkin, and Ronald Green. On the one hand, MacIntyre observes that the search for the foundations of ethics is frustrating precisely because reason alone can not deliver an ethic, or at least a concrete ethic. We live in a time in which the original foundations of our prevailing moral intuitions are not any longer taken seriously. The point was, for example, brought out in this volume by the discussions between James Gustafson and Hans Jonas. Their analysis of how strong the role of religious views can and should be in shaping our culture shows in fact how the cultural importance of religion has changed and has in fact lost its previously controlling role for science and ethics. It has, however, remained bound up with metaphysical and cosmological views about the ultimate reality and meaning of things—and the place and purpose of man in the cosmos. These persist as haunting questions, even if unanswerable. They are indeed increasingly unanswered questions as religion discovers the time-bound nature of its images and is increasingly reticent to offer, or even support, general metaphysical views. As it is, we are, with respect to our own culture, in the position, as MacIntyre shows, of philosophers who would be trying to reconstruct the taboos of Cook's Hawaii. One can give an account of the rules or the grammar involved in the prohibitions, but not defend their rationale. A general rationale for much of our social conduct, he argues, is no longer forthcoming and awaits a future historical synthesis. On the other hand, both Dworkin and Green contend that further attention to the nature of rationality can indeed illuinate the moral predicament.

As a consequence, the attempt to understand the foundations of ethics and its relationship to the sciences has led to comparisons of disputes and controversies in ethics with those in science that have an ethical or political overlay. Even where an investigation has only disclosed fragmentation, confusion, and disarray, there have been similarities among the dynamics of fragmentation. Which is to say, the analyses of the foundations of ethics and its relationship to the sciences have led to analyses of the processes of evaluation and the processes of explaining, and to comparisons of the similarities between these two endeavors. What becomes of note, as a result, is the character of the controversies in ethics and science, and the ways in which they interact and are similar. As this last volume in this series shows, there is not only a borrowing of concepts between science and ethics, but similarities of goals and similarities of problems.

As the complexity of these analyses indicates, they cannot be contained within any particular disciplinary boundary. Nor will it do to isolate the issues within numerous distinct, but in principle independent, areas of analysis. Rather, it has become clear that the investigation of these issues best occurs in a truly interdisciplinary fashion, for at least four reasons: (1) the questions at issue are not confined within strict disciplinary boundaries, they concern how reason functions and gains content with which to work; (2) the investigation of the interplay of facts and values requires insights and methods from those disciplines dealing with facts and from those dealing with values; and (3) the nature of the issues bearing on either facts or values taken in isolation is such as often to raise basic issues in one discipline, which then raise secondary issues in other disciplines; thus questions about facts can raise questions about values, and the reverse. In addition (4) an understanding of the similarities and dissimilarities in the natural history of controversies in ethics and science requires cross-disciplinary comparisons.

Many of the conclusions of these four years of reflections are thus programmatic. They lead as much to better understanding of how one should go about analyzing the foundations of ethics and its relationship to sciences, as to discovering these foundations and their particular relationships. Consequently, this volume contains reflections on both the unity and the fragmentation that human reason discloses in its enterprise of explanation and evaluation. As Neruda suggests in his poem, we may at least learn to ask the right questions, to know the kinds of things that ethics and the sciences are, even if we cannot be assured of the right answers. Which is to say, we can at least come to know something about the processes of our reasoning in ethics and in science, even if final answers in ethics and in science may resolutely elude us. It is here that the focus of these four years culminates in this volume: the search for the common roots of knowing and valuing—*cuando conversan las raices*—when do the roots converse? We have come at least to see how those roots are put down and at times intertwine. Even when these accounts are incomplete, they illumine the human condition, which is itself incomplete. This is the modest but irreplaceable contribution of the humanities.

NOTES

1. When do roots converse?

. . .

What we know is so little,
and we presume so much,
and learn so slowly
that we ask questions, then die.

Pablo Neruda, "Through a Closed Mouth the Flies Enter," in *A New Decade, Poems 1958–1967*, translated by Ben Belitt and Alastair Reid (New York: Grove Press, 1969), p. 40–41.

2. Sigmund Freud, *Moses & Monotheism*, in *The Complete Psychological Works of Sigmund Freud*, vol. 23, trans. and ed. by James Strachey (London: The Hogarth Press, 1953); and B.F. Skinner, *Beyond Freedom and Dignity* (New York: Alfred A. Knopf, 1971).

3. E. O. Wilson, ed., *Sociobiology: The New Synthesis* (Cambridge, Mass.: Harvard University Press, 1975), and *On Human Nature* (Cambridge, Mass.: Harvard University Press, 1978).

4. John Ladd, "Are Science and Ethics Compatible?" in *Science, Ethics and Medicine*, ed. H. Tristram Engelhardt, Jr. and Daniel Callahan (Hastings-on-Hudson, N.Y.: Hastings Center, 1976), pp. 49–78.

5. Marc Lappé, "The Non-neutrality of Hypothesis Formation," in *Science, Ethics and Medicine*, pp. 96–113.

6. E. D. Pellegrino, "Commentary: Science and Moral Neutrality: Some Notes on Ladd's Method of Logical Negation," in *Science, Ethics and Medicine*, pp. 84–95; also, "Commentary: Hypothesis Formulation: Another 'Inviolate' Realm Open for Eth-

ical Inquiry?" in *Science, Ethics and Medicine*, pp. 114–19.

7. H. Tristram Engelhardt, Jr., "Human Well-being and Medicine: Some Basic Value-Judgments in the Biomedical Sciences," in *Science, Ethics and Medicine*, pp. 120–39; also, "Doctoring the World, Treating the Disease, Helping the Patient: Some of the Works of Hygeia and Panacea," in this volume.

8. Stephen Toulmin, "Ethics and 'Social Functioning': The Organic Theory Reconsidered," in *Science, Ethics and Medicine*, pp. 195–217.

9. H. Tristram Engelhardt, Jr. and Daniel Callahan, eds., *Science, Ethics and Medicine* (Hastings-on-Hudson, N.Y.: Hastings Center, 1976).

10. H. Tristram Engelhardt, Jr., "Human Well-being and Medicine: Some Basic Value-Judgments in the Biomedical Sciences," in *Science, Ethics and Medicine*, pp. 120–39.

11. Lester S. King, "Values in Medicine," pp. 225–41; Guenter B. Risse, "Commentary: Historical Notes on Value Systems in Medicine," pp. 242–47; and Marx W. Wartofsky, "The Mind's Eye and the Hand's Brain: Toward an Historical Epistemology of Medicine, pp. 167–94, all in *Science, Ethics and Medicine*.

12. Michael Scriven, "The Science of Ethics," in *Science, Ethics and Medicine*, pp. 15–43.

13. H. Tristram Engelhardt, Jr. and Daniel Callahan, eds., *Knowledge, Value and Belief* (Hastings-on-Hudson, N.Y.: Hastings Center, 1977).

14. David Burrell and Stanley Hauerwas, "From System to Story: an Alternative Pattern for Rationality in Ethics," pp. 111–52; and E.D. Pellegrino, "Commentary: Rationality, the Normative and the Narrative in the Philosophy of Morals," pp. 153–68, both in *Knowledge, Value and Belief*. See also Edmund Pincoffs, "Quandary Ethics," *Mind*, 80 (1971), 532–71.

15. Thomas Nagel, "Commentary: The Fragmentation of Value," in *Knowledge, Value and Belief*, pp. 279–94.

16. Gunther S. Stent, "The Poverty of Scientism and the Promise of Structuralist Ethics," in *Knowledge, Value and Belief*, pp. 225–46.

17. Bernard Towers, "Toward an Evolutionary Ethics," pp. 207–24.; and Patrick Heelan, "Commentary: Deep Structures and an Evolutionary Ethics," pp. 247–53, both in *Knowledge, Value and Belief*.

18. See the interchange among Paul Ramsey, "Commentary: Kant's Moral Theology or a Religious Ethics?" pp. 44–74, Alasdair MacIntyre, "Commentary: A Rejoinder to a Rejoinder," pp. 75–78, and Corinna Delkeskamp, "Commentary: Another Response to MacIntyre, Tragedy, Reason, Religion, and Ramsey," pp. 79–99 in *Knowledge, Value and Belief*.

19. H. Tristram Engelhardt, Jr. and Daniel Callahan, eds., *Morals, Science and Sociality* (Hastings-on-Hudson, N.Y.: Hastings Center, 1978).

20. Loren R. Graham, "Attitudes Toward Eugenics in Germany and Soviet Russia in the 1920s: An Examination of Science and Values," in *Morals, Science and Sociality*, pp. 119–49.

21. Stephen Toulmin, "The Moral Psychology of Science," in *Morals, Science and Sociality*, pp. 48–67.

22. Stephen Marcus, "The Origins of Psychoanalysis Revisited: Reflections and Consequences," in *Morals, Science and Sociality*, pp. 73–92.

23. Richard Alexander, "Natural Selection and Societal Laws," in *Morals, Science and Sociality*, pp. 249–90.

24. Gerald Dworkin, "Moral Autonomy," pp. 156–71, Gregory Vlastos, "The Rights of Persons in Plato's Conception of the Foundations of Justice," pp. 172–201, and Eric Cassell, "Self Conflict in Ethical Decisions," pp. 215–33, all in *Morals, Science and Sociality*.

25. Alasdair MacIntyre, "Objectivity in Morality and Objectivity in Science," in *Morals, Science and Sociality*, p. 37.

26. Gerald Dworkin, "Moral Autonomy," in *Morals, Science and Sociality*, pp. 156–71.

27. David Burrell and Stanley Hauerwas, "Commentary: Rationality, the Normative and the Narrative in the Philosophy of Morals," in *Knowledge, Value and Belief*, pp. 153–68; and Loren R. Graham, "Attitudes towards Eugenics in Germany and Soviet Russia in the 1920s: An Examination of Science and Values," in *Morals, Science and Sociality*, pp. 119–49.

28. Ludwik Fleck, *Entstehung und Entwicklung einer wissenschaftlichen Tatsache: Einführung in die Lehre vom Denkstil und Denkkollektiv* (Basel: Benno Schwabe, 1935).

29. Thomas Kuhn, *The Structure of Scientific Revolutions* (Chicago: University of Chicago Press, 1969).

1

A Crisis in Moral Philosophy: Why Is the Search for the Foundations of Ethics So Frustrating?

Alasdair MacIntyre

THE NEED TO INQUIRE about the foundations of ethics arises intermittently; when it does arise, it generally represents a point of crisis for a culture. In different periods in the past of our own culture the oracles that have been resorted to in such situations have been of various kinds: Hellenistic cults, the *imperium* of Augustus, and the rule of St. Benedict all represent responses to such crises. But at least three times it has been the moral philosophers who have been summoned: in the twelfth century when "Ethica" took on the meaning transmitted to our word "ethics"; in the eighteenth and nineteenth centuries when a shared, secular rational form of moral justification was required to fill the place left empty by the diminution of religious authority; and now.

The ability to respond adequately to this kind of cultural need depends of course on whether those summoned possess intellectual and moral resources that transcend the immediate crisis, which enable them to say to the culture what the culture cannot— or can no longer—say to itself. For if the crisis is so pervasive that it has invaded every aspect of our intellectual and moral lives, then what we take to be resources for the treatment of our condition may turn out themselves to be infected areas. Karl Kraus's famous remark that psychoanalysis is a symptom of the very disease of which it professes to be the cure may turn out to have application to other disciplines.

I am going to argue that Kraus's remark applies to a good deal of work in recent and contemporary English and American moral philosophy. (Note that I am not at all suggesting that outside the Anglo-Saxon world they order these things better; *au contraire*.) I shall proceed in the following way: First I shall describe what I take to be the symptoms of moral crisis in our culture and their historical roots; secondly, I shall describe what I take to be the key features of recent moral philosophy; thirdly, I shall conclude from my description that such moral philosophy is essentially a reflection of our cultural condition and lacks the resources to correct its disorders; and finally, I shall inquire why this is so.

Symptoms of Moral Crisis

The superficial symptoms of moral disorder are not difficult to identify: what can be going on when the *New York Times* announces that ethics is now fashionable? What can be said of a culture in which morality is periodically "rediscovered"? Why is instant but short-lived moral indignation endemic among us? What are we to make of a society in whose *liberal* iconography a few years ago the diabolical face of Richard Nixon was counterbalanced by the angelic benignity of a Sam Ervin, it being for that purpose obliterated from consciousness that Senator Ervin had voted against every piece of civil rights legislation ever proposed in the Congress? What are we to make of those politicians and academics who have already so successfully forgotten what they did during the Vietnam War? Who now remembers the present President's response to Lieutenant Calley's courtmartial conviction?

What the answers to such questions establish is that overt moral stances in our culture tend to have a temporary and a fragile nature. These characteristics are, I suggest, rooted in the character of contemporary moral debate and contemporary moral conviction. It is a central feature of contemporary moral debates that they are unsettlable and interminable. For when rival conclusions are deployed against one another—such as "All modern wars are wrong," "Only anti-imperialist wars of liberation are justified," "Sometimes a great power must go to war to preserve that balance of power which peace requires," *or* "All abortion is murder," "Every pregnant woman has a right to an abortion," "Some abortions are justified, others not"—they are rationally defended by derivation from premises that turn out to be incommensurable with each other. Premises that invoke a notion of a just war derived from medieval theology are matched against premises about liberation and war derived partly from Fichte and partly from Marx, and both are in conflict with conceptions that count Machiavelli as ancestor. Premises about the moral law with a Thomistic and biblical background are matched against premises about individual rights that owe a good deal to Tom Paine, Mary Wollstonecraft, and John Locke; and both are in conflict with post-Benthamite notions of utility.

I call such premises incommensurable with each other precisely because the metaphor of weighing claims that invoke rights against claims that invoke utility, or claims that invoke justice against claims that invoke freedom, in some sort of moral scale is empty of application. There are no scales, or at least this culture does not possess any. Hence moral arguments in one way terminate very quickly and in another way are interminable. Because no argument can be carried through to a victorious conclusion, argument characteristically gives way to the mere and increasingly shrill battle of assertion with counterassertion. This is bad enough, but it is not all.

For if I have no adequately good reasons to give you to convince you that you should exchange your premises for mine, then it follows that I should have adopted my premises rather than yours, when I originally adopted my position. The absence of a shared rational criterion turns out to imply an initial arbitrariness in each one of us—or so it seems.

This conjunction of an inability to convince others and a sense of arbitrariness in ourselves is a distinctive characteristic of the American present. It provides a background against which rapid shifts of feeling become an intelligible phenomenon, against which it is less surprising to find so much moral self-consciousness combined with so little moral stability. It is unsurprising also that a need to inquire about the foundations of ethics arises, independently of any special concerns with particular areas of the moral life. What produced this condition?

Part of the answer is clear, even if only part: our society stands at the meeting-point of a number of different histories, each of them the bearer of a highly particular kind of moral tradition, each of those traditions to some large degree mutilated and fragmented by its encounter with the others. The institutions of the American polity, with their appeal to abstract universality, and to consensus, are in fact a place of encounter for rival and incompatible outlooks to a degree that the consensus itself requires should not be acknowledged. The image of the American is a mask that, because it must be worn by blacks, Indians, Japanese and Swedes, by Irish Catholics, New England Puritans, German Lutherans, and rootless secularists, can fit no face very well. It is small wonder that the confusions of pluralism are articulated at the level of moral argument in the form of a mishmash of conceptual fragments.

Key Features of Modern Moral Philosophy

There are three central features of modern moral philosophy: its appeal to intuitions, its handling of the notion of reason, and its inability to settle questions of priority between rival moral claims. I shall only be able to give a few examples to illustrate my claims, but I shall therefore take care to use examples that have a certain typicality and that enjoy a certain prestige. My final suggestion will be that modern analytical moral philosophy is essentially a ghost discipline; its contemporary practitioners are pale shadows of eighteenth- and nineteenth-century predecessors and their failures simply reiterate the failures of those predecessors.

One of the key ancestors of modern moral philosophy is of course Henry Sidgwick. It is Sidgwick whose use of the word "intuition" bridges the gap from its nineteenth-century to its twentieth-century usage. And it was Sidgwick who took it to be the task of moral philosophy to articulate, to systematize, and to bring into a coherent rational whole our prephilosophical moral intuitions, as does John Rawls nowadays—and as does J. O. Urmson and as did Sir David Ross. What is surprising is that, even when such authors acknowledge a debt to Sidgwick, they never notice his own conclusion: where he had hoped to find Cosmos, he had found Chaos. That is, they do not face the possibility that our prephilosophical intuitions do not form a coherent and consistent set and therefore cannot be systematically and rationally articulated as a whole. Yet the evidence is close at hand. Rawls constructs what he takes to be *the* concept of justice in terms of a set of principles of patterns of distribution; Nozick retorts with arguments starting from premises that are certainly as widely held as are Rawls's. From this he then is able to show that if his premises are conceded, the concept of justice cannot be elucidated in terms of any pattern of distribution. The structure of the debate between them is thus for all its philosophical sophistication at once reminiscent of the modes of everyday moral argument. Why should I accept Nozick's premises? He furnishes me with no reasons, but with a promissory note. Why should I accept Rawls's premises? They are, so he argues, those that would be accepted by hypothetical rational beings whose ignorance of their actual position in any social hierarchy enables them to plan a type of social order in which the liberty of each is maximized, in which inequalities are tolerated only insofar as they have the effect of improving the lot of the least well-off, and in which the good of liberty has priority over that of equality.

But why should I in my actual social condition choose to accept what those hypothetical rational beings would choose, rather than for example Nozick's premises about natural rights? And why should I accept what Rawls says about the priority of liberty over equality? Many commentators have identified a weakness in Rawls's answer to this latter question; but the weakness of Rawls's position is as clear when we consider the former question.

Rawls might suggest that if I do not accept his premises, I myself will fail as a rational person. This type of consideration has been central to the work of a number of other moral philosophers and notably to that of R. M. Hare, who has deplored

Rawls's appeal to intuitions and has urged that in the conception of moral reasoning alone can we find adequate means for discriminating those principles that we ought to accept from those that we ought to reject. But Hare is only able to carry through his project—which turns on the fact that I cannot consistently apply universal principles to others that I am not prepared to apply in like circumstances to myself—by excluding from it a class of agents whom he calls "fanatics," a class that includes Nazis who are prepared to embrace such principles as "Let all Jews be put to death and let this be done even if it is discovered that I am a Jew."

It follows that we do not discriminate moral principles, even on Hare's view, by logic or reason alone, but only—at best—by conjoining the requirements of logic or reason with the nonlogical requirement that moral agents shall not be, in Hare's special sense, fanatics. And there seem no good arguments for accepting this latter point and at least one good argument against it; surely to want political office-holders to hold such principles as "Let all incompetent political office-holders be deprived of office and let this be done even if it is discovered that I am incompetent." It is difficult not to see in this part of Hare's position a covert, even if mistaken, appeal to intuitions as clear as any in Rawls.

The moral that I want to draw is simple and twofold; intuitions are no safe guide, and the conception of reason—usually a conception of consistency, sometimes eked out by decision theory—employed in moral philosophy is too weak a notion to yield any content to moral principles. What is wrong with being morally unprincipled is not primarily that one is being *inconsistent* and it is not even clear that the unprincipled *are* inconsistent, for it seems to be the case that in order to be practically inconsistent one first needs to have *principles*. (Otherwise what is it about one that is inconsistent?) Consider those two charming scoundrels who lounge insolently at the entrance to modernity, Diderot's *Lui* in *Le Neveu de Rameau* and Kierkegaard's 'A' in *Enten-Eller*. Both boast that they abide by no rules. What have Rawls and Hare to say to them? Rawls and Hare might well answer—and I sympathize with their answer—that it is not required of a moral theory that it be able to convince scoundrels, no matter how intelligent. A certain seriousness in the hearer is also required.

But if this was to be their reply—and I must not put words in their mouths—it does suggest that their arguments will only find a starting-point with hearers who are already convinced that it is right to lead a principled life—for what else is it to be serious—where by "principled" we mean something much more than any notion of rationality can supply. And indeed I take it that just this *is* generally presupposed in modern moral philosophy.

One outcome of this weakness in the central conceptions of such moral philosophy is that it presents us with no way of dealing with conflicts of rules or principles. Methods of justification for individual rules or principles are overabundant: we have utilitarian justifications, contractarian justifications, universalizability justification, intuitionist justifications, and each of these in more than one variety. But from Ross to Rawls the treatment of priority questions is notoriously weak. For it always presupposes some prior unargued position about how our values are to be organized. Here arbitrariness becomes visible.

These failures have historical roots. Analytical moral philosophers, who have often treated the history of philosophy as an optional extra for philosophers (much like dancing lessons at a private school, they lend a touch of elegance, but are scarcely essential), have often recognized their particular debts to Kant, who is clearly the ancestor of the concept of reason in Hare, or to Hume or to Mill or to whomever. What they have not recognized is that they have been systematically retreading the ground of the great eighteenth- and nineteenth-century debates and now emerge with no greater success than their predecessors. Kant's notorious failure to derive substantial moral principles from a purely formal concept of practical reason has simply been repeated by his successors; and Hume and Mill have had their ghosts too.

One feature of the eighteenth-century debate that has reappeared is the superiority of negative over positive argument. What we owe to Hume, Smith, Diderot, Kant, and Mill are good arguments *against* the positions of their rivals; each destroys the pretentions of the others, while failing to establish his own position. Similarly with recent moral philosophy—instead of myself adverting to its weaknesses, I might simply have quoted each author against some other; Hare against Rawls, Warnock against

Hare, Harman against Nagel, and so on. There is indeed a striking consensus against modern analytical moral philosophy concealed within it: every modern moral philosopher is against all modern moral philosophers except himself and his immediate allies. There is scarcely a need for any external attack.

Moral Philosophy and Modern Culture

What is striking then is the concordance between the ordinary contemporary moral consciousness and the condition of analytical moral philosophy. Precisely at those points at which the ordinary moral consciousness reveals arbitrariness and instability analytical moral philosophy discovers problems insoluble by it with any of the means available to it. It is difficult to resist the conclusion that such moral philosophy is a mirror-image of its age; and this conclusion is reinforced by attention to detail. Just as the inability of the adherents of each contemporary moral standpoint to convince the protagonists of other standpoints is reflected in the inability of moral philosophy to provide agreed rational criteria by which to judge moral argument, so a number of particular moral positions are mirrored in some moral philosopher's account. Not all, for moral philosophers are characteristically middle-class liberals, and it is unsurprising therefore that the moral stance presented in philosophical guise is normally that of such liberalism. But even that liberalism has its varieties and so the contemporary political liberals of *Time* can inspect their portraits in Rawls's theory of justice, while the contemporary economic liberals of *Newsweek* can inspect *their* portrait in Nozick's theory. There is therefore a case to be made that analytical moral philosophy is one of the many ideological masks worn by modern liberalism. But to pursue that case would be to overemphasize a merely negative polemic. Instead I want to try to gain a new perspective both on the predicament of contemporary morality and on the related predicament of contemporary moral philosophy. One way to do this is to alienate oneself from the present by adopting some external standpoint: what standpoint more external than that of Polynesia in the late eighteenth century?

In the journal of Captain James Cook's third voyage, Cook

records the first discovery by English speakers of the Polynesian word *taboo*. The English seamen had been astonished at what they took to be the lax sexual habits of the Polynesians and were even more astonished to discover the sharp contrast with the rigorous prohibition placed on such conduct as that of men and women eating together. When they enquired why men and women were prohibited from eating together, they were told that that practice was *taboo*. But when they enquired further what *taboo* meant, they could get little further information. Clearly *taboo* did not simply mean *prohibited*; for to say that something—person or practice or theory—is *taboo* is to give some particular sort of reason for its prohibition. But what sort of reason? It has not only been Cook's seamen who have had trouble with that question; from James Frazer and Edward Tylor to Franz Steiner and Mary Douglas the anthropologists have had to struggle with it. From that struggle two keys to the problem emerge. The first is the significance of the fact that Cook's seamen were unable to get any intelligible reply to their queries from their native informants. What this suggests is that the native informants themselves did not really understand the word they were using, and this suggestion is reinforced by the ease with which and the lack of social consequences when Kamehameha II abolished the taboos in Hawaii forty years later in 1819.

But how could the Polynesians come to be using a word which they themselves did not really understand? Here Steiner and Douglas are illuminating. For they both suggest that taboo rules often and perhaps characteristically have a two-stage history. In the first stage taboo rules are embedded in a context that confers intelligibility upon them. So Mary Douglas has argued that the taboo rules of Deuteronomy presuppose a cosmology and a taxonomy of a certain kind. Deprive the taboo rules of their original context and they at once are apt to appear as a set of arbitrary prohibitions, as indeed they characteristically do appear when the initial context is lost, when those background beliefs in the light of which the taboo rules had originally been understood have not only been abandoned but forgotten.

In such a situation the rules have been deprived of any status that can secure their authority and, if they do not acquire some new status quickly, both their interpretation and their justification become debatable. When the resources of a culture are too meager to carry through the task of reinterpretation, then the task of justification becomes impossible. Hence the relatively easy, although to some contemporary observers astonishing, victory of Kamehameha II over the taboos (and the creation thereby of a moral vacuum in which the banalities of the New England Protestant missionaries were received all too quickly). But had Polynesian culture enjoyed the blessings of analytical philosophy it is all too clear that the question of the meaning of *taboo* could have been resolved in a number of ways. *Taboo*, it would have been said by one party, is clearly the name of a nonnatural property; and precisely the same reasoning which led Moore to see *good* as the name of such a property and Prichard and Ross to see *obligatory* and *right* as the names of such properties would have been available to show that *taboo* is the name of such a property. Another party would doubtless have argued that "This is taboo" means roughly the same as "I disapprove of this; do so as well"; and precisely the same reasoning which led Stevenson and Ayer to see "good" as having primarily an emotive use would have been available to support the emotive theory of *taboo*. A third party would presumably have arisen, which would have argued that the grammatical form of "This is taboo" disguises a universalizable imperative prescription.

The pointlessness of this imaginary debate arises from a shared presupposition of the contending parties, namely that the set of rules whose status and justification they are investigating provides an adequately demarcated subject-matter for investigation, provides the material for an autonomous field of study. We from our standpoint in the real world know that this is not the case, that there is no way to understand the character of the taboo rules, except as a survival from some previous, more elaborate cultural background. We know also and as a consequence that any theory that makes the taboo rules of the late eighteenth century in Polynesia intelligible without reference to their history is necessarily a false theory; the only true theory can be one that exhibits their unintelligibility as they stand at that moment in time. Moreover the only adequate true theory will be one that will *both* enable us to distinguish between what it is for a set of taboo rules and practices to be in good order and what it is for a set of such rules and practices to have been fragmented and thrown into disorder *and* enable us to understand the historical transitions by which the latter state emerged from the former. Only the writing of a certain kind of history will supply what we need.

And now the question inexorably arises in the light of my earlier argument: why should we think about real analytical moral philosophers such as Moore, Ross, Prichard, Stevenson, Hare, and the rest in any way different from that in which we were thinking just now about their imaginary Polynesian counterparts? Why should we think about *good, right* and *obligatory* in any different way from that in which we think about *taboo*? The attempt to answer this question will at once raise another: why should we not treat the moral utterances of our own cultures as *survivals*? But from what then did they survive?

The answer is in surprisingly large part that the patterns of common moral utterance in our culture are the graveyard for fragments of culturally dead large-scale philosophical *systems*. In everyday moral arguments in bars and boardrooms, in newspapers and on television, in which rival conclusions about war are canvassed, we find, as I already noted, remnants of the medieval doctrine of the just war contending against cut-down, secondhand versions of utilitarianism, both being confronted in turn by amateur Machiavellianism. And in a precisely similar way debates about abortion, about death and dying, about marriage and the family, about the place of law in society and about the relationship of justice to equality, to desert, and to charity become encounters between a wide range of variously truncated concepts and theories out of our different pasts.

It is because of this that the procedures of piecemeal philosophical analysis are so inadequate. They become in practice a kind of unsystematic conceptual archaeology whose practitioners possess no means of distinguishing the different aspects of our past of which our present is so very largely composed. So it produces, piece by piece, as *what we would say* or as *the concept of x* or as *our commonsense beliefs* what are in fact survivals from large-scale philosophical and theological systems that have been deprived of their original context.

It is unsurprising as a result that the contemporary moral philosopher has so little to say to the crises of contemporary morality. For he fails to understand either himself or that morality historically; and in so failing he condemns himself to handling systematically rival positions without that context of systematic thought that was and is required even to define the nature of such rivalries, let alone to decide between the contending positions. Consider just one such juxtaposition: that of modern consequentialism to its absolutist rivals and critics.

Every moral scheme contains a set of injunctions to and prohibitions of particular types of action on the one hand ("Do not murder," "Do not bear false witness," "Honor thy father and thy mother") and a general injunction to do good and to avoid and frustrate evil on the other. But the different relationship between these two elements is one of the principal differences between rival and alternative moral schemes. For on the one hand Thomists and Kantians make what they take to be the injunctions and prohibitions of the moral law absolute and exceptionless; it follows that our duties to promote the good of others and of ourselves and to prevent harm to others and to ourselves are bounded and limited by the injunctions and prohibitions of the moral law. On no occasion whatsoever may I disobey a precept of the moral law in order to promote the general good or to avoid any degree of ruin whatsoever; and there can be no question of weighing or balancing the beneficial consequences that might be reasonably predicted to result from such a breach on a particular occasion against the importance of obeying the precept.

A utilitarian by contrast sees any injunction to or prohibition of any particular type of action as having only provisional and conditional force. Rules of conduct, wrote Mill, "point out the manner in which it will be least perilous to act, where time and means do not exist for analyzing the actual circumstances of the case," but when circumstances permit us to carry through such an analysis, any rule, may be suspended or modified or replaced in the interests of promoting the greatest happiness or the least pain. Thus the precepts of morality are bounded and limited by our calculation of the general good.

Between the Kantian position and the act utilitarian position a number of others are ranged. At the utilitarian end of the spectrum a rule utilitarian may treat rules with a less conditional and provisional respect than does the act utilitarian, although he will hold that the rules themselves must be subject to an evaluation of the consequences of their being generally followed; and, since contingent circumstances change, even the rules that seem to offer the best possible reason to respect may have to be reevaluated from time to time. Consequently, the rule utilitarian can never assert of any specific type of action that it is forbidden irrespective of circumstances any more than the act utilitarian can; and this would remain true, even if David Lyon's argument that rule utilitarianism collapses into act utilitarianism were not as successful as I take it to be.

Nearer the Kantian end of the spectrum—although still abhorrent to Kant—would be any moralist who holds that in some situations all choices of action involve the doing of some evil, but that some evils are lesser than others. Such a moralist would resemble the utilitarians in holding that sometimes it is necessary to do evil, but unlike a utilitarian would still see the best possible action open to him as evil.

Nonetheless, although these intermediate positions are important, I believe that we can evaluate their claims upon our allegiance only if we first consider the conflict between those who hold that certain types of action ought to be done or not done irrespective of circumstances and consequences and those who deny this. I wish for the moment, although only for the moment, to consider these contentions in forms in which they are least entangled with the variety of philosophical contexts in which they have been at home. After all, moralists as different as Aristotle, St. Paul, and Aquinas hold the former absolutist position as stringently as do Kantians; and consequentialists, to borrow G.E.M. Anscombe's term for them, are of many varieties also. It is enough to remember the contrast between the Benthamites and the followers of G.E. Moore.

What is striking is the way in which the stauncher adherents of both views find their own position apparently obviously true and their opponents equally obviously false. So Anscombe once wrote that "if someone really thinks, *in advance*, that it is open to question whether such an action as procuring the judicial execution of the innocent should be quite excluded from consideration—I do not want to argue with him; he shows a corrupt mind." (*Modern Moral Philosophy*, Philosophy, Vol. XXXIII, No. 126, p. 17.) Whereas Jonathan Bennett thinks it equally obvious that if predicted consequences of harm are recognized as a reason for not acting in certain types of case, then no prohibition of any type of action whatsoever irrespective of consequences can be rationally defensible and to uphold together such a recognition and such a prohibition can only be the consequence of "muddle" (*Whatever the Consequences*, Analysis, 26, p. 102) or, even perhaps worse, "conservatism."

But what is it about which the rival protagonists are in fact disagreeing? There are at least, so I suspect, three major areas of disagreement involved. One centers around the concepts of causality, predictability, and intentionality and involves the relationship of consciousness to the world. Another is concerned with the concepts of law, evil, emotion, and the integrity of the self. A third focuses upon the relationship of individual identity to social identity and involves the question of the relation of ethics to politics. Let me consider each in turn briefly.

What is an action? What is the connection between, what is the distinction between an action and its effects, results or consequences? Can causal connections be established without a knowledge of law-like generalizations? Can causal relationships be established where one term of the relationship has to be characterized nonextensionally, that is, in terms of an agent's beliefs and intentions? This group of questions is conventionally allocated to the philosophy of action or to the philosophy of mind; but an answer to them—or at the very least some theories about why we do not need an answer to them—is presupposed by any account of morality. For what an agent is or can be depends upon what the answers are.

The force of this consideration can be brought out by considering the answers presupposed by some novelists. Dickens's world is one of brisk practical effects where sentiments can become deeds the moment the material in which the deeds can be embodied, money and persons, becomes available and in which harm and benefit are matters of immediate human agency. Proust's world by contrast is one in which the inaccessibility of each consciousness to others—that range of illusions that constitutes a hall of distorting mirrors—makes the character of our actions in the external world ("in what?" one is sometimes disposed to say in Proustian moments) essentially ambiguous. The irrefragable realities are pain, disillusionment, and art. In Tolstoy's world art is one of the illusions and the notion of large-scale contrivance is equally illusory: victories in war and the rise and fall of empires are not made or unmade, they happen. All that is to hand is the immediate moral deed.

It is crucial to recognize that in answering the questions or evaluating the answers of an Anscombe, a Quine, a Davidson, or a Wisdom on the philosophy of causality, action, and mind, we are deciding the case between Dickens, Tolstoy, and Proust, deciding it perhaps against all of them. What is not open to us is to leave the case undecided. In our actions, even if we choose not to acknowledge it, we have to inhabit some such world. Thus ethics requires a *systematic* connection with the philosophy of causality, mind, and action.

A second set of questions concerns law, evil, emotion, and the integrity of the self. Stoics, Thomists, and Kantians perceive the self as situated in a cosmic order in which it can receive fatal or near fatal wounds. Utilitarians perceive the self as always able to choose the most beneficial or least harmful course of action open to it, *whatever* that may involve the self in doing. No deed is morally beyond the self; there are no limits. But from this standpoint, as Bernard Williams has noted, the traditional notion of a virtue of integrity disappears; for integrity consists precisely in setting unbreakable limits to what one will do. For Stoics, Thomists, and Kantians therefore my passions must be educated by reason, lest they betray my integrity; and this requires a thesis about the relation of reason to the passions and of both to law and to breaches of law. For a central distinctive emotion in the Thomist and Kantian schemes at least has to become that of remorse, the embodiment in feeling of repentance. Whereas a Utilitarian scheme may have some room for emotions of regret, but none surely for emotions of remorse or repentance. Moreover Stoics, Thomists, and Kantians believe that they confront a timeless moral order, whatever the variations in human psychology, while for Bentham and his successors the moral order can vary only within the limits imposed by a timeless psychology. Here once again it is clear that *systematic* answers to metaphysical questions are presupposed by rival moral outlooks. And so it is also with the third group of questions.

Who am I? In what role do I act? Whom do I represent in acting? Who is answerable for what I do? If I am a German now, how can I stand in relationship to a Jew now? If my father burnt his grandparents? If my father stayed home and did nothing while his grandparents were burnt? Liberal political theory has envisaged all the political and social, familial and ethnic characteristics of a moral agent as contingent and inessential except insofar as he chose them himself. Abstract, autonomous humanity has been its subject matter. But the deeds of individuals are often corporate deeds: I am my family, my country, my party, my corporation, as it presents itself to the world. Their past is my past. Hence the question arises: how is moral identity related to political identity? Aristotle, Kant, Hegel, and Marx all give different answers. Each answer presupposes a particular view of the state and of the relationship of state and citizen. So that I cannot solve the problems of ethics without making a *systematic* connection with political theory.

The implications of my earlier thesis are now clear. Ours was once a culture in which the systematic interrelationship of these questions was recognized both by philosophers at the level of theory and in the presuppositions of everyday practice. But when we left behind us the ancient, medieval, and early modern worlds, we entered a culture largely and increasingly deprived of the vision of the whole, except at the aesthetic level. Each part of our experience is detached from the rest in quite a new way; and the activities of intellectual enquiry become divided and compartmentalized along with the rest. The intellectual division of labor allocates problems in a piecemeal and partial way; and the consequent modes of thought answer very well to the experience of everyday life.

The consequences for moral philosophy are clear; it reflects in its modes the society and the culture of which it is a part. It becomes a symptom rather than a means of diagnosis. And it is unable to solve its own problems because it has been isolated as

a separate and distinct form of enquiry and so has been deprived
of the systematic context that those problems require for their
solution.

The Fate of the Moral Sciences

The history of how moral philosophy underwent its transition
from large-scale systematic enquiry to piecemeal analysis—and
therefore the explanation of why the search for the foundations of
ethics is so frustrating—needs to be supplemented in at least
three ways, if it is to be adequately characterized. First, of
course, there are the parallel intellectual transformations within
adjacent enquiries. Not only has philosophy been subdivided, but
the rest of the moral sciences have been similarly reapportioned.
Hence arises that peculiarly modern phenomenon, the intellectual
boundary stone jealously guarded by professionals and signalled
by such cries as "But that's not philosophy!" or "You are really
doing sociology." Adam Smith by contrast, when he published
the second part of his course at Glasgow as *The Theory of the
Moral Sentiments* and the fourth part as *The Wealth of Nations*,
was not aware that he was contributing to more than one discipline. So moral philosophy since the eighteenth century has
become partially defined in terms of what it is not or rather what
it is no longer. And consequently, the history of the changes in
moral philosophy will be partially unintelligible, unless it is
accompanied by a history of what used to be the moral sciences
and their subsequent fate. This fate is symbolized by the fact that
when Mill's translator came to translate the expression "the moral
sciences," he had to invent the German word *Geisteswissenschaften*, a word taken over by Dilthey and others for their
own purposes; when in this century Englishmen came to translate
such German writers, they proclaimed that *Geisteswissenschaften*
is a word without any English equivalent.

Second there are significant questions of genre. It is far from
unimportant that up to the early nineteenth century moral philosophy is written almost exclusively in books, whereas now it is
written primarily in articles. The length, and therefore, the possible scope of an argument is part of what is affected by this

change; but it also reflects a change in the continuities of reading of the public to which the philosophical writer addresses himself. Hume, Smith, and Mill still presuppose a generally educated public whose minds are informed by a shared stock of reading which provides both points of reference and touchstones. They seek in part, sometimes in large part, to add to the stock and alter these points of reference and touchstones. This is a very different endeavor from the contemporary professionalized contributions to a dialogue to be shared only by professors. Philosophy becomes not only piecemeal, but occasional. (It is perhaps worth noting here that part of the destruction of the generally educated mind is the sheer multiplication of professional philosophical literature. From this point of view the increase in the number of philosophical journals—and the pressure to write that produces that increase—are almost unmitigated evils. The case for making nonpublication a prerequisite for tenure or promotion is becoming very strong.)

Finally it would be necessary to reflect upon the *ideological* functions served by recent moral philosophy's reflection of the liberal *status quo*. What is clear at the very least is that a moral philosophy which aspires to put our intuitions in order is going to be protective of those intuitions in one way, while a moral philosophy that claims to derive its tenets from an analysis of *what it is to be rational*, but that in fact has a large unadmitted component whose roots are quite other, is likely to be protective of them in another way. That recent moral philosophy should function in this protective way is scarcely surprising if I am right in identifying that philosophy as the heir of the eighteenth century; for the morality that it protects is the heir of the eighteenth century too. But the eighteenth century claimed for its liberalism epistemological foundations of a kind philosophy has since had to repudiate; *we* hold no nontrivial truths to be self-evident, *we* cannot accept Bentham's psychology or Kant's view of the powers of reason. Thus liberalism itself became foundationless; and since the morality of our age is liberal we have one more reason to expect the search for the foundations of ethics to be unrewarded.

Ethics, Foundations, and Science: Response to Alasdair MacIntyre

Gerald Dworkin

> . . . The foundations of ethics . . . those universal principles, from which all censure or approbation is ultimately derived.
>
> Hume
>
> Foundations of morality are like all other foundations; if you dig too much about them the superstructure will come tumbling down.
>
> Butler

To a philosopher the only sight less cheering than MacIntyre's portrait of philosophers attacking the views of other philosophers is that of a philosopher attacking philosophy. I propose to defend moral philosophy against MacIntyre's critique. I shall focus on the work of John Rawls, both because I believe that MacIntyre's criticisms are incorrect, and because I believe that a proper understanding of Rawls's theory can throw some light on issues concerning the foundations of ethics as well as their relationship to science. It is strange that so little philosophical attention has been paid to specifying what might be meant by reference to the foundations of ethics, and I shall make some initial attempts to clarify that question.

I

MacIntyre criticizes three central features of modern moral philosophy: its reliance on intuitions, its use of the notion of reason, and its inability to settle priority questions involving rival moral claims. Let us consider each of these features as they arise in Rawls's work.

The starting point for moral theory, according to Rawls, is our considered moral judgments, i.e., those moral judgments (which can be about particular actions or institutions or about principles or reasons for action) that we are most confident about and that have been formed under conditions most conducive to sound judgment. The first task of moral theory is to formulate a set of principles or rules that accounts for these judgments. MacIntyre points out that we have no reason to suppose this set is consistent and, therefore, capable of being systematically and rationally articulated but whether this is so is an empirical question and it is reasonable from a methodological standpoint to assume consistency until we find otherwise.

The methodological device Rawls uses to generate the principles of distributive justice is that of a hypothetical social contract.[1] MacIntyre asks why we should accept as correct, principles chosen by these contractors rather than, say, Nozick's views about natural rights. It is essential to recognize that it is only part of Rawls's defense that the principles chosen account for our considered judgments. If this were the whole story then we would, at most, have explained our moral judgments, not justified them. We would be doing moral psychology not moral philosophy. What is needed is what Kant called a "deduction," i.e., establishing a claim to legitimacy. This is why Rawls's own analogy to the task of the theoretical linguist is faulty.

Rawls argues for the correctness of the principles chosen in terms of the independent plausibility of the contractual scheme. It is obvious that such a scheme makes many assumptions about the nature of the choice situation. There are assumptions about the list of principles from which the contractors are to choose (a small set suggested by the history of moral theory), the formal constraints on the nature of the principles (no proper names), the rationality of the contractors (nonenvious), the information available to them (no knowledge of their social class), the procedures governing the choice (unanimity), the domain that the principles are supposed to regulate (the basic structure of the society), and others. These assumptions are in turn justified in terms of a large number of complex theoretical considerations. These include a theory of the nature of persons (autonomous individuals who assume responsibility for their fundamental projects), a theory of the function of principles of justice (to provide an ordering of conflicting claims concerning the division of the products of social cooperation), a theory about the range of application of moral principles (cases likely to arise given the circumstances that human beings are in), a theory of fair procedures (which facts it is morally relevant for the contractors to know), a theory of moral motivation (the contractors have, and view themselves as having, a sense of justice, and their desire to act on this conception normally determines their conduct), and more. The justification of a set of moral principles is an enormously complicated matter of seeing how the principles both account for considered judgments and cohere with, follow from, are made plausible by (these are quite distinct relations of support) a large body of other theories, views, and assumptions.

Let me now enumerate what I consider to be mistakes in MacIntyre's accounts of Rawls. First, it is misleading to speak of Rawls constructing "*the* concept of justice" implying a moral imperialism. Rawls distinguishes between the concept of justice (which is a purely formal notion characterized by the absence of arbitrary distinctions between persons and by rules determining a proper balance among competing claims) and conceptions of justice which consist of the substantive principles which provide the content for the concept. The disagreement between Rawls and Nozick is over conceptions of justice, not concepts. Second, Rawls does not deny that our "intuitions" may be incoherent. He starts with them, he does not end with them, and he explicitly admits that even after reaching what he calls "reflective equilibrium," different persons may "affirm opposing conceptions." Third, it is not an answer that "Rawls *might* give" (assuming consistency) to why we should accept his premises that those who do not cannot be considered rational. Rawls agrees with MacIntyre that no conception of reason is sufficient to yield moral principles with substantive content.

MacIntyre need not worry about putting words in Rawls's mouth when he suggests that Rawls's arguments assume persons "who are already convinced that it is right to lead a principled life." As I indicated above, Rawls explicitly assumes the contractors have a sense of justice. But why does MacIntyre think that this is a "weakness" that prevents moral theory from dealing with conflicts of rules or principles? What does working out priority questions have to do with assumptions about moral motivation?

Finally, I disagree with the claim that Rawls's treatment of priority questions is "arbitrary." It may not be correct but it is argued for in terms of a conception of the person as autonomous, i.e., as desiring to retain the capacity to change his system of final ends and to be active in choosing his own conception of the good. Such a person will, if rational, seek to preserve access to information and the power to shape his political and cultural environment. He ought, therefore, to accord a priority to the liberties of citizenship over more material goods (at least once a certain level of abundance has been reached). Perhaps this argument only applies to persons who conceive of themselves in a way that has been shaped by social and historical circumstances. But this fact by itself does not show that the claim of priority for liberty is arbitrary.

Let me conclude my direct commentary by noting how much of Rawls's work runs counter to the diagnosis MacIntyre gives of the state of contemporary moral philosophy. It is a *book*, not an article, and a *big* book. It is not addressed only to professional philosophers nor does it respect narrow intellectual boundaries. It is informed by and contributes to decision theory, economics, and moral psychology. It is linked in the most direct way to the history of philosophy. The debt to Kant is most obvious, but Aristotle, Marx, Rousseau, Mill, and Sidgwick all have their influence. It is not piecemeal, but systematic and comprehensive. Lest it be thought I am arguing from the isolated case, it should be noted that there are a number of philosophers who have, in recent years, written books that share many of the above features—Fried, Donagan, Nozick, Gewirth, Brandt, and Richards.

II

Does Rawls's theory, if correct, provide us with foundations for ethics? What is the relationship of such a theory to science?

An answer to either of these questions requires some specification of what is meant by the idea of ethical foundations. Philosophers have meant very different things by this obscure phrase.

Some philosophers have thought of it as a question about motivation. Why should any rational person do what is morally correct? Do we have good reasons to do what is right? Do moral principles have, by themselves, motivational force? Are there considerations that can convince all rational persons to accept certain moral principles as correct? Notice that all these questions presuppose that we know very well what is right and what is wrong; which principles are correct and which faulty. The issue is either how to convince others or get ourselves to do what we know to be right. I shall call this set of issues that of motivational foundations.

Other philosophers have worried about questions of justification. How do we tell which principles are correct? Is there a decision procedure for resolving moral problems? How do we prove that courage is a virtue? What priority rules can we justify? What are the starting points for moral reasoning? Is there a class of self-evident or a priori truths that can be used as premises to support less fundamental propositions? Let us call this set of questions that of the epistemological foundations of ethics. It is, I suppose, this set of issues that occurs to most people as foundational.

Still other philosophers have worried about the role of objectivity and truth in moral theory. Are the statements of ethics bearers of truth-values? Are values part of the world, out there, in the way that physical objects are? Do we discover values or choose them? Can we reduce moral judgments to nonmoral ones? Call this the question of ontological foundations.

With respect to each of these types of foundational issues, I want to say something about how Rawls's theory bears on them and about their relationship to science (which I understand to be any general, systematic, theoretically and empirically grounded knowledge about the natural and social world).

Rawls does not attempt to show that *any* rational person has good reason to develop or maintain a sense of justice. We cannot simply decide to alter our character at will. We always begin from where we are, and what we have reason to develop depends in large part on our existing preferences. Rawls does assume that there is psychological evidence that people raised under conditions of a just society will have a sense of justice and that all of us have, at least, the capacity to develop such a sense. He does, moreover, argue that for most persons (not all) we can give good reasons why they ought to affirm and maintain their sense of justice; why it is good *for* the person to be just. This argument relies on contingent truths of moral psychology. Unlike the argument that Nagel gives in *The Possibility of Altruism*, Rawls does not claim to show on a priori grounds that ethical requirements have motivational force for rational agents. Thus the findings of psychology or theories of biological motivation, such as reciprocal altruism or the results of game-theoretical work on the Prisoners Dilemma and coordination problems, are all relevant to questions of motivational foundations. I say relevant but not dispositive, for all such knowledge has to be mediated by philosophical investigation of concepts such as "good reason," "rationality," "prudential," and so forth.

With respect to the ontological issues, Rawls's view is that the theory is neutral with respect to the question of the objectivity of moral judgments or, at least, that an answer to these questions will be forthcoming only after we have studied in a systematic fashion various alternative moral theories. He suggests that it may be a necessary condition for the existence of objective moral truths that there be sufficient convergence among the various moral conceptions that are developed in reflective equilibrium. My own view is that intersubjective agreement is neither necessary nor sufficient for establishing objectivity. One must always know why there is agreement or lack of it. Is the agreement accidental or does it reflect essential features of human nature? Has the agreement been manipulated or is it the product of processes that we believe are related in rational ways to the securing of agreement? The argument for objectivity has to be one about the best explanation of intersubjective agreement.

If, for example, the correct explanation of such agreement is that the favored set of principles provides a solution to coordination problems that any creatures living in a complex society would face, or if the explanation is in terms of reproductive fitness à la Alexander, then we will be relying on certain objective features of the world. We would be making the claim that creatures constructed with certain features and facing certain problems in given circumstances would arrive at the following beliefs. This seems to me as much objectivity as we can get and as much as we need. Obviously, the findings of decision theory, evolutionary biology, and moral anthropology are all relevant to such a claim.

Finally we come to the issue of epistemological foundations. On a number of interpretations of this question a theory such as Rawls's suggests a negative answer. There are no self-evident moral truths that have substantive content. If "murder is wrong" is self-evident that is because we are defining murder as wrongful killing. If, on the other hand, murder is defined in terms of the deliberate killing of the innocent, then only a theory will give content to the notion of innocence. There are no incorrigible intuitions that provide a safe starting point for ethical reflection. In Neurath's metaphor we are always rebuilding the ship while we are sailing. There is no "faculty" (not even Harvard's) which perceives the truth of moral claims. No analysis of the nature of moral concepts can establish a priori the truth of ethical claims. Nor can we reduce the moral to the nonmoral. As an examination of Rawls's system shows, there are moral assumptions present in the theory from the start. At most one may be able to make partial reductions in the sense that one may be able to reduce rights to ideals or rules to virtues.

It may be that, as similar investigations of scientific and common-sense knowledge seem to show, all justification is ultimately circular. What one is looking for is as large a circle as possible.

Again, however, it is clear that if justification is going to take the kind of coherence form suggested by Rawls's theory, then scientific knowledge will be relevant. Such knowledge will enter into the argument at rather different levels. Some knowledge will be relevant to the feasibility of various moral and political principles. Thus, one way of arguing for or against a principle of positive responsibility to render aid to others is in terms of the constraints on liberty and autonomy which such principles pose, and to ask whether we can commit ourselves to such constraints and expect to act in accordance with them.

Some knowledge will be relevant to questions of theory construction. For example, some recent work in social choice theory has shown that given plausible assumptions one can prove an analogue of Rawls's difference principle. But the analogous principle violates the mathematical requirement of continuity. While Rawls does not take this as a refutation, he recognizes it as an objection to his theory and seeks to explain the anomaly.

Some knowledge will be relevant to the stability of various principles, i.e., whether they tend to generate (psychologically) their own support or to undermine it. The latter is what Marxists call the "contradictions" of a social system.

Lest it be thought that the relationship between moral philosophy and science is, in the words of Kolakowski, like the relationship between the city and the countryside—the former receiving life-giving sustenance and giving back in return garbage—it should be noticed that the interaction proceeds in both directions. Rawls's theory has stimulated work in social psychology, economics, and social choice theory.

One last point. It is not clear to me whether MacIntyre intends to suggest that whatever moral crises we face would or could be alleviated by discovering foundations for ethics. Such a hope would be as false in its way as the fear that Frege expressed when Russell pointed out a contradiction in the system Frege invented as a foundation of arithmetic. Frege wrote to Russell that "arithmetic totters." But we no more need foundations in order to count correctly than we need them in order to act correctly.

NOTES

1. For the most recent development and elaboration of Rawls's theory see his "Reply to Alexander and Musgrave," *Quarterly Journal of Economics*, November, 1974. "The Independence of Moral Theory," Proceedings and Addresses of the American Philosophical Association, vol. 48, 1974–75, pp. 5–22. "The Basic Structure as Subject," *American Philosophical Quarterly*, vol. 14, no. 2, April, 1977.

2

How Can We Reconnect The Sciences with the Foundations of Ethics

By Stephen Toulmin

ANYONE FAMILIAR WITH THE contemporary literature on the philosophical foundations of ethics—say, from John Rawls's *Theory of Justice* (1972) up to Alan Donagan's *Theory of Morality* (1977) and Ronald Dworkin's *Taking Rights Seriously* (1977)— will know how little attention such books give to "science," or at least to "the natural and social sciences," as they are conceived of at the present time in the English-speaking world.[1]

The question is, "How far does this lack of attention reflect some immutable verities about the *essential* relations between science and ethics? And how far is it, rather, a temporary—even, transient—fact about their *actual* relation in our own day?" At other times, certainly, both "science" and "ethics" have been conceived of in other ways, and their interactions have been both more obvious and more vigorous. By recognizing how those interactions have been minimized over the last 100 or 150 years, we should be able to recognize also how they might be re-established and reactivated. Even to agree on that diagnosis would be to achieve something substantial. The arguments in this paper will therefore be partly historical and partly diagnostic.

The Purist View of Science

From a strict philosophical point of view, all attempts to insulate the sciences from ethics can easily be undercut. This is

44

true whether our focus of discussion is intellectual, sociological, or psychological: the basic concepts of the sciences, the institutions and collective conduct of the scientific profession, or the personal motives of individual scientists.

As to the concept of science: so long as we restrict ourselves to the physicochemical sciences, our basic notions and hypotheses (e.g., hadron, field gradient, and amino acid) may have no obvious evaluative implications. But the physiological, to say nothing of the psychological and social sciences, employ whole families of concepts, for instance, those associated with functionality and adaptedness, and their cognates, which raise evaluative issues directly, both within the relevant scientific theories and in their broader implications.[2]

As to the scientific profession: the codes of good intellectual practice, and the criteria of professional judgment in the sciences, may once upon a time have looked to the needs of effective inquiry alone, rather than to broader "ethical" considerations. But it is by now no longer possible to draw so clear or sharp a line between the intellectual demands of good science and the ethical demands of the good life. The increasingly close links between basic science and its practical applications expose working scientists more and more to ethical problems and public accountability of sorts that are commonplace in service professions such as medicine and law.[3] A strong case can also be made for seeing the professional enterprises of natural science as creating, and even defining, certain basic ethical modes of life and conduct having their own characteristic virtues, duties, and obligations.[4]

Finally, as to the individual motives that operate for scientists in their work: though the "ideal" spring of action for scientific inquiry may be a pure respect for the rationality of the inquiry itself, such a "pure respect" is at best an aspiration, and a *moral* aspiration at that. Furthermore, it is something that can be developed in the course of any individual's lifetime, only as a somewhat refined product of moral education.[5]

Yet, despite these powerful objections, the notion that the intellectual activities of science are carried on at a level that sets them, if not above, then at any rate beside and on a par with the moral law, continues to have its charms; and we must try to understand its seductive power. One potent source, I suggest, has been scientists' fear of relativism. During a period when exploration and anthropology were encouraging a sense of *pluralism* in human affairs, and so generating a kind of moral relativism and subjectivism that put the very foundations of ethics in doubt,* it was understandable that scientists should have resisted the intrusion of ethics into the business of science; and that, in return, they should have insisted that the concerns of science—unlike those of ethics—were entirely objective, and in no sense "matters of taste or feeling." Furthermore, the fact that scientific issues could plausibly be depicted as public and intersubjective (rational) made it possible, also, to define the intellectual demands of the scientific life in a similarly objective way. So, both the collective conduct of the scientific profession and the personal choices of individual scientists were apparently freed from the existential arbitrariness and ambiguity of the ethical realm.

At this point, it might have been better if philosophers and scientists alike had emphasized the similarities between science and ethics, and had used the "rational objectivity" of science as a model in seeking to reestablish the claims of moral objectivity, as well. The argument that ethical issues are, in their own proper ways, as public and intersubjective as scientific issues (and so equally "rational") was thus abandoned too quickly and lightly. But many scientists, lacking any sense of joint intellectual responsibility and interest with the moral philosophers, were happy enough to disown relativism in science and bolt for cover on their

---

*In discussion, Paul Ramsey queried whether the natural sciences have in fact been affected by the debate about subjectivism and relativism carried on *within philosophy* over the last fifty or one hundred years. That, of course, would be highly questionable. The point of my present argument is that the recognition of anthropological diversity led, by around 1800, to a widespread sense—not by any means confined to philosophers—that ethical beliefs and practices vary arbitrarily from culture to culture. Earlier in the eighteenth century it had still been possible for Voltaire to declare, "There is only one morality, as there is only one geometry"; but, from 1800 on, cultural relativism became a force to reckon with in general thinking about ethical matters. The corresponding doubts about "objectivity" in natural science did not become serious until the present century: first, following the collapse of the classical Newtonian/Euclidean synthesis on which Kant had rested his case, and more recently with the widespread adoption of Thomas Kuhn's theory of "paradigms" as justifying a similar diversity in "views of Nature."

own. For so long as relativism and subjectivism remained viable options in philosophical ethics, most scientists understandably felt that it was more important to emphasize the distinctively intellectual—and so, presumably, "value-neutral"—character of their own enterprises. Provided they could preserve the autonomy of the scientific community against all outsiders, they did not mind letting the moral philosophers sink or swim by themselves.

By now, however, the "rationality" of science—the objectivity of scientific issues, the autonomy of the scientific professions, and the categorical claims of the scientific life—can no longer be used to differentiate science entirely from the rest of thought and morality. We are faced, on every level, not by a hard and fast distinction, but by a spectrum.

- The basic concepts of the sciences range along a spectrum from the effectively "value-free" to the irretrievably "value-laden";
- The goals of the scientific enterprise range along a spectrum from a purely abstract interest in theoretical speculations to a direct concern with human good and ill;
- The professional responsibilities of the scientific community range along a spectrum from the strictly internal and intellectual to the most public and practical.

Nonetheless, as recently as the 1930s, when I first acquired my ideas about "science," the most characteristic mark of the scientific attitude and the scientific task was to select as one's preferred center of attention the purest, the most intellectual, the most autonomous, and the least ethically implicated extreme on each of these different spectrums.

No doubt this "puristic" view of science was an extreme one, and by no means universally shared by working scientists, to say nothing of the outside social commentators who wrote about the scientific scene. Yet it is a view that had, and continues to have, great attractions for many professional scientists. Since "rational objectivity" is an indispensable part of the scientific mission, and the intrusion of "values" into science had come to be regarded as incompatible with such objectivity, all concern with values (or other arbitrary, personal preferences) had to be foresworn in the higher interest of rationality. Certainly, the professional institutions of science tended to be organized on this basis. The memberships of scientific academies, for instance, have for the last 75 or 100 years been increasingly recruited on the basis of the narrowly defined intellectual contributions of candidates alone,* without regard to their social perceptiveness, ethical sensitivity, or political wisdom. Indeed, the puristic view is still powerful today: consider, for instance, Arthur Kantrowitz's current proposals for a Science Court, whose duty would be to pronounce on the "factual implications" of science and technology for issues of public policy, without reference to the "values" at stake in each case.[6]

Accordingly, the purism of the views about science into which I was initiated was not merely a feature of the particular culture and time of my youth: one more local and temporary characteristic (so to say) of the factual, unemotional, antiphilosophical, class-structured, and role-oriented attitudes of the English professional classes between the two world wars. In part, the nature of that culture may have accentuated the larger tendency toward purism. Perhaps, if I had grown up in the United States rather than Britain (or even in Britain thirty years later) I would have acquired different views, both about science itself, and about its ethical significance. Certainly, there have not always been the kinds of barriers between ethics and science that I grew up with; nor need there always be such barriers in the future. Still, I seriously doubt whether this attitude was solely a local and temporary oddity of twentieth-century English upper-middle-class life and social structure. For many of the considerations advanced to explain and justify scientific purism have a force that carries them across national boundaries. These considerations—the intellectual reaction against ethical relativism, the collective desire for professional autonomy, the personal charms of an ethically unambiguous life plan—may have been felt with a special strength in the England of my youth, but they were by no means confined to it.

---

*Even in the second half of the nineteenth century, it was still accepted as a matter of common form that a poet such as Alfred Tennyson should be a Fellow of the Royal Society, and sit on important Royal Society committees. The restriction of membership in National Academies of Science to expert, full-time working scientists is thus largely a twentieth-century development.

The Professionalization of Science

What deeper explanation should we look for, then, to account for the emergence of this puristic view of science? Granted that, by the early twentieth century, relativism and subjectivism were beginning to pose an implicit threat to the objectivity of science as well as to ethics, how was it that scientists perceived and defined their own collective interests and self-image so clearly? How did they come to suppose that they could see science as capable of being the stronghold of reason by itself and on its own, in contradistinction to ethics, which had seemingly been unmasked as the plaything of emotion?

In part, these questions are issues for the history of ideas: in part, they will carry us deeper into the sociology and philosophy of science. Certainly, the distinction between an objective science and a subjective ethics may be traced back at least as far as the scientific positivism of Comte, in the early nineteenth century; and the same contrast helped to encourage the revival of scientific positivism in Vienna in the 1920s. But why was scientific positivism itself able to carry conviction from the early nineteenth century on, in a way that it had not done earlier? At this point, we should go behind the history of ideas, and consider these changes in "ideas" against their larger human background.

For our present purposes, I believe, the crucial development in the history of nineteenth-century science was the establishment of distinct scientific disciplines, professions and roles: that is, the process by which individual, sharply delimited special sciences began to crystallize from the larger and less-defined matrix of eighteenth-century natural philosophy. As a result of this change, scientific workers divided themselves up into new and self-organized collectivities, and acquired a collective consciousness of their specialized intellectual tasks, as contrasted with the broader concerns of philosophical, literary, and theological discussion more generally. In this way, it at last became possible to define the new individual role of "scientist." (This familiar word was coined as recently as 1840 by William Whewell, on the model of the much older term "artist," for his presidential address to the British Association for the Advancement of Science.)

In all these respects, scientific roles and writings, organizations

and arguments dating from before 1830 differ sharply from anything to be found after around 1890. In the hands of the most
distinguished eighteenth-century authors, scientific issues were
always expanding into, and merging with, broader intellectual
questions. In the writings of a John Ray or a Joseph Priestley,
the doors between science, ethics, and religion are always open.
"And why not?" they would have asked; "for natural philosophy
must surely embrace within itself, not just mathematical and
experimental philosophy, but also natural theology and natural
morality." (Their sentiments were also those of Isaac Newton
himself, for whom "to discourse of God" from a study of His
Creation "does certainly belong to natural philosophy."[7]) Indeed,
it took a series of deliberate and collective decisions to restrict
the scope of scientific debate before these larger issues of philosophy and theology were effectively excluded from the professional debate about scientific issues. One such example was the
resolution adopted by the Geological Society of London in 1807
to exclude from its Proceedings all arguments about the origin,
antiquity, and creation of the earth, as being merely speculative,
and to confine the Proceedings to papers based on direct observations of the earth's crust.[8] This is simply one early illustration of
a trend that rapidly became general. During the rest of the
nineteenth century, the intellectual concerns of the different special sciences were identified and defined in progressively sharper
terms, setting them apart from the broader interests of philosophers, theologians, and the general reading public.

At this point, it would be helpful to develop a fuller understanding of the manner in which natural philosophy, as conceived
in the seventeenth and eighteenth centuries, fell apart into its
component elements, and the sciences (and scientists) were led to
set up shop on their own. Even as late as the 1820s, Joseph
Townsend could still present significant contributions to geological science in the guise of an argument vindicating *The
Veracity of Moses as an Historian*.[9] By the end of the century,
biblical history and geochronology had become entirely distinct
disciplines, pursued by quite separate communities of scholars.
Yet, even in this case, the transitions involved were protracted,
hard-fought, and painful. Similarly, one major reason for the
hostile reception that greeted Darwin's *Origin of Species* was the

threat it seemingly posed to the traditional association between natural history and sacred history. Acknowledging a presentation copy of the book, Darwin's teacher Adam Sedgwick expressed sorrow and alarm at Darwin's disregard of the "essential link" between the moral and material order of the world. If natural historians no longer showed us how the hand of the Creator was exemplified in the living creatures that were his handiwork, how then could the human race be expected to retain its confidence in divine wisdom and providence?

In addition, it would be helpful to have more detailed studies of the institutional changes during the nineteenth century by the leading scientific academies and societies that had originally been founded from 1650 on. How did they move from being general associations of scholars, clerics, and gentlemen to being specialized organizations of professional experts, with a narrowly defined scope and strict entrance qualifications? Before 1830, the Royal Society of London was still largely an association for the general discussion of issues in natural philosophy. By the 1890s, it had become the mode to pursue, not just art for art's sake, but also science for science's sake: even, electrical theory for electrical theory's sake, organic chemistry for organic chemistry's sake, botanical taxonomy for botanical taxonomy's sake. This was so because, by 1890, the self-defining disciplines and autonomous professions with which we are familiar today—each of them devoted to the special aims of one or another science—had finally established an existence independent of each other.

Once again, however, these institutional changes did not come automatically or easily. On the contrary, the intellectual and institutional claims of the special sciences faced continued resistance from the churches and elsewhere. So the collective experience, interests, and self-perceptions of, for example, cell physiologists, historical geologists, and electromagnetic theorists led them to defend their newly won territories with some real jealousy, to act protectively toward the intellectual goals of their disciplines, and to resist any countermoves aimed at reabsorbing them into some larger system of philosophy or theology. Ernst Haeckel, the German zoologist and a leader of the German Monistic Alliance, is an interesting figure in this respect. He was perhaps the last representative of the older tradition, comprised of scientists who could maintain an acceptable balance between generalism and specialism, combining genuine expertise in a restricted field of study with a talent for larger-scale philosophical synthesis and exposition.

In short, if we are to understand how science came to part company from the foundations of ethics, we need to focus attention on the history of scientific specialization. It was the development of specialization and professionalization that was responsible for excluding ethical issues from the foundations of science, and so, though inadvertently, destroyed most of the links between science and the foundations of ethics, as well. During the hundred or so years beginning around 1840, the concepts and methods, collective organization, and individual roles of science were progressively sharpened and defined, in ways designed to insulate truly "scientific" issues and investigations from all external distractions. So defined, the task of "positive science" was to reveal how and in what respects, regardless of whether we like them or not, discoverable regularities, connections, and mechanisms are manifest in, or responsible for, the phenomena of the natural world.

This "positive" program for science was sometimes associated, but was never identical, with the philosophy of scientific positivism. It rested on a number of significant assumptions, which are worth spelling out here.

A scientific picture of the world differs radically from a metaphysico-religious picture. The former is realistically confined to demonstrable facts about the natural world: the latter embeds those demonstrable facts within a larger conceptual system, structured according to prejudices that are (from the scientific standpoint) arbitrary, externally motivated, and presumably wish-fulfilling.

A realistic view of the natural world is one that is kept free of irrelevant preferences and evaluations, and so depicts Nature as it is, "whether we like it or not."

If scientific work is to be effectively organized and prosecuted, questions of "demonstrable fact" must be investigated quite separately from all arbitrary, external, wish-fulfilling notions. Only in this way can we carry forward the technical inquiries of science proper, without being sidetracked into fruitless and inconclusive debates about rival values or *Weltanschauungen* to which individual scientists may happen (like anyone else) to be attracted for personal reasons, external to science, but which are not part of the collective agenda of science.

Thus, the deeper reasons for defining the scope and procedures of the special sciences in ways that keep ethical issues out of their foundations were connected with the basic methodological program of the modern scientific movement. In particular, they reflect the steps which have been taken over the last 100 years to give institutional expression to the maxims and ambitions of the founders of the Royal Society, through the professionalization of the scientific enterprise. Given the care and effort that the community of professional scientists has taken in this way to insulate the foundations of science from ethics, we should not therefore be surprised if they have made it that much the harder to preserve clear and significant connections between science and the foundations of ethics, as well.

Philosophical Justifications for Separating Ethics and Science

My argument* is aimed at showing how natural scientists worked to keep ethical considerations and preferences from operating within "the foundations of science"; so that, for instance, the tests for deciding whether one scientific theory or concept was "better" or "worse" than its rivals, from the scientific point of view, should be wholly divorced from issues about what was ethically "better" or "worse." It was a matter of great importance for scientists to be able to make the choice between alternative theories or concepts turn solely on "objective" or "factual"

---

*Against this background, it will be easier to analyze and deal with the points of difference between my own position in this paper and Loren Graham's, as presented in his commentary on my argument. For Professor Graham claims to find a far livelier and healthier interaction between science and ethics during the last hundred years than I here allow. Yet on closer examination (I believe) even his best and most carefully expanded example—that of the English astrophysicist and cosmologist, A.S. Eddington—will be found to support my conclusion.

considerations: they hoped to avoid having to face the question whether one theory or concept is morally preferable to, or more objectionable than, rival theories or concepts. (Can this divorce be preserved absolutely in psychiatry, for example? May it not be legitimate to raise moral objections to one or another theoretical formulation in the psychiatric field? Leaving aside all questions about their other rights and wrongs, we may still approve of Thomas Szasz's arguments for simply raising that issue.)

That kind of value neutrality is, of course, quite compatible with particular scientists adopting all sorts of ethical views and positions on their own responsibility. It is even compatible with one rather more general, collective view: namely, that we must begin by drawing a sharp line between matters of pure or real science and matters of applied science or—more precisely—of technology, after which it will become clear that questions of ethical desirability can arise only in the latter, technological area. (To put it crudely, anatomy is value-free, clinical medicine value-laden.) Above all, it is compatible with all sorts of philosophical discussions, as professional scientists seek to rationalize or justify their particular ethical positions, and square their personal views about ethics with their scientific interests and methodologies.

That is what seems to me to be happening in most of the cases that Loren Graham discusses in his commentary (see pp. 70–72). His exemplary scientists are not people who went out of their way to bring ethical considerations into their scientific work, to the detriment of the intellectual detachment at which professional scientists had aimed for so long. Rather, they were people with idiosyncratic views about the philosophical relevance of science to ethics, and vice versa. And, interestingly enough, several of them are people whose philosophical positions are ones that justify divorcing science from other realms of experience.

In this respect, Arthur Eddington in Britain resembles Pierre Duhem in France. Duhem combined a scientific expertise in the field of thermodynamics with a religious commitment to Roman Catholicism. He was anxious not merely to avoid, but actually to prevent, any conflict between those two parts of his thinking. So, he adopted early in his career a "phenomenalist" attitude toward scientific theories and ideas. In his view, it is not the business of scientists to aim at discovering the nature of reality, but only to formulate mathematical schematisms capable in practice of "saving the phenomena": this posture allowed him to reserve questions about reality to the pronouncements of the metaphysicians and theologians. For instance: when J.J. Thomson first argued for the existence of "electrons" less than 1/1000 as massive as the lightest chemical atoms, Duhem was very scornful. To publish speculative arguments of that sort was to take the pretensions of the atomistic manner of talking far more seriously than they deserved. (Thermodynamics was, of course, almost totally "phenomenalistic" in its methods of analysis.) And he went on to pursue his learned and classic researches into the history of astronomy—researches whose motto might well have been, *Osiander was right.* Finally, he published an essay in which he made his underlying program entirely clear, with the revealing title, *Physique d'un Croyant*, or *The Physics of a Believer*.

Both Duhem and Eddington were thus seeking to provide philosophical justifications for keeping science and ethics, or science and theology, at arm's length. Far from their example refuting my position, it tends only to confirm it. Both of them were in this respect people of their time, armed with a program for defining and pursuing the proper work of science in separation from ethical or religious thought. If they differed from the majority of their colleagues of the time, it was only in being more than wholly devout in their personal commitments to Catholicism or Quakerism. But their other commitments played their part in other areas of their lives, not within their science. They were, in short, both professional scientists and also religiously devout; not "religiously devout" in their actual ways of thinking about scientific issues. And, if that is a correct diagnosis, they were concerned to scrutinize the relations between science and ethics only for the sake of keeping them more securely apart.

The Limits of Positivism

In our own day, the accumulated successes of the "positive" methodology have carried science—and scientists—up against the limits of that program's validity, and in some places across them. As a preparation for answering my central question—"How can we set about reconnecting the sciences with the foundations of ethics?''—I can usefully begin by identifying certain points at which, during the last few years, the location of those limits has become apparent.

> To begin with, the positive program for science normally took for granted a sentimental view of ethics: this was used to justify excluding ethics—which was assumed to deal with labile and subjective matters of taste or feeling—from the systematic investigation of "demonstrable facts." It was assumed, in other words, that human values, valuations and preferences have no place within the world of nature that is the scientist's object of study.

During the twentieth century, by contrast, science has expanded into the realms of physiology and psychology, and in so doing has shown the limits of that assumption. As physiology and psychology have succeeded in securing their own positions as sciences, human beings have ceased to be onlookers contemplating a natural world to which they themselves are foreign and have become parts of (or participants within) that world. As a result, the makeup, operations, and activities of human beings themselves have become legitimate issues for scientific investigation. At the very least, the biochemical and physiological preconditions of *normal* functioning, and so of *good* health, can accordingly be discussed nowadays as problems for science, as well as for ethics.* With this crucial incursion by science into the foundations of ethics, we can recognize that not all *human* evaluations must necessarily be regarded, from the scientific point of view, as *irrelevant* evaluations. On the contrary, some of the processes and phenomena studied by natural sciences carry with them certain immediate evaluative implications for the "good and

---

*Notice, in this connection, John Stuart Mill's remark early on in *Utilitarianism* about the "goodness" of health. Health is in fact, for Mill, one of those paradigmatic "goods" about which utilitarian questions do not have to arise: it is "desirable," just because there would be something clearly paradoxical about people's not "desiring" it. (It should not have to be underlined that Mill was *not* committing G.E. Moore's "naturalistic fallacy" by this association of the "desirable" with "what is actually desired": on the contrary, what Mill sees is that any ethical system must rest on the existence of *some* things that anybody *may be presumed to* regard as "desirable," since they are the prerequisites—like health—for all other potentially "good" human experiences.)

ill" of human life. With this example before us, we are ready to take the first step in the direction hinted at earlier in this paper: that of using the "rational objectivity" of science as a model for reestablishing the claims of moral objectivity, as well.

> Given the increasingly close involvement of basic science with its applications to human welfare, notably in the area of medical research, it is meanwhile becoming clear that the professional organization and priorities of scientific work can no longer be concerned *solely* with considerations of intellectual content and merit, as contrasted with the ethical acceptability and social value, either of the research process itself, or of its practical consequences.

The very existence of the bioethics movement generally, is one indication of this change. The work of the National Commission for the Protection of Human Subjects, and of institutional review boards to review research involving human subjects, is another.

This being the case, the doors between science and the foundations of ethics can no longer be kept bolted from the scientific side, as they were in the heyday of positive science. Neither the disciplinary aspects of the sciences, their basic concepts and intellectual methods, nor the professional aspects of scientific work, the collective organization of science, and its criteria of professional judgment, can ever again be insulated against the "extraneous and irrelevant" influence of ethics, values, and preferences.

On what conditions, then, can we set about reestablishing the frayed links between science and ethics?

1. We should not attempt to reestablish these links by reviving outworn styles of natural theology. The kind of syncretistic cosmology to be found in Teilhard de Chardin, for example, is no improvement on its predecessors: this is indeed an area in which "demonstrable facts" are in real danger of being obscured by a larger wish-fulfilling framework of theological fantasies.[10] Instead, we should embark on a critical scientific and philosophical reexamination of humanity's place in nature, with special reference to the use of such terms as "function" and "adaptation," by which the ethical aspects of our involvement in the natural world are too easily obscured.

2. We should not attempt to force the pace, and insist on

seeing ethical significance in all of science, let alone require that every piece of scientific investigation should have a demonstrable human relevance. Though the enthusiasms of the 1960s "counter-culture" were intelligible enough in their historical context, that would be going too far in the opposite direction, and would land us in worse trouble than the positivist program itself.[11] Instead, we should pay critical attention to the respects in which, and the points at which, ethical issues enter into the conduct of scientific work, including its immediate practical consequences. The ethical aspects of human experimentation, and of such enterprises as sex research, are only samples, from a much larger group of possible issues.

3. We should not see this renewed interaction between science and ethics as threatening, or justifying, any attack on the proper autonomy of scientists within their own specific professional domains. The recent debate about recombinant DNA research generated rhetoric of two contrary kinds: both from scientists who saw the whole affair as a pretext for outside interference in the proper affairs of the scientific professions, and from laypersons who genuinely believed that those affairs were being carried on irresponsibly.[12] Instead, we should reconsider, in a more selective way, just what the proper scope and limits of professional autonomy are, and at what points scientists cross the line separating legitimate professional issues from matters of proper public concern, whether political or ethical.

4. We should not suppose that renewing diplomatic relations between science and ethics will do anything to throw doubt on the virtues, duties, and obligations of the scientific role or station. During the last decade, the antiscientific excesses of the radicals have sometimes made it appear necessary to apologize for being a scientist; and, as a reaction against this radical rhetoric, some professional scientists have developed, in turn, a kind of resentful truculence toward public discussions about the ethical and political involvements of the scientific life. Instead, we need to set about understanding better, both how the line between the narrowly professional and broader social responsibilities of scientists runs in the collective sphere, and also how individual scientists can balance their obligations within the overall demands of a morally acceptable life, as between their chosen

professional roles as neurophysiologists, for example, and the other obligations to which they are subject in other capacities as citizens, colleagues, lovers, parents, religious believers, or whatever.

Renegotiating the Connection between
Science and Ethics

I have suggested that changes in the social and historical context of science could easily end the divorce of science from the foundations of ethics; and even that such changes may, already, in fact, be underway. There is indeed some evidence that this is already happening. During the last few years, the "purist" view of science—as a strictly autonomous intellectual enterprise, insulated against the influence of all merely human needs, wishes, and preferences—has lost its last shreds of plausibility. Whether we consider the basic concepts of the sciences, the collective enterprises of professional science, or the personal commitments and motivations of individual scientists, we can maintain a strictly value-free (or rather, ethics-free) position only by sticking arbitrarily to one extreme end of a long spectrum.

From that extreme point of view, the ideally scientific investigation would be a piece of strictly academic research on some application-proof project in theoretical physics, conducted by a friendless and stateless bachelor of independent means. There may have been a substantial body of science approximating this idea as recently as the 1880s and 1890s, but that is certainly not the case any longer. On the contrary, we can learn something about the foundations of ethics by reconsidering the character and content of the scientific enterprise on all three levels.

1. As a collective activity, any science is of significance for ethics on account of the ways in which it serves as an embodiment or exemplar of applied rationality. In this respect, the very objectivity of the goals at which scientists aim, both collectively and individually, provides us with the starting point for a counterattack against relativism and subjectivism in ethics, too; while the manner in which the sciences themselves, considered as "forms of life," define individual roles, with their own specific virtues, can

also be taken as a starting point for a much broader reconstruction of ethics.[13]

2. Correspondingly, the moral character of the scientist's personal motivation, particularly the way in which the Kantian "pure respect for rationality as such" grows out of the wider life of affect or "inclination"—what I have elsewhere called "the moral psychology of science"[14]—can teach us something about the nature of personal virtue and commitment in other areas of life as well.

3. Finally, the actual content of the sciences is at last contributing to a better understanding of the human locus within the natural world. This fact is well recognized in the physiological sciences, where the links betwen *normal* functioning and *good* health are comparatively unproblematic. But it is a matter of active dispute in several areas just at this time: for example, in the conflict over the relations between social psychology and sociobiology. And there are some other fields in which it should be the topic of much more active debate than it is: for example, in connection with the rivalry between psychotherapeutic and psychopharmacological modes of treatment in psychiatry.

This done, it should not be hard to indicate the points at which issues originating in the natural sciences can give rise to, and grow together with, evaluative issues—and not merely with issues that involve the values "intrinsic to" the scientific enterprise itself, but also larger human values of a more strictly ethical kind. For as we saw, the new phase of scientific development into which we are now moving requires us to reinsert human observers into the world of nature, so that we become not merely onlookers, but also participants in many of the natural phenomena and processes that are the subject matter of our scientific investigations. This is true across the whole spectrum of late twentieth-century science: all the way from quantum mechanics, where Heisenberg's Principle requires us to acknowledge the interdependence of the observer and the observed, to ecology, where the conduct of human beings is one crucial factor in any causal analysis of the condition of, say, Lake Erie, or to psychiatry, where the two-way interaction between the psychiatrist and his client is in sharp contrast to the one-way influence of nature on the human observer (but not *vice versa*) presupposed in classical nineteenth-century science.[15]

One likely outcome of this novel phase of science could well be the revival of interest in quasi-Stoic systems of ethics and philosophy, not to say, natural theology. The purist, or positivist, conception of science discussed earlier has a certain significant analogy with the Epicurean philosophy of late antiquity: both attempted to justify equanimity, or *ataraxia*, by pointing to the essential indifference ("value neutrality") of natural phenomena toward human affairs, and vice versa. By contrast, any improved understanding of the human locus *within* the natural world will presumably undercut this assumption of mutual indifference, and encourage people to move in a neo-Stoic direction—seeing human conduct as subject to ethical principles that must harmonize with the principles of the natural world.[16] Just as good health and physiological functioning are intrinsically linked together, so too human beings can presumably contribute to, or impair, the welfare of the natural ecosystems, or chains, within which they are links or elements.

Recognizing the interconnectedness of human conduct and natural phenomena may not by itself, of course, determine the direction in which those interconnections should point us. Acknowledging the need to establish some harmony between human conduct and natural processes is one thing: agreeing on what constitutes such a harmony is another, harder task. There was, for instance, a disagreement between Thomas Henry Huxley and his grandson, Julian, about the relations between human ethics and organic evolution.[17] (T.H. saw it a basic human obligation to fight against the cruelty and destructiveness of natural selection, whereas Julian saw the direction of human progress as a simple continuation of the direction of organic evolution.) What both Huxleys agreed about, however, was the need to see human ethics as having a place in the world of nature, and to arrive at a rational understanding of what that is.

It was with this need in mind that I referred, at the outset, to such concepts as function and adaptation as requiring particular scrutiny at the present time. For the question, "What is the true *function* of human beings?", is potentially as much a topic of debate today as it was in classical Athens, when Plato had Socrates raise it in the *Republic*. Likewise, the question, "How should our ways of acting change, in order to become *better adapted* to the novel situations in which we are finding ourselves?" is a question that also invites answers—sometimes, overly simple answers—based on a reading of contemporary biology and ecology. We are probably ripe for a revival of the organic theory of society and the state. And, though this is a topic that must be taken seriously, it is also one that is going to need to be handled with great caution and subtlety, if we are to avoid the crudely conservative emphases of earlier versions of the theory.[18] Starting from where we do, the answers we give to such questions will certainly need to be richer and more complex than those available in Plato's time; but, sharing Plato's questions, we are evidently back in a situation where our view of ethics and our view of nature are coming back together again.

To conclude: if there is one major field of discussion within which we should most urgently renegotiate the relations between the sciences and the foundations of ethics, that has to do with the concept of responsibility. There is a certain tension in all the sciences of human behavior at the present time, which I have discussed elsewhere under the heading of Townes's Paradox.[19] In thinking about the behavior of their research subjects, as objects of scientific study, psychologists and psychiatrists, neurophysiologists and the rest, are inclined to interpret their observations in a systematically *causal* manner. In thinking about their own behavior, as psychologists, psychiatrists, neurophysiologists or whatever, they are inclined to do so always in *rational* terms. They are prepared, that is, to take credit on their own behalf for a kind of rationality—a freedom to think, act, and write as they do for good reasons—that is missing from their accounts of the thoughts, actions, and expressions of their research subjects. And, since the human capacity to act "for good reasons" is a basic presupposition of all ethics (just as it is of any truly rational science) arriving at a satisfactory resolution of this tension between the causal and rational way of interpreting human conduct is a matter of some urgency, both for science and for the foundations of ethics.

NOTES

1. The point cannot be stated quite so crisply in French or German: Dworkin, at any rate, is certainly contributing to *Rechtswissenschaft*, or

les sciences du droit. But the differences in scope and sense between the English "science," French *science*, German *Wissenschaft*, Greek *episteme*, Arabic *'ilm* etc., provide too large and complex a topic to pursue here.

2. See, for instance, my paper, "Concepts of Function and Mechanism in Medicine and Medical Science," in *Evaluation and Explanation in the Biomedical Sciences*, ed. H.T. Engelhardt, Jr. and S.F. Spicker (Dordrecht: 1975), pp. 51-66.

3. See, for instance, my paper, "The Meaning of Professionalism," in *Knowledge, Value and Belief*, ed. H.T. Engelhardt, Jr. and Daniel Callahan, (Hastings-on-Hudson, N.Y.: The Hastings Center, 1977), pp.25ff.

4. Cf. Alasdair MacIntyre, "Objectivity in Morality and Objectivity in Science," in *Morals, Science, and Sociality*, ed. H.T. Engelhardt, Jr., and Daniel Callahan (Hastings-on-Hudson, N.Y.: The Hastings Center, 1978), pp. 21-39.

5. See, for instance, my paper, "The Moral Psychology of Science," in *Morals, Science and Sociality*, pp. 48-67.

6. Arthur Kantrowitz, "The Science Court Experiment: An Interim Report," *Science*, 193 (1976), pp. 653 ff.

7. Cf: John Ray, *The Wisdom of God*, which is an indispensable source for the early history of botanical and zoological systematics; Joseph Priestley, *Disquisitions concerning Spirit and Matter*; and Isaac Newton, particularly his *Four Letters to Richard Bentley*.

8. Charles Gillispie's fascinating book, *Genesis and Geology* (New York: Harper & Row, 1959), is the classic source for this episode in the relations between geological science and natural theology.

9. See Gillispie, *Genesis and Geology*.

10. I have discussed this topic at greater length in an article about Teilhard de Chardin in *Commentary*, 39 (1965), 50 ff.

11. See for instance, my paper, "The historical background to the anti-science movement," in *Civilization and Science*, a Ciba Foundation Symposium, Amsterdam, 1972, pp. 23-32.

12. Cf. the National Academy of Science report on recombinant DNA research in February 1977.

13. Cf. Alasdair MacIntyre, "Objectivity in Morality and Morality in Science," and his forthcoming book, *Beyond Virtue*.

14. Cf. Toulmin "The Moral Psychology of Science."

15. Cf. Karl Popper's striking arguments in *On Clouds and Clocks*, (St. Louis: Washington University, 1966.)

16. It is interesting to consider Arthur Koestler's scientific writings as a kind of neo-Stoic reaction against the supposed Epicureanism of behaviorist psychology, neo-Darwinist biology etc. See, e.g., his *Janus* (London and New York: 1978).

17. The contributions of both men to this topic are conveniently printed together in the book, *Evolution and Ethics 1893-1943* (London: 1947), which comprises T.H. Huxley's original Romanes Lecture together with Julian's subsequent Herbert Spencer lecture.

18. See, for instance, my paper, "Ethics and Social Functioning," in *Science, Ethics and Medicine*, ed. H.T. Engelhardt, Jr. and Daniel Callahan (Hastings-on-Hudson N.Y.: The Hastings Center, 1976), which discusses the role of physiological analogies in the writings of such social theorists as Emile Durkheim and Talcott Parsons.

19. See my paper on "Reasons and Causes," in *Explanation in the Behavioural Sciences*, R. Borger and F. Cioffi, eds. (Cambridge, England: 1970). Hans Jonas has recently drawn my attention to similar arguments in his own writings: see, e.g., *The Phenomenon of Life* (New York: 1966), pp. 124-25, and his earlier paper in *Social Research* 20 (1953).

Commentary

The Multiple Connections between Science and Ethics: Response to Stephen Toulmin

By Loren R. Graham

STEPHEN TOULMIN'S ATTEMPT to answer the question, "How can we reconnect the sciences with the foundations of ethics?" contains a great many observations with which I entirely agree. His belief that we have recently passed through a period (a generation or two) in which an extreme and historically conditioned effort was made to achieve a complete divorce between science and values is, in my opinion, correct. His observation (and prediction) that this era is now coming to an end, and will not soon be repeated, is supported by current controversies in many scientific fields. Equally helpful is his suggested alternative of a "series of spectra" to the "value-free" picture of science that has reigned in much of Western Europe and America in past decades.

He drew our attention to several points on these spectra which he thinks we should study more carefully, such as the scientific terms "function," "adaptation," the ethical aspects of human experimentation, the proper scope and limits of "professional autonomy," and the concept of "responsibility." Finally, Toulmin issued several crucial warnings about how *not* to go about the effort to investigate links between science and ethics: do not try to revive outworn styles of natural theology; do not engage in such examinations in order to attack or defend the professional autonomy of scientists within their own specific domains.

With all of the above points I am in agreement. And yet, I must admit that I am troubled by what I see as a striking discrepancy between the actual, historical interaction of science and ethical values during our century and the relationship which he described. Is the century described by Toulmin the one in which I have been living? While he sees few connections between science and ethics in past decades, I see a multiplicity of such contacts. Indeed, I maintain that the interaction of science and ethics has been particularly intense through this century and that, at the present moment, it is probably greater than at any time in history.

Part of the explanation of this paradox can be found in the distinction between ethics as an academic discipline and ethics as the principles of conduct of an individual or a group. Toulmin is undoubtedly correct when he says that ethics as an academic discipline has recently been little affected by science. He began his essay by referring to the works of John Rawls, Alan Donagan, and Ronald Dworkin; he correctly noted that these works give scant attention to science. It would be a mistake, however, to consider ethics only as an academic field; our dictionaries give us various definitions of "ethics," and several of the main definitions place ethics squarely in a broad social rather than a narrow academic context. An example would be "the rules of conduct recognized in respect to a particular class of human actions or a particular group, culture. . . ."

I maintain that within the framework of this definition of ethics there has been during recent decades a massive influence of science upon ethics and *vice versa*. If the leading academic writers on the foundations of ethics have not wrestled adequately with this vigorous interaction, then an appropriate response would be "Why not?" instead of "Why are there so few contacts between science and ethics?" Or, returning to Toulmin's essay, it seems to me that a more helpful title would be, "How can we analyze the existing connections between the sciences and the foundations of ethics?" The problem we face is not in creating connections that earlier did not exist, but in recognizing and interpreting connections that have been there all along.

Ideally, an analysis of the connections of science and ethics or values should be broad enough to include most of the interactions we have observed in the history of modern science. Only in that way can we hope to understand how science has influenced our values and how values have influenced science. It is true that by casting our net so widely we will include within our analysis instances in which the concepts of science are connected with ethics and values by processes of poor reasoning and bad logic, but if these historical events had actual effects, they must be considered in order to meet our goal of understanding how society has been affected by science-value interactions. We cannot dismiss these cases by maintaining that individual authors were guilty of committing the "naturalistic fallacy." Scientific theories have often interacted with ethical and value systems at moments when a rigorous philosophical examination might result in the conclusion that the interaction was illegitimate. But just as illegitimate children need to be taken seriously by those who conceive them, so also must the interactions of the supposedly aloof systems of science and values be taken seriously by those who wish to understand history.

Throughout the history of science a great many attempts have been made to draw conclusions about ethical or socio-political values on the basis of science, and these attempts have differed greatly in approach and in quality of argument. Without attempting to classify exhaustively all of these efforts, I would like to point to two distinctly different classes of arguments about the relationship of science and values which I will call Expansionism and Restrictionism.

The Expansionist Approach

By Expansionism I mean that type of argument which cites evidence within the body of scientific theories and findings which can supposedly be used, either directly or indirectly, to support conclusions about ethical, sociopolitical, or religious values. I call this approach Expansionism because its result is to expand the boundaries of science in such a way that they include, at least by implication, value questions. A historically well-known type of interpretation in this category is an "argument by design" for the existence of God; the architecture of the universe, the structure of organisms, or the form of individual organs may be cited as evidence for the existence of some sort of a Supreme Architect. Numerous examples could easily be given, from Newton to Paley. A critic of religion who argues in the opposite direction— as, say, Clemence Royer did in the introduction to her French translation of Darwin's *Origin of Species*—is also using an Expansionist approach, for evidence found in the body of science is brought to bear on value questions.

Within Expansionism several different types of subclasses of arguments exist, which I will not be able to discuss in detail here. I will merely mention that the linkage between science and values constructed by Expansionist authors can be either direct or indirect. A direct linkage is one where the science is supposed to relate to values in a way that is not merely by suggestion or implication, but in a logical, confirming or denying fashion. Charles Gillispie's *Genesis and Geology* contains much discussion of this sort of argument. If a person is a Biblical literalist who takes the Genesis story as factually true—or even merely its main assumption of a historically describable divine creation— then the sciences of geology and biology should speak to that person in a direct way. On a more sophisticated and contemporary level, psychological behaviorists who believe that values are environmentally formed and can be created and controlled at will—once science is refined—are clearly Expansionists who are making direct linkages between science and values. An example of such a linkage is this statement of B.F. Skinner's:

> When we say that a value judgement is a matter not of fact but of how someone feels about a fact, we are simply distinguishing between a thing and its reinforcing effect. . . . Reinforcing effects of things are the province of behavioral science, which to the extent that it is concerned with operant reinforcement, is a science of values.[1]

E.O. Wilson in his *Sociobiology* opened the door leading to direct Expansionist linkages when he called for a "biologicization of ethics" but one remarkable aspect of that book was that, by and large, Wilson did not walk through the door; he only opened it and pointed through it. The reason, however, that the fields of sociobiology and animal behavior have excited interest among the educated lay public is that the members of that public correctly see these academic fields as efforts to expand natural science further into at least a partial explanation of human behavior, including ethics.

Expansionist authors may belong to a second subclass, that of indirect linkages. These are people who do not try to bring a particular piece of scientific evidence into immediate logical relationship with values, but instead work indirectly with the instruments of analogy, simile or metaphor. Social Darwinists who made apologies for industrial capitalism by pointing to the analogy between the struggle for existence in the biological world and competition in the economic world were following the line of argument of indirect linkage within the Expansionist approach. So was Friedrich Engels when he pointed to similar dialectical laws in chemistry and economics in his *Anti-Dühring*. And the astronomer James Jeans playfully pursued a similar type of argument in his popular writings when he spoke of the "finger of God" that started the planets in their orbits.

The Restrictionist Approach

The logical alternative to Expansionism is Restrictionism, an approach that confines science to a particular realm or a particular methodology and leaves values outside its boundaries. Although there are many types of values other than religious ones, Restrictionism is best known in debates about religion; Restrictionists often say "science and religion cannot possibly conflict, because they talk about entirely different things."

A strict adherence to this approach would mean that the relationship of science to ethical, sociopolitical, and religious values is neutral. Science can be used to support neither human selfishness nor human altruism, nor can it affirm or deny either religious belief or atheism. Science is simply neutral with respect to values.

Returning now to the analysis of recent attitudes toward science-value interactions given by Stephen Toulmin, we see that the view of science that he described as the attempt "to choose the purest, the most intellectual, the most autonomous, and the least ethically implicated extreme" on the spectra of science-value interactions was simply an unusually vigorous Restric-tionism. Toulmin implies (and I agree) that the main error of this Restrictionism was not that it *never* is correct, but that it ignored almost everything that was happening at the other ends of the spectra, those topics in science, particularly in the biological and social sciences, where the basic concepts are irrevocably value-laden.

Before discussing why this view of science is now breaking down, I would like to examine one of its paradoxical features. As we have seen, strictly speaking, the adherence to Restrictionism that reigned in the thirties and forties should not have supported any particular value system, for it was based on the assumption that science and values belong to separate realms. But in order to understand the function of Restrictionism, we need to turn from abstract analysis to chronological and social analysis. Histor-ically, the Restrictionism of those decades had a considerable impact on values, for its actual function was to protect two systems of values: the professional values of scientists and the predominant nonscientific ethical and sociopolitical values of so-ciety. For if science and values could not interact, then scientists were safe from incursions by critics who tried to submit scientific ideas and the scientific profession to social criticism; and ethicists and spokesmen for political or religious values were safe from attempts by scientists to show the relevance of science for their concerns. With the realms of science and values effectively insu-lated from each other, the historical effect of this demarcation of boundaries was to support existing institutional expressions of positions on science and values. Since I am a supporter of the scientific enterprise and also believe that society cannot exist without value systems, I believe that at least some of the effects of this demarcation were positive, but I also agree with Toulmin that it was a temporary historical product based on assumptions no longer tenable. Indeed, the negative effects of this compro-mise are now increasingly clear.

Let us look briefly at one well-known scientist who wrote extensively in the middle of the period between the two world wars, the generation upon which Toulmin concentrated in his description of the "value-free" era of science. The great British astrophysicist Arthur Stanley Eddington supported Restrictionism strongly and yet, simultaneously, he found it a useful foundation on which to support existing social values. He was well aware of the naturalistic fallacy and—contrary to the opinions of several of his critics—he never tried to support religion directly with the findings of science. He wrote:

> I repudiate the idea of proving the distinctive beliefs of religion either from the data of physical science or by the methods of physical science.[2]

Eddington realized that to give scientific arguments in favor of ethics or religion was simultaneously to provide the theoretical base for scientific arguments pointed in the opposite direction. Thus, he affirmed that "The religious person may well be content that I have not offered him a God revealed by the quantum theory, and therefore liable to be swept away in the next scientific revolution."[3] Eddington found Restrictionism a source of great security, for it left his religious preferences undisturbed.

His motivation for relying on Restrictionism emerges in the following quotation:

> . . . If you want to fill a vessel with anything you must make it hollow. . . . Any of the young theoretical physicists of today will tell you that what he is dragging to light on the basis of all the phenomena that come within his province is a scheme of symbols connected by mathematical equations. . . . Now a skeleton scheme of symbols is hollow enough to hold anything. It can be— nay, it cries out to be—filled with something to transform it from skeleton into being, from shadow into actuality, from symbols into the interpretation of symbols.[4]

Eddington was trying to create a thirst in his readers for values derived from nonscientific realms, and he was accomplishing that purpose by maintaining that science was merely a system of symbols with no relevance to the major questions of human existence. Far too sophisticated and subtle a person to engage in proselytizing for his own religion of Quakerism, he nonetheless pointed out that "Quakerism in dispensing with creeds holds out a hand to the scientist." Eddington confined science to a small realm of man's concerns and he then invited his readers to fill the remaining space with value systems based on religion. We thus see that in Eddington's hands Restrictionism was turned in on itself and became a justification for certain kinds of values.

It is my opinion that Eddington is only one example of a number of writers on science during the twenties and thirties who found the principle that science is value-free useful in defending their own value preferences. If science tells us nothing about values, then every person is free to defend values without fearing that science will interfere. I should add, of course, that the use of the value-free principle in this "value-laden" way says nothing about the particular values being defended, because the principle could be used to justify any values at all. In historical reality, however, the principle tended to support societal values already dominant.

In his paper Toulmin tends to discount the relevance of people such as Eddington for an understanding of the relationship between science and values in the last generation or two. Eddington, he says, was a person "with idiosyncratic views about the philosophical relevance of science to ethics; and *vice versa.*" For the moment I will leave aside the fact that Eddington was probably the most influential and popular writer on physics (for the educated English-speaking public, not for professional philosophers) of the middle decades of this century, and I will agree with Toulmin that Eddington was indeed idiosyncratic. However, I think that the example of Eddington is still instructive for us in our effort to understand the relationship between science and values in recent generations. Eddington made explicit in a specific and idiosyncratic way the social relevance of Restrictionism that was, in a more general and less idiosyncratic fashion, widely accepted elsewhere. That view can be summarized as follows: if you insist that science and values do not mix, then the antecedent values of society are protected.

This position can be defended until that point in time when the relevance of new scientific knowledge to antecedent social values becomes so overwhelming that their separation becomes obviously artificial. After several generations of brave efforts to keep the two realms separate we have now reached that point of artificiality and the whole question of the relationship of science to values has to be raised anew.

I agree with Toulmin that a historical reconstruction or reinterpretation of the ways in which science came to part company with ethics "needs to focus attention on the history of scientific specialization." However, too narrow a concentration on professionalization and specialization could be misleading, for they are merely the *modes* by which science was separated from ethics, they are not the *reasons*, or, as a biologist might say, they do not reveal the "adaptive value" of the separation. Restrictionism (a term I prefer to "Separationism," since a pure separation was never possible) protected science, but not only science. Restrictionism also protected society by making its values imperturbable by science.

Links of Science to Values

The move toward Restrictionism came not because of specialization but because the relevance of science to values seemed to be changing in a way that made such protection desirable. In the eighteenth century, science could be rather easily used as an apologia or justification of the values most widely accepted in society at large. "Arguments by design" were essentially the employment of science for the buttressing of orthodox value positions. When this kind of argument was readily available and fairly persuasive, it was in the interests of scientists (natural philosophers) to advance such views in an explicit fashion. However, when science began to undermine existing values (for example, historical geology versus Creationism; Darwinian evolution versus *a priori* moral systems), the motivation for being explicit about links between science and values disappeared. Professional societies restricted their memberships increasingly to working scientists who avoided value questions because it was much safer that way. However, implicit links between science and values continued to pile up, as in some secret bank account, as science continued to develop. One day the dimensions of the reserve would demand discussion. Twentieth-century science moved heavily into the fields of behavioral psychology, human genetics, biomedicine, and ethology; the impossibility of keeping the links between science and values outside the concerns of scientists and their institutions became increasingly apparent. We now must reckon with the account that was gradually accumulated, as well as define our position on its future growth. Viewing the situation from this standpoint, I think the need is not so much to "reconnect" the links of science to values as it is to evaluate the links that have been multiplying for decades.

The exaggeration of the value-free nature of science which reigned in the interwar period (1918-39) had many causes, both intellectual and social, and a full analysis of them will not be possible here. One important intellectual stimulus, however, was the revolutionary developments in physics in the first thirty years of this century. Physics was seen in these decades as the science *par excellence*; when many scientists and philosophers talked about "science" they often meant "physics." And one of the important effects of the crisis in physics leading to the emergence of relativity theory was the stress on the extreme value-free and assumption-free end of the spectrum of science-value interactions that Toulmin described. Not only did most people agree, then and now, that the concepts of physics are far from value considerations, but even *within physics* the effect of the advent of relativity was to push thinkers back to the absolute minimum of assumptions about the natural world. Einstein had insisted that each physical quantity be defined as the result of certain operations of measurement, and he showed that by examining these operations more closely than anyone before had done a logical opening appeared through which a new concept of time, or simultaneity, could be drawn. Scientists and philosophers of science were understandably impressed by the fruitfulness of this approach, and a generation of writing followed in which physics was the major influence in the philosophy of science, driving it toward an analogous minimum of value-free assumptions.

Our more recent concerns about the relationship of science and values have been shaped by events in scientific disciplines on the other end of the spectra of science-value interactions, those where the connections between science and values seem unavoidable, probably intrinsic. Increasingly the attempt in the interwar years to build a value-free concept of science based on physics seems constricted, even quaint, to our ears. The areas of science that have treaded most closely on human values in the last decades are not ones in which quantitative approaches or measurement theory are crucially important. To take one example, the science of animal behavior, recognized by the award of Nobel Prizes to three of its leading practitioners in 1973, attempts to explain animal and human behavior in ways that have obvious value significance. What would Konrad Lorenz—who rarely made measurements, once boasted that he had never drawn a graph in his life, and found mathematics largely incomprehensible—say to the assertions of a number of scientists and philosophers of the interwar years that the division between scientific and extrascientific realms is the same as the cleavage between the metrical and the nonmetrical? And in other areas where science-value interactions are currently important, as in behavioral psychology, human genetics, neurophysiology, the concepts of philosophy of science, which came largely from physics, are not very helpful in solving our problems.

We are obviously now in a new era in our understanding of science-value relationships, and this new period brings with it both novel opportunities and novel dangers. We must live in the middle range of the science-value spectra, recognizing the erroneousness of the value-free conception of science so prevalent in the previous generation, and the equal erroneousness of the countering view that "all of science" is value-laden.

We now recognize more openly than before that at least some of the concepts of science, especially those of the social and behavioral sciences, contain value elements. We also know that scientific theories and findings in areas such as psychology, genetics, neurophysiology, and animal behavior can have important value effects. It seems, furthermore, increasingly likely that some of the aspects of human behavior that were previously assigned to the ethical realm are influenced by genetic and physiological bases. As we learn more about what sociobiologists and others have called the "emotive centers of the hypothalamic-limbic system" we will probably see more clearly that genetics and physiology are relevant to discussions of ethics. And as our knowledge of these areas increases, our power of intervention often grows.

In chronological terms the most dangerous period of the development of a science is when enough is known to advance the first fruitful speculations and to try a few interventions, but not enough is known to bring discipline to those speculations or to predict the possible side effects or aftereffects of intervention. When the science of human genetics first began to develop at the end of the nineteenth century and the first decades of the twentieth it was so inexact and contained so many flawed conceptions, such as beliefs in single-gene determination of behavioral and psychological characteristics, that it allowed room for a rash of pseudo-scientific eugenic theories and practices in which social and political prejudices played important roles. As we move into the newer areas of science-value interactions on the basis of such still fairly recent sciences as sociobiology a little conservatism about accepting all the claims advanced by advocates is entirely warranted.

As we learn that aspects of our behavior which earlier seemed to be based solely on nonscientific ethical values are actually conditioned genetically, we should be cautious about shifting the entire weight of our attention to that sort of explanation. Some important part of our ethical values may not be well-explained genetically, and these cultural aspects of ethics may play valuable roles of which we are still unaware. Just as we wish to preserve our genetic reserves, so we should preserve our cultural ones as well. Human beings are probably wiser than they know; *both* the genetic bases of their behavior *and* the cultural, ethical bases of their behavior have been selectively tested throughout the evolution of civilization. This cultural and biological evolution has been successful (in the sense of reproductive success and its surrogates), but its mechanisms are not fully understood.

Anthropologists tell us that the beliefs and superstitions of primitive peoples, at first glance irrational, often serve very practical goals in preserving the security of the particular primitive society although the society itself may not be aware of the value of their customs. Our traditional value systems, hopelessly nonscientific, may still work in some similar ways. Despite the injustices of contemporary civilization, it works fairly well, and we should not attempt to change its underlying assumptions in a wholesale way when we are operating on the basis of very partial scientific knowledge. There is an argument for gradualism even when irrationality is being replaced by rationality.

Perhaps a somewhat simple analogy will help a bit here. A grade-school child is often superb at riding a bicycle even though he or she knows nothing of the principles of physics that permit one to ride a bicycle and that govern what can be done with it. Later he or she may learn the necessary physics at school. If the youth would on some fine day decide to relearn how to ride a bicycle on a scientific basis, applying these principles, his riding would at first gain nothing, and he might even have a wreck. Accumulated experience is more important here than science. In a similar way, it is quite likely that some of the values necessary for the continuation of civilization were learned on a nonscientific basis and are now encased in nonscientific or even irrational beliefs; as we learn what the scientific explanations for some of these values and ethical systems are, we should be intelligently cautious about attempting a sudden new way of keeping our equilibrium. Indeed, we are so far from having a scientific explanation of ethics that genuine skepticism about a "biologicization of ethics" is warranted.

We have left behind the view that science is value-free. We recognize the links that exist between many areas of science and our values and ethics. We are ready to benefit from the insights that science can bring to our understanding of these values. We know that we must live in the middle range of science-value interactions, seeing that the pure poles of "value-free science" and "science-free values" are diminishing in strength. But living on this particular slippery slope will require extreme caution. The major flaw in the view of the past generation described by Toulmin was to refuse to see where science was affected by values; we should guard against a possible future period in which we might fall into one of two possible different errors: the attempt to explain values exhaustively in terms of a science that is always incomplete, or the attempt to attack all science as being intrinsically value-laden.

Avoiding these extremes, much valuable work remains to be done. We need to examine the internal concepts of science, as Toulmin has suggested, to find how we might analyze the connections of the sciences with the foundations of ethics. We need to study more thoroughly the importance of genetic evolution for understanding our social behavior. We also need to re-examine the history of science to see where science-value interactions have occurred with important social effects, even though some of the concepts were, from our present point of view, faulty (the history of eugenics, the attempts to link quantum mechanical indeterminacy with concepts of free will, the relationship between Marxism and science, the relationship between religion and science). And of course we need to explore the ethical dimensions of present scientific research procedures and technological practices. By pursuing these different approaches we will learn much more about the great variety of ways in which science and values can interact.

NOTES

1. B.F. Skinner, *Beyond Freedom and Dignity* (New York: Alfred A. Knopf, 1971), p. 104.

2. A.S. Eddington, *The Nature of the Physical World* (Cambridge: Cambridge University Press, 1928), p. 333.

3. Eddington, *The Nature of the Physical World*, p. 353.

4. A.S. Eddington, *Science and Religion* (London: Friends Home Service Committee, 1931), pp. 9–10.

Science and Morality as Paradoxical Aspects of Reason

Gunther S. Stent

As RONALD GREEN POINTS OUT, the theme of "The Foundations of Ethics and Its Relationship to the Sciences" comprises a highly diverse set of issues and problems.[1] First, there are several different interpretations of the phrase "foundations of ethics." Second, under any one of these interpretations, there are several different senses in which these foundations can be said to be "related" to the sciences. The particular interpretation of "foundation that I address in this essay is that which, as Green mentioned, was explored by Kant, and which has most interested philosophers since Kant: the rational basis of morality. And the "relation" to the sciences that I address arises from the fact that the sciences too have a rational basis, i.e., from the joint grounding of morality and science in human reason. As I will claim here, the set of basic postulates about the world that reason intuits, and thanks to which it constructs reality from experience, is paradoxical. Consequently, because of their common paradoxical source, morality and science would be related via a fundamental resemblance: both are internally inconsistent (in addition to being mutually incompatible). These internal inconsistencies are not so grave that they prevent us from building a superficially coherent picture of reality for a rational conduct of everyday life. They become apparent only when scientists and philosophers

79

pursue the analysis of that picture to the bottom of the night. Then, once the analysis has proceeded far beyond a certain depth, basic incompatibilities or ambiguities come into view that cannot be resolved unless some fundamental, intuitive postulates about the world are altered. Such alterations may reintroduce "local" coherence, but making them has grave cognitive and affective consequences: they alienate man from the reality that he constructs in the service of everyday, sane human life.

Inconsistencies, or paradoxes, embedded in the rational foundations of science and ethics have certainly come to light in these Hastings Center Conferences. As for ethics, Alisdair MacIntyre found that it is characteristic of contemporary moral debates that they are unsettleable and interminable.[2] According to MacIntyre this state of affairs is due to the failure of our moral intuitions to form a coherent and consistent set. Hence moral philosophy cannot systematically and rationally articulate that set of intuitions as a whole. However, MacIntyre attributed this incoherence to a historical evolution of moral concepts, which has left us with a graveyard of disemboweled ideas, rather than attributing it, as I do in this essay, to the paradoxical nature of human reason. And as for science, in an essay "The Moral Psychology of Science" Stephen Toulmin illuminated the defects of the generally held notion that science is an objective exercise of pure reason whose judgments are free of moral considerations.[3] As Toulmin points out, science, being an activity of real persons driven by their affects, cannot, in fact, possess that quality. According to Hume, "reason is, and ought to be the slave of the passions." Hence the acceptability of scientific arguments depends not so much on their intrinsic intellectual merits as on their capacity to move the audience to which they are addressed. That capacity to move is, in turn, dependent on factors extrinsic to the arguments, such as the historical and sociological context in which they are produced and the moral psychology of individual scientists. And, in considering the nature of that moral psychology, Toulmin observes that, "when we ask ourselves what there is in Science for scientists, it is not enough to answer—whether ingenuously or disingenuously—Why—Truth and Rationality, of course." No, to answer that question one must resort to the techniques of psychoanalysis and probe the depth of the subconscious. What one is likely to find there is not so clear, but Toulmin thinks that of the motivational infrastructure of the scientist, love of truth and rationality can have only a small part. Hence Toulmin's paper presented us with a paradox. Although the generally held notion of science as a wholly rational search for truth, in which truth itself provides also the main value, appears to be what Toulmin calls "a pious fraud," it is at the same time an *essential* fraud. For the belief in the objective, purely truth-seeking character of scientific judgments, on which no moral consideraions are to be brought to bear, is so integral a part of the very concept of science that without it science would not be science. Accordingly, a person standing in a laboratory dressed in a white coat and doing experiments directed to the understanding of nature would not *be* a scientist unless he *thought* that his judgments were uncontaminated by moral considerations. It is generally recognized, of course, that there have been cases—particularly in biology—in which the acceptability of arguments about nature *was* clearly influenced by moral considerations, but to keep the faith such cases have to be seen as pathological exceptions that prove the rule.[4] Thus to accept the general validity of Toulmin's proposition would be tantamount to admitting that the unavoidably contaminating influence of moral affects makes science an impossible pipe dream.

Another example of a troublesome foundational inconsistency emerged from Gerald Dworkin's essay "Moral Autonomy."[5] Dworkin's essay illuminated the defects of the view that the moral agent is autonomous. Dworkin points out that although this view is generally shared across the board by moral philosophers of otherwise most divergent views, it is difficult to see in what meaningful sense of "autonomy" morals can, in fact, be autonomous. If the concept of autonomy implies that each person is free to create or invent on his own any moral principles whatever, then autonomy is impossible on both empirical and conceptual grounds. On *empirical* grounds, it is clear that we are born into a given environment, with a given set of biological endowments. This fact, when considered in a scientific perspective, cannot help but lead to the conclusion that our moral principles are not freely invented, but subject to biological determination. On *conceptual* grounds, it is clear that the essentially interpersonal character of moral principles—what one person chooses to do depends upon his expectation of what other persons will do—requires a mutual congruence of moral principles that their free, individual invention would preclude. Thus, on both grounds it would, according to Dworkin, make "no more sense to suppose that we invent the moral law for ourselves than to suppose that we invent the language to speak for ourselves."

But the concept of autonomy is also not tenable if it implies, not the free invention of moral principles, but merely the personal choice to accept or reject an existing moral framework. For instance, Dworkin cites Sartre's exemplary story of a young man who must decide between joining the French Resistance and staying home with his aged mother. Contrary to Sartre's interpretation, the young man is not "obliged to invent the law for himself." Rather, he is faced with a tragic moral dilemma precisely because he is *not* free to reject either filial duty or patriotism as a binding moral principle: he is bound to both of them. Finally, what is left of the concept of autonomy is the notion that even if we are not free to choose our own moral principles, at least the moral judgments we make based on those principles are our own, freely arrived at on rational grounds. But this notion conflicts with another essential aspect of morality, namely the implicit belief in the possibility that moral judgments can be objectively correct or incorrect. As Dworkin points out, our view of morality demands that some inferences, such as "that Gandhi was a better person than Hitler" must be objectively true, independently of my will or decision. Accordingly, the belief in objectivity would lead to the conclusion that I am constrained by reason to arrive at a judgment that is not genuinely my own, but simply a logical consequence of my contextual situation. Furthermore, this last concept of autonomy conflicts also with the notion of moral obligation. For to act in accord with one's obligations means precisely to be limited in the scope of exercise of one's will. In particular, according to Dworkin, "from the temporal perspective, the commitments of my earlier self must bind (to some degree) my later self. It cannot always be open for the later self to renounce the commitments of an earlier self . . . . The difference between my earlier self and later selves is only quantitatively different from that between myself and others."

There is of course a good reason why the belief in moral autonomy (in Toulmin's terms, another "pious fraud") is so widely held: the very notion of morality seems indissolubly wedded to the notion of responsibility. Without responsibility, morals would not be morals. And the view of the moral agent as being responsible for his acts demands, in turn, that his judgments be his own, in the sense that he make a genuine choice. Thus to accept the general validity of Dworkin's critique of autonomy would be tantamount to admitting that the mutual incompatibility of its central concepts of autonomy, objectivity, and responsibility make also morality an impossible pipe dream.

To move beyond examples supplied by the Hastings Center Conferences, we may consider one of the most extensively discussed paradoxes encountered thus far in the pursuit of rationally constructed pictures of reality to the bottom of the night: the "complementarity" of alternate descriptions of quantum physical events. The notion of complementarity was first presented by Niels Bohr at the 1927 International Congress of Physics in Como. In that initial presentation, Bohr limited his attention to the attempt to harmonize the conflicting views taken by different physicists regarding recent developments in quantum physics. In later years, however, Bohr gradually extended the complementarity concept to a much wider domain, and it presently took on the character of a general theory on the nature of human knowledge, sometimes called the "Copenhagen Spirit."[6] Unfortunately, Bohr never published a well-developed application of complementarity to any problem outside of physics. Thus the working out of his broad epistemological critique still remains to be done, guided only by sketchy outlines provided by Bohr in his various lectures, in his correspondence, and in his recorded personal discussions. Under the eventual, full unfolding of the Copenhagen Spirit, the notion of complementarity came to comprise three related, yet significantly different aspects. The first and most readily understood of these aspects, to which I shall refer as the *instrumental* aspect, pertains to a limitation placed on our knowledge of the world arising from the unavoidable perturbation of any observed system by the observer. This aspect of complementarity, so Bohr realized, is of high antiquity, since it addresses the same "kind of epistemological problems with which thinkers like Buddha and Lao Tse have been already confronted, when trying to harmonize our position as spectators and actors in the great drama of existence."[7] The modern paradigmatic case of the instrumental aspect, however, is presented by Heisenberg's "Uncertainty Principle" of quantum mechanics (which states that because of the momentum exchange between an electron and the agency used to observe it, the product of the error of simultaneous measurements of its position and its momentum cannot be less than the value of Planck's constant). Later, Bohr extended the instrumental aspect of complementarity beyond quantum physics. He expressed the view that complementarity is likely to be encountered also in biology, where the necessity to kill an organism in order to study its finest details is bound to place a limitation on our understanding of life.[8] Similarly, in psychology, the fact that "mental content is invariably altered when attention is concentrated on any special feature of it" is bound to place a limitation on our understanding of the mind. The instrumental is the least controversial aspect of the Copenhagen Spirit. (It should be noted, however, that in his 1962 lecture, "Light and Life Revisited," Bohr acknowledged that meanwhile the success of molecular biology has transcended the instrumental limits on the understanding of life that he had foreseen thirty years earlier).[9] The validity of the instrumental aspect was granted by Einstein in his arguments with Bohr regarding the philosophical implications of quantum physics that began in 1927 and continued through the 1930s.[10]

What Einstein was not willing to grant, however, was the validity of the second aspect of complementarity, to which I shall refer as the *metaphysical* aspect. This second aspect goes beyond statements about the limits of observation and addresses the very essence of reality. Viewing reality from the metaphysical aspect of complementarity, standard quantum mechanics alleges that there is no such thing in the world as an electron with definite position and momentum. Moreover, the dynamics of an individual electron, if left to itself, are not subject to the conventional cause-effect chains with which we are familiar in the macroscopic world but are governed by intrinsically probabilistic, indeterminate laws. Einstein could not bring himself to accept this view, because of his unwillingness to grant that "God plays at dice." Accordingly, in his arguments with Bohr, Einstein conceived a series of hypothetical experiments designed to eliminate the metaphysical aspect (while allowing the instrumental aspect), but each of these experiments was in turn successfully refuted by Bohr. It may be noted that, in line with their bent for defining all deep metaphysical problems out of existence, the philosophers of logical positivism, such as Philipp Frank, tried to blow away the troublesome metaphysical aspect of complementarity. Frank claimed that the very notion of the "state" of an electron is merely the product of "idealistic philosophy," and maintained that "position" or "momentum" of a particle refer to nothing other than data gathered by particular types of experiments.[11] Accordingly, the concept of complementarity would be descriptive, neither of knowability, nor of reality, but merely of a relation between mutually exclusive observational arrangements. But since, as we shall see, belief in the existence of objects with characteristic states inheres in human reason, rather than being a mere figment of "idealistic philosophy," Frank's positivistic casuistry is hardly a satisfactory approach to the deep problems raised by Bohr.

The third and, in the context of a discussion of the relation of science and ethics, most relevant aspect of complementarity, transcends even considerations of the nature of reality and addresses the nature of human reason. This aspect, to which I shall refer as the *intuitional* aspect, revealed, according to Bohr, "hitherto unnoticed presuppositions in the rational use of the concepts on which the communication of experience rests." As far as science is concerned, Bohr pointed out that since its goal "is to augment and order our experience, every analysis of the conditions of human knowledge must rest on considerations of the character and scope of our means of communication. Our basis (of communication) is, of course, the language developed for orientation in our surroundings and for the organization of human communities. However, the increase of experience has repeatedly raised questions as to the sufficiency of concepts and ideas incorporated in daily language".[12] These concepts include the elementary dimensions of space, time, and mass, in terms of which scientists describe the events for which explanations are sought. As was pointed out by Kant, the meanings that these terms have for us are not inferred from experience; being intuitive, or a priori, they are brought to, rather than inferred from, experience. Accordingly, the models that modern science offers as explanations of reality are pictorial representations built on these a priori concepts. This procedure was eminently satisfactory as long as explanations were sought for phenomena that are commensurate with events that are the subject of our everyday experience (give or take a few orders of magnitude). But this situation began to change when, at the turn of the century, physics had progressed to the stage where problems could be studied involving either tiny subatomic or immense cosmic events on scales of time, space, and mass billions of times smaller or larger than those of our direct experience. Now, according to Bohr, "there arose difficulties of orienting ourselves in a domain of experience far from that to the description of which our means of expression are adapted."[13] For it turned out that the description in ordinary, everyday language of phenomena belonging to that transcendent domain leads to contradictions, or mutually incompatible pictures of reality. In order to resolve these contradictions, time, space, and mass have · to be denatured into generalized concepts by eliminating from them some hidden presuppositions, with the results that their meaning no longer matches that provided by intuition.

As Bohr repeatedly reminded him in their discussions, it was Einstein who had himself taken an earlier, giant step toward showing the inadequacy of the rational use of intuitive concepts.[10] Einstein had denatured the intuitive concept of time in his development of the special relativity theory, long before the Copenhagen Spirit had done the, to him unacceptable, violence to our intuitive notion of the existence of objects with characteristic states, governed by deterministic natural laws. For Einstein had discovered contradictions when applying the ordinary concept of time to objects moving with velocities close to the speed of light. These contradictions arose from the hidden presupposition in the rational use of the concept of time that the flow of time is absolute. So Einstein resolved these contradictions by eliminating that hidden presupposition and thus allowing a counterintuitive dependence of the relative time of occurrence of events on the frame of reference of their observer.

Probably the most profound example of the inconsistency of rational intuition to have surfaced thus far is Gödel's proof of the existence of undecidable propositions in the theory of numbers, and in any other axiomatic logical system of comparable or higher complexity. The notion of number is another fundamental intuitive concept that we bring to experience. Here, the hidden presuppositions, or axioms, underlying the rational use of the number concept are so subtle and complex that it took the work of some of the leading nineteenth-century mathematicians to uncover them and make them explicit. In any case, the concept of number served man well for his everyday affairs (and then some), just as did the concept of time, as long as he did not try to follow its implications too far. But once the scope of mathematical inquiry had transcended certain limits, it turned out that, when followed to the bottom of the night, the intuitive concept of number is unexpectedly open-ended. Whereas common sense would seem to demand that any proposition concerning a relation between numbers must be either true or false (just as it demands that an object is either here or there, or that two events either are or are not simultaneous, or, indeed, that a moral judgment is either correct or incorrect) Gödel demonstrated the counterintuitive, paradoxical existence of propositions beyond truth and falsity.

In the late 1920s, at the very time that the inadequacy of our intuitive epistemological concepts for dealing with phenomena dimensionally remote from everyday experience came to be recognized by Bohr, the process by which these concepts arise in our minds in the first place came under study by Jean Piaget. For Kant's claim that these concepts are a priori, and hence immanent in human reason, does not necessarily mean that they are already present, full blown, at birth. On the contrary, according to Piaget, they are *not* present at birth and are built up only gradually during childhood as the result of an orderly process of "genetic epistemology." This process of gradual construction of the elements of rational thought passes through a series of clearly recognizable stages and depends on the sensory-motor interactions of the child with its environment. Thus at an early stage the child first builds elementary forms of concrete classificatory and relational systems, such as the notion of an object with a characteristic state, which at a yet earlier stage it still lacks. That is to say, the very young child does not yet attribute constant size, or even identity, to the objects of its surroundings. It is out of such concrete notions that the more abstract linguistic, logical, and mathematical modes of thought later develop. For instance, Piaget found that before the child can use words to refer to definite objects, or have access to the concept of number, it must first build the notion of invariance.[14]

As far as the abstract Kantian categories of space and time are concerned, Piaget found that they take on their mature form at a relatively late stage. Prior to that stage the child's ability to make purely temporal or purely spatial judgements is quite rudimentary, since the notions of time and space still appear to be intertwined. The importance of Piaget's work for this discussion lies in his empirical demonstration that our epistemological concepts arise autonomously during the early childhood of every normal human being, as a result of a dialectic between the developing nervous system and the physical world. These concepts are not, therefore, the products of culture, let alone of the teachings of idealistic philosophy. They are, instead, truly intuitive; constructing them is what it means to grow up into a sane human being.

But the scientific approach to the world, by means of which we construct and seek to understand a reality of objects governed by causal relations, is only one of two aspects of the global, intuitive ideology by means of which we structure our experience. The other aspect is the ethical approach, by means of which we construct and seek to provide norms for the interpersonal relations of a reality of human subjects. This global ideology with its twin aspects has found a variety of concrete realizations, some religious, some secular, in various cultures. In many, or even most of these realizations, however, the distinction between the scientific and ethical approaches is either not recognized or expressly denied. The failure to make this distinction has the virtue of permitting a global ideology relatively free of conflicts both within and between science and ethics. It has the drawback, however, of preventing the development of science as an autonomous intellectual activity and thus presents an insurmountable obstacle to getting very far toward understanding, and therefore gaining mastery over, the world of objects. In Western culture by contrast, the distinction between the two approaches has been emphasized since the time of the Greeks. It made possible the eventual flowering of science, and led to a version of the global ideology that is replete with unresolvable conflicts and contradictions. It appears to me that these conflicts and contradictions are one further instance of the paradoxes inhering in rationality. That is to say, in my view the intuitive notions underlying the ethical approach embody hidden presuppositions that lead to a picture of reality that is internally inconsistent as well as mutually incompatible with the picture built on the scientific approach.

Just as it took the work of the physicists and mathematicians to uncover the presuppositions hidden in our concepts of time, causality, and number, so it has taken the work of moral philosophers to explicate the presuppositions embedded in our concepts of morals. One of these fundamental presuppositions is the moral autonomy of persons illuminated by Dworkin's essay. And, as we saw, it is difficult to see just how our moral judgments can, in fact be autonomous, without conflicting with other essential presuppositions, such as objectivity and responsibility. Another presupposition flows from our intuitive concept of the good. Guided by the notion of the good, reason constructs the laws that are to govern judgments made by a freely willing, autonomous person. Unfortunately, moral philosophy has not yet advanced very far toward its central task of explicating the intuitive concept of the good. In that regard moral philosophy seems to lag behind mathematics and its successful explication of the central intuitive concept of number. But analysis of the rational consequences of the notion of the good has proceeded far enough to permit the recognition that when pursued to the bottom of the night the moral concepts that are to govern good will are found to lack consistency, just as do the concepts of science. Indeed, Bohr pointed to one well-known paradox of moral law as an example of complementarity in the domain of ethics: "Though the closest possible combination of justice and charity presents a common goal in all cultures, it must be recognized that any occasion which calls for the strict application of law has not room for the display of charity, and that, conversely, benevolence and compassion may conflict with all ideas of justice."[15]

According to Isaiah Berlin, it was Machiavelli who first drew attention to the inconsistent character of our moral intuition.[16] Berlin sees as the central message of *The Prince* Machiavelli's discovery that we are beholden to two fundamentally different sets of values, of which Berlin calls one "Platonic-Hebraic-Christian," and the other "pagan," that are incompatible not merely in practice but in principle. The Platonic-Hebraic-Christian morality intuits the existence of some single principle—an impersonal Nature, a cosmic purpose, a divine Creator—that not only regulates the course of the sun and the stars but also prescribes man's proper behavior. Thanks to that principle, the world—human society included—is a single intelligible structure. Hence reason can find, at least in principle, universally correct and final answers to questions of moral conduct (e.g., "Gandhi *was* a better person than Hitler"). Pagan morality, by contrast, does not envisage any universal principle as the ultimate source of moral law. Instead, its fundamental intuition is that human beings, by their nature, are made to live in communities, and that their communal purposes are the ultimate values from which the rest are derived. Here, there are no final and universally correct answers to moral questions, since the moral values on which these answers are based depend on the purpose and character of the *polis*, i.e., are contingently dependent. From this it would follow "that the belief that the correct, objectively valid solution to the question of how men should live can in principle be discovered is itself, in principle, not true".[17] But since reason does not seem to allow most of us to accept only one of these two fundamentally inconsistent approaches to moral values to the exclusion of the other—to choose either a good, virtuous, private life or a good, successful, social existence—we are faced with a lifelong dilemma. Thus Machiavelli would qualify as an early discoverer of the complementarity of moral intuition, for having shown that the City of God cannot be realized on earth, not because of human frailties or imperfections but because that City is meant to incorporate mutually incompatible goals, among which are not only Bohr's complementarity of justice and charity, but also the fundamentally antagonistic values of humility versus *virtú*, happiness versus knowledge, glory versus liberty, and magnificence versus sanctity. Berlin thinks that it is for broadcasting this spiritually subversive message that Machiavelli has appeared as Old Nick, the devil incarnate, to all those who have a dream, across the whole spectrum of Western religious, philosophical, and political thought.[18]

Further conflicts and contradictions arise when the presuppositions of the scientific and ethical approaches are examined jointly. As noted by Toulmin, the essential belief that science is objective and purely truth-seeking, uncontaminated by moral judgments, is vitiated by the fact that it is carried out by persons with moral affects. And as Kant recognized, our a priori attribution of freedom of will to the person appears to contradict our a priori attribution of causal necessity to nature. And since, as rational beings, we cannot abandon the idea of moral freedom any more than we can abandon the idea of scientific causal necessity, Kant concluded that this contradiction must be illusory. According to Kant, the contradiction vanishes once we realize that the relationship between the person and his action is fundamentally different when we think of the person either as a moral agent or as a natural object. Thus Kant anticipated the Copenhagen Spirit, in maintaining that apparently paradoxical attributes of a phenomenon arise merely from the differences in the viewpoints from which it is regarded. Thus Kant sees man unavoidably stuck with a dualistic global ideology. Under that ideology man must think of himself as existing simultaneously in two worlds: on the one hand, man, the scientist, is conscious of himself as a material object forming part of the causally determined events of the natural world; on the other hand, man, the moralist, is conscious of himself as an intelligent subject forming part of the world of thought that is independent of the laws of nature. As another forerunner of intuitional complementarity, Kant held that to ask which of these worlds is the "real" one is, indeed, to pose a genuine question, but one that lies beyond the capacity of human reason to answer. Thus Kant must be included among those who would alienate man from his reality; for however logically compelling philosophical dualism may be, it is hardly a serviceable world view in support of a sane, everyday life.

By way of an example of the troublesome consequences for everyday life of the dualistic philosophy, we may consider the radical criticism directed by Thomas S. Szasz against psychiatry.[19] Szasz argues that mental illnesses are not genuine diseases and that psychiatry is not a bona fide medical speciality. According to him, insanity is not attributable to "an abnormality or malfunctioning of [the] body. . . . Strictly speaking . . . disease and illness can affect only the body. Hence there can be no such thing as mental illness. The term 'mental illness' is a metaphor." At first it seems quite incredible that Szasz could claim that the abnormal behavioral symptoms associated with insanity do not derive from a malfunctioning of the body. Does he, a professor of psychiatry in the State University of New York, not know that complex aspects of human behavior are generated by an organ of the body called the brain, that the advances in neuroanatomy and neurophysiology of the past century have provided extensive insights into just how the brain manages to do its work, and that certain well-defined abnormalities or malfunctions of that organ produce behavioral abnormalities? For instance, there exist persons afflicted with periodic manias that are characterized by immoral behavior during the manic phase and hyper-moral (or guilt-ridden) behavior during the depressive phase.[20] Whereas the highly regular, endogenous (quasicircadian) two-or-three-day cycle of these manias is quite uninfluenced by the person's day-to-day experience, his psychotic symptoms disappear immediately upon treatment with lithium salts. It is, therefore, difficult to escape the conclusion that the rhythmic, insane, moral judgments of such persons are, in fact, attributable to an endogenous (neurophysiological) abnormality or malfunctioning of the body. I imagine that Szasz does know all this, but the moral implications of that knowledge are simply unacceptable. In fact, Szasz makes plain the philosophical source of his moral rejection of psychiatric practice by accusing Freud, whom he holds (falsely) responsible for creating the metaphor "mental illness" in the first place, of a "systematic strategy for reifying and personalizing pseudomedical labels, and for stigmatizing and depersonalizing persons." Szasz evidently holds to the dualistic doctrine that the person, the free and responsible moral agent, is not the body but an incorporeal self. And since the self belongs to the world of thought, behavioral abnormalities or deficits ordinarily associated with insanity cannot be bodily ills and hence are outside the realm of science. Thus, to treat insane people as if they were sick is, according to Szasz, to confuse medicine with morals: "Hence, if and insofar as it is deemed that 'mental patients' endanger society, society can, and ought to, protect itself from the 'mentally ill' in the same way it does from the 'mentally healthy'—that is by means of criminal law." Although Szasz's claim that scientifically established malfunctions of the brain cannot impair the quality of moral judgments appears ludicrous on empirical grounds, and common sense makes his recommendation to apply the criminal law indiscriminately to the insane seem a barbaric throwback to a prescientific age, it is not obvious how his argument is to be rejected on philosophical grounds. For once it is admitted that "abnormal" brain function can result in impaired moral judgments, it would be unreasonable to deny that "normal" brain function does not, in turn, have a determinative effect on moral judgments, albeit with a different outcome. That is to say, the sane would be no more free, and hence no more responsible, for their moral judgments than would be the insane.

At the outset of his studies of the ontogenetic development of our concepts on which the scientific approach to the world is based, Piaget also addressed the nature of the processes by which the child gains competence to make moral judgments.[21] In line with his notion that the child does not "learn" the fundamental epistemological concepts from experience, but rather constructs them as theories about the world that are tested and modified as a result of interaction with the surroundings, Piaget similarly views moral development, not as learned or socially conditioned behavior, but as a constructivist and interactional process. Thus the growth of moral competence is seen as an integral part of a general cognitive development, under which, from a relatively young age, an individual forms theories about morality that, like its scientific theories, are tested and become transformed. And, according to Piaget, just as is the case for the acquisition of general epistemological concepts, the growth of moral competence also passes through successive, clearly identifiable stages. Piaget recognized only two such stages, of which he designated the first (generally corresponding to ages three to eight and following a "premoral stage") as the *heteronomous* stage. During the heteronomous stage the child's morality is based on respect for adult authority. Piaget designated the second of the stages as the *autonomous* stage, during which the child's morality of unilateral respect becomes reorganized into a morality of cooperation and mutual respect.

After a long hiatus, Piaget's early studies on moral development were eventually resumed by L. Kohlberg, who extended the original two-stage system into a more finely differentiated six-stage system.[22] A number of cross-cultural studies based on these stage formulations have found a very similar sequence of moral development in the most diverse social settings. Although the rates and extent of development were seen to vary in different cultures, the sequential ontogenetic transition from one stage to the next was found to be generally invariant. It would appear, therefore, that there is indeed some innate directionality in human moral development.

Both Piaget and Kohlberg viewed the development of the capacity for making moral judgments as a specialization of a more general capacity to make nonmoral judgments. As an early step in this judgmental process there is the appearance of the child's ability to act in conformity with the social conventions of its surroundings. And this ability is thought to mature only later into a state of autonomous and principled moral reasoning. Full-blown moral maturity would finally be reached when the demands of justice have come to weigh more than the demands of social convention. More recent studies by E. Turiel suggest, however, that the capacity for moral judgments does *not* arise ontogenetically out of a respect for authority-imposed social convention.[23] This conclusion stands to reason, since moral judgments are not, in fact, specializations or refinements of the appreciation of social conventions. Instead, there is a fundamental difference: moral judgments are based on factors intrinsic to actions, whereas social conventions refer to the relation of actions to explicit (or implicit) regulations. As Turiel has found, very young children are already capable of distinguishing these two, basically different types of normative prescriptions. For instance, by recognizing the physical harm and pain caused to one child hit by another child, four- to five-year-old children are able to judge this act as a moral transgression, quite in the absence of any culture-specific information. By contrast, the judgment as transgressions of talking out of turn or of not gathering up one's toys is tied to the awareness of the existence of certain social regulations. Maturing humans are able to make the fundamental distinction between moral and social-conventional judgments across all developmental levels, from preschool age through adolescence to young adulthood. Thus Piaget's autonomous stage would not be a successor to the heteronomous stage; instead both "stages" would develop in parallel, ontogenetic progress in both being reflected in an increase of the sublety and logical coherence with which both types of judgments can be made. In any case, these findings lend support to the view implied by Kantian moral philosophy that our ethical approach to the world reflects a biological given, rather than a contingent product of social or philosophical convention. Hence moral principles are immanent in reason, and constructing them is what it means to grow up into a sane human adult.

How can these paradoxes arising from the intuitionally complementary aspects of human reason be resolved? As Bohr had realized, for this purpose we may look to Far Eastern philosophy, and in particular to its "Three Teachings" of Buddhism, Taoism, and Confucianism.[24] Evidently, the supposedly innate character of the notion of "object" and its immanence in "normal" human ontogeny notwithstanding, the Chinese managed to develop a global world view from which the troublesome separation of subject and object is largely absent. As conceived by the Three Teachings, the world is an organismic whole of which each person forms an inseparable part. Hence, being on their inside rather than on their outside, each person is thought to have as its birthright the potential power and insight (expressly denied by Kant) to penetrate things-in-themselves. This power to gain direct knowledge of reality derives from intuition, rather than logical reasoning or inference. Accordingly, knowledge of the world is not viewed as a cognitive grasp of a given structure of objective truths; rather it is an understanding of one's own mental states and an appreciation of one's inner feelings. Thus to gain sagehood is to know oneself; and with sagehood comes the knowledge of the Way, or *Tao*, that allows the person to harmonize itself constantly with an ever-enlarging network of relationships.

The belief in the superiority of intuition over logical reasoning and inference as instruments for the acquisition of knowledge caused Chinese science to take a course very different from that of Western science. Because Taoism, of the Three Teachings that are most interested in man's relation with Nature and hence the main intellectual fountainhead of Chinese science, regards the workings of nature as inscrutable for the theoretical intellect and lacks the (Babylonian) concept of natural law, Chinese science developed along mainly empirical lines. This empirical development was slow but steady, and by Renaissance times Chinese science and the technology it inspired were considerably more advanced than anything that had been achieved in the West. But lacking the spiritual incentive to integrate its empirical discoveries, Chinese science remained an intellectually fragmented enterprise. By contrast, Western science began its meteoric rise, leaving Chinese science far behind, with Galileo's discovery that models built on mathematically expressible natural laws can give a workable account of reality. As it turned out, contrary to the Taoist doctrine, the workings of nature are not all *that* inscrutable for the intellect. Provided that the questions one asks of nature are not too deep, satisfactory answers can often be found. Difficulties arise only when, as Bohr had noted, the questions become too deep and their answers are no longer fully consonant with some of our intuitive concepts of reality. So Taoism, though wrong in the short run, turned out to be right in the long run. According to Joseph Needham, "with their appreciation of relativism and the subtlety and immensity of the universe [the Chinese] were groping after an Einsteinian world-picture without having laid the foundations for a Newtonian one."[25] For that Chinese science, Toulmin's exposition of the paradox generated by the "moral psychology of science" has no relevance. In Chinese science the role of reason is not even that of "a slave of the passions"; reason is to be distrusted as an obstacle to getting to know the Way. And on that Way, there are no objective truths to be found. So Chinese science cannot be based on the "pious fraud" of love of truth and rationality that underlies Western science.

And just as the Three Teachings have given rise to a fundamentally different form of science, so have they also engendered a view of the moral life that is very different from that of the

West.[26] Just as the Chinese tradition does not regard scientific knowledge as a corpus of objective truths, so does it not regard virtue as the capacity to make objectively correct moral judgments. Indeed moral behavior is not seen primarily as involving choice and responsibility at all, since the (normative) Way to social harmony is not thought of as having any crossroads. One may start and stop along the Way, or even deviate from it, but there are no alternative directions open to choice. Therefore the central moral issue is not the responsibility of a man for deeds he has by his own free will chosen to perform, but the factual questions of whether a man is properly taught the Way and whether he has the desire to learn diligently.

Instead, since the good, or knowledge of the Way, is already within us, virtue derives from self-knowledge. Although existentially, human beings may not be what they ought to be, they can perfect themselves through self-cultivation. From this Far Eastern perspective the problem of "moral autonomy" considered by Dworkin is not in sight. Not only is the concept of objectively correct moral judgments absent here, but so is its mutually incompatible notion of the autonomous moral agent. The self, far from representing an isolated and boxed-up individual, signifies a shareable commonality accessible to every member of the Family of Man. Hence the socially necessary congruence of the moral notions held by different persons, to which Dworkin draws attention, is made possible here by the self forming part of an organismic whole.

It is instructive to note in this connection how Dworkin, writing within the Western philosophical tradition, finally attempts to resolve the paradoxical character of moral autonomy. He points out that most of our judgments, in the moral as well as in the scientific sphere, are, in fact, based on the acceptance of the authority of other persons. Naturally, there are many good reasons why such a policy is rational, the benefits of a division of labor being foremost among them. And so what remains of the autonomy concept is that it corresponds merely to the right (but not, so far as I can make out from Dworkin's essay, the duty) of the moral agent to make occasional critical reflections on the goodness of the authority that he accepts. This limited notion of autonomy is a far cry from the view of the moral agent as a sovereign Lone Ranger who, west of the Pecos River, is a law unto himself, responsible only to God. But it permits, according to Dworkin, "one reasonable ideal of a moral life." It acknowledges that some of us may be better at moral reasoning than others, and, most importantly, admits the relevance of tradition to moral life. By opening the possibility of moral sagehood and reducing the role of choice in Everyman's morality to the occasional reflection on the goodness of the authority he accepts, Dworkin has moved well toward the concept of the Way and its reflection in tradition.

Finally we may consider the Far Eastern attempt to resolve the paradoxes inherent in human reason in the light of the findings of Piaget and his followers. How is it possible for the Chinese to have groped for an "Einsteinian" (or, more appropriately, "Bohrian") world picture for more than two millennia and to hold the Confucian view of morality, when, according to the studies of developmental psychologists, the cognitive concepts on which the Newtonian universe of objects and the Kantian universe of morals are based arise "naturally" as products of normal human development? In order to resolve this quandary (without invoking an improbable hereditary divergence of the psychological structures of the Mongolian race) we may note that developmental studies usually take as their endpoint the cognitive status of young adults. But it is not excluded—indeed it seems likely—that genetic epistemology is a lifelong "natural" process. That is to say, the last developmental stages ordinarily considered by Piagetian research could be followed by yet later stages which entail a further "maturation" of the elements of rational thought. It is these later stages that would form the epistemological substratum of the Three Teachings and permit the attainment of sagehood in old age. Seen in this light, the rise of Chinese philosophy would appear as an acceleration of cognitive development engendered by cultural evolution. Thus, in the philosophically more highly evolved Chinese cultural context, the "natural" stages and their concepts on which the Newtonian and Kantian universes are based would still arise during childhood. But the successor stages, which provide the foundations for the "Bohrian" and Confucian world pictures, develop at a much earlier physiological age than in less evolved human societies such as ours. This speedup of the biologically given developmental sequence takes some doing, however, as indicated by the arduous efforts of the inmates of Ch'an (or Zen) monasteries, and the rigorous mental discipline demanded by their masters. Apparently it is possible to achieve *satori*, i.e., to repress reason, after having already acquired it in childhood, and thus transcend the troublesome paradoxes of the human condition arising from rationality. But this precocious freedom from conflict appears to be bought at an unreasonably high price: the demolition of the foundations of ethics and the sciences.

Acknowledgement: I am indebted to Max Delbrück and Allen Wheelis for helpful comments on earlier drafts of this paper.

NOTES

1. R. M. Green. "Should We Return to Foundations?" This volume.
2. A. MacIntyre. "Why is the Search for the Foundations of Ethics so Frustrating?" This volume.
3. S. Toulmin, "The Moral Psychology of Science," in *Morals, Science and Sociality*, ed. H. T. Engelhardt, Jr. and D. Callahan (Hastings-on-Hudon, N.Y.: The Hastings Center, 1978). pp. 48-67.
4. The most recent such case is presented by the summary rejection of sociobiological arguments on the grounds that they could be used (or have already been used) to support immoral or nefarious social policies. Although on first sight this morally inspired put-down of sociobiology seems "unscientific," on second sight it actually *might* have some merit. In view of the evident impossibility of describing the social behavior of animals (not to speak of the social behavior of humans) without the use of terms, such as pain, hunger, aggression, queen, workers, courtship, slave, rival, or soldier, that connote functions, roles, and values, sociobiological propositions not only state what is the case but, *volens nolens*—the "naturalistic fallacy" notwithstanding—they imply also what ought to be the case. Hence, sociobiological work has an ethical content and is, therefore, open to criticism on moral grounds. That is not to say, however, that past antisociobiological criticism was necessarily legitimate. Cf. G. S. Stent, "You Can Take the Ethics Out of Altruism But You Can't Take the Altruism Out of Ethics," *Hastings Center Report*, December, 1977, pp. 33-36.
5. G. Dworkin, "Moral Autonomy," in *Morals, Science and Sociality*. pp. 156-71
6. N. Bohr. *Atomic Physics and Human Knowledge* (New York:

Science Editions, 1961). See also G. Holton, "The Roots of Complementarity," *Daedalus* 99 (1970): 1015-55.

7. N. Bohr, *Atomic Physics and Human Knowledge*, p. 20.

8. N. Bohr, "Light and Life," *Nature* 131 (1933): 421-23, 457-59. Also in N. Bohr. *Atomic Physics and Human Knowledge*, pp. 3-12.

9. N. Bohr, "Lighting and Life Revisited," in *Niels Bohr: Essays 1958-1962* (New York: Interscience, 1963), pp. 23-29.

10. N. Bohr, "Discussions With Einstein on Epistemological Problems in Atomic Physics," in *Albert Einstein Philosopher Scientist*, ed. P. A. Schilpp. (La Salle, Ill.: Open Court, 1949), p. 201-41. Also in N. Bohr, *Atomic Physics and Human Knowledge*, pp. 32-66.

11. P. Frank, "Philosophical Misinterpretations of the Quantum Theory," in *Modern Science and Its Philosophy*, ed. P. Frank (Cambridge, Mass: Harvard University Press, 1949), pp. 158-71.

12. N. Bohr, *Atomic Physics and Human Knowledge*, p. 88.

13. Ibid., p. 85.

14. J. Piaget and B. Inhelder. The Psychology of the Child. (New York: Basic Books, 1969).

15. N. Bohr, *Atomic Physics and Human Knowledge*, p. 81. Also, in his critique of the first draft of this paper Paul Ramsay stated that the justice-compassion paradox is only one of many "conflict-of-value" problems that "have various solutions within ethical analysis," short of admitting any inconsistency or "complementarity" of moral reason. One of these solutions, according to Ramsay, is a "hierarchy of values," and another is Rawls's "lexical ordering." These solutions are supposed to be applicable to specific conflict cases, in which it can be asked "which particular judgment overrides another, e.g., to save a life or to keep a promise?" But surely the demands of saving a life and keeping a promise (or of filial piety and patriotism, for that matter) are not in inherent logical conflict. Moral dilemmas arise from them only under particular circumstances (such as those that obtained for Sartre's young, would-be *résistant*). By contrast, the demands of seeing to it that justice is done and of compassion for the perpetrator of an injustice *are* in inherent logical conflict and produce inevitable rather than contingent moral dilemmas. That the practical (and morally desirable) result of the justice-compassion conflict may be, as Ramsay suggests, to keep justice "just" would merely add to rather than detract from its fundamentally paradoxical character.

16. I. Berlin, "The Question of Machiavelli," *New York Review of Books*, November 4, 1971, pp. 20-32. Berlin points out that Machiavelli has been traditionally misinterpreted from Ramsay's "conflict-of-value" perspective as justifying immoral acts—murder, lying, cheating—when required under exceptional circumstances for the good of the state. For,

so Machiavelli is falsely alleged to have reasoned, the survival of the state is necessarily paramount in the "hierarchy of values" because the state provides the indispensable institutional framework for all other values. However, according to Berlin, Machiavelli regarded the *raison d'état* as a system of moral values wholly separate from private morality and found otherwise heinous acts committed on its behalf as entirely moral.

17. Ibid., p. 28

18. In his oral comments on this paper, Alisdair MacIntyre stated that Machiavelli scholars generally reject (though have not troubled to refute in writing) Berlin's interpretation of the meaning of Machiavelli's texts. Rather, MacIntyre said, they find that Berlin has merely projected his own philosophical notions onto the pages of *The Prince*. But for the purpose of this essay it is not essential whether Berlin has or has not interpreted Machiavelli correctly. What *is* essential is whether the notions that Berlin attributes to Machiavelli are, as I believe them to be, meritorious in their own right. In any case, to me they do not seem to be all that different from the lack of coherence of moral intuitions that MacIntyre himself attributes to the graveyard of disemboweled ideas.

19. T. S. Szasz, "Mental Disease as a Metaphor," *Nature*, 242 (1973): 305-7.

20. F. A. Jenner, "Psychiatry, Biology and Morals," in *Morality as a Biological Phenomenon*, ed. G. S. Stent (Berlin: Dahlem Konferenzen, Abakon, 1978). pp. 141-69.

21. J. Piaget, *The Moral Judgment of the Child*. (Glencoe, Ill.: The Free Press, 1952).

22. L. Kohlberg, "Moral Stages and Moralization: the Cognitive-Developmental Approach," in *Moral Development and Behavior: Theory Research and Social Issues*, ed. T. Lickons (New York: Holt, Rinehart and Winston, 1976), pp. 31-53.

23. E. Turiel, "Distinct Conceptual and Developmental Domains: Social Convention and Morality," in *Nebraska Symposium on Motivation* (Lincoln, Nebraska: Nebraska University Press, 1979) vol. 25, pp. 77-116.

24. When, in 1947, Christian X made Bohr a Knight of the Royal Danish Order of the Elephant, Bohr designed for himself a coat of arms that bore the Taoist symbol of Ying and Yang as its central heraldic device and *Contraria Sunt Complementa* as its motto.

25. J. Needham. *The Grand Titration* (London: George Allen & Unwin, 1969), p. 311.

26. H. Fingarette. *Confucius–The Secular as Sacred*. (New York: Harper & Row, 1972).

Commentary

Stent's Moral Paradoxes: To Be Resolved or Deepened? Response to Gunther Stent

Paul Ramsey

"THE MAN WHO SEES the consistency in things is a wit," G.K. Chesterton once remarked; "the man who sees the inconsistency in things is a humorist." Gunther Stent, however, is a serious philosopher. To lay down a broad challenge to the views he presents would require an exact and exhaustive examination of his use of the words "paradox," "incompatible," "ambiguity," "inconsistency," "complementarity," "contradiction," "dilemma," "troublesome separation" (of subject and object), the "troublesome paradoxes of the human condition arising from rationality," even *alienation* from the reality we construct. A complete analysis would require an appraisal of whether Stent uses these terms and their cognates consistently, whether they are actually interchangeable terms, whether another meaning oɪ ordinary usage of one or another term is not to be preferred in some contexts, and in particular whether such terms can be ascribed the same meaning in the philosophy of morality as in the philosophy of science.

I shall not undertake that sort of fundamental response. To the point of our need to differentiate among these terms in meaning and usage, I remark only that Stent's chapter paradoxically falls in line with the centuries-old attempt to demonstrate the unity of the sciences, physical and moral. This unity used to be sought by reducing our moral knowledge to "scientific" knowledge, or by showing both physical and moral sciences to exhibit the same model, or way of knowing the world. Stent's view is a paradoxical form of the latter. My sole observation concerning his projected unitary interpretation of the physical and moral sciences is that such an achievement is unlikely, since it is a *prima facie* incredible to believe that our knowledge of morality can be found so far remote from ordinary experience as Stent describes this remoteness in physical science: "involving either tiny subatomic or immense cosmic events on scales of time, space and mass billions of times smaller or larger than those of our direct experience."

As an ethicist, my response is properly a limited one. I propose, first, to show that several of the data Stent adduces in support of deep contradictions in the nature of morality as we know it are conflicts that can be resolved, or admit of possible resolution. Then, secondly, I tack in the opposite direction to show that if Stent probed deeper still—to the borderline between morality and religion—he could find in human experience deep enough contradictions to be labeled "intuitional" complementarity, perhaps even "metaphysical" complementarity.

On the matter of resolution of some of Stent's moral paradoxes, four points are to be considered: (a) the supposed necessary conflict between personal autonomy and ethical principles that are known, true, and binding; (b) whether moralities in some areas may be incompatible without frontal contradiction; (c) the conflict betwen subject and object, participant and observer; and (d) the conflict between justice and compassion. I myself believe that many, indeed most, of Stent's moral dilemmas are resolvable. But a softer claim will do as well: one need only show that reputable philosophers, theologians, or moralists have proposed solutions in order to demonstrate that until each is dealt with in turn, Stent is too ready to find evidence for contradictions in the nature of moral reason itself; and that he is generalizing without sufficient reason from physical science and from the existence of undecidable propositions in the theory of numbers.

(a) What is the meaning of *genuine* choice, of one's judgments and actions being "one's own"? I suggest that Stent casts up a false alternative by his assumption that there is a necessary conflict between "one's own" personal choice and adherence to the right or the good. He casts up a false alternative between freedom and ethical objectivity or moral responsibility.

This grand canyon is dug by contradictions in the nature of moral reasoning itself. However, such incoherence in the demands of morality arises because, and only because, Stent assumes an arbitrary freedom to be the nature of true choice, choices that are one's own. An arbitrary freedom to choose to *invent* one's moral principles is, of course, incompatible with moral responsibility, or with any objective moral truths. In response, I must point out that such "modern prevailing notions of that freedom of will which is supposed to be essential to moral agency, virtue and vice, reward and punishment, praise and blame," Jonathan Edwards undertook to run out of the world— and for persons who have reason in exercise, rather succeeded in running it out of the world—in 1754.[1]

By an arbitrary freedom I mean a supposed freedom to act while having in that action a characterless, contextless freedom to have done otherwise had one chosen to do so. To perform gratuitous actions from a "freedom of indifference," without reason and unbounded by moral responsibility. Such notions of freedom are, indeed, prevalent, viz., in avant-garde medical and public policy discussions, among psychologists testifying in courts about a defendant's irresistible impulses, and in patients' rights movements—leading to suggestions that there are no limits to a patient's right to refuse treatment or for families to define death as they please, or of a woman's right to use the institutions of amniocentesis for the choice of the sex of a child she brings to birth. Such a freedom of autonomy does demand to invent moral principles, to choose the choice of bringing oneself under any moral framework, to deliver moral verdicts in unbounded freedom from the constraints of moral reason or one's past promises[2]—else (the claim is) moral agents have no power to make genuine choices and their choices are not their own.

Every ten years or so, some graduate student proposes to write yet another doctoral dissertation on free will and determinism. At the oral defense of these dissertations, I regularly present the author with the following verse:

Here's a question; if you can, sir,
Please supply a simple answer.
Was your novel dissertation
Product of predestination,
Result of native drive and knowledge
Effect of home and school and college?
Why, if so, should *you* have credit
Even though your name may head it?
Why not graduate some actor
Who died ere you became a factor?
If, however, no causation
Accounts in full for its creation,
Why should *you* be made a doctor,
And not some other don or proctor?

The answer is not simple. It may be "paradoxical." But it is certainly not "inconsistent" or "incoherent" to distinguish between compulsion and rational determination of the mind one way rather than another. The more convincing the reasons, the more a judgment or a science becomes one's own. The more we cannot choose otherwise than within a moral point of view—the more our moral judgments are based on principles deeply entrenched in the self—the more are these moral judgments one's own.

Suppose one holds, with Jonathan Edwards, that the will "*is* as *is* the last dictate of the understanding," or "*is* as *is* the greatest good apprehended," or "the greatest *apprehension* of the good" or "*is* as *is* the strongest motive to good."[3] On such a view there is room for a tradition of ethics. There is room for discourse about it. There is room for moral nurture. There is room for definitive influences—rational determinations—of every sort. A moral agent does not arbitrarily or out of the blue "autonomously" choose principles to live by. Yet his will, choices, and actions are truly "his own." He was not compelled—for example, by conventions learned from parental instruction; nor can he himself compel choice to come forth. If he wills in accord with moral nurture, or the contrary, his will is as is the last dictate of *his* understanding, *his* greatest apprehension of the good, *his* strongest motive to good. To cite one of Edwards' (dated?) illustrations: the more virtuous a woman is the more she cannot commit adultery. Her actions are continuously in accord with a "moral necessity," although there is no "natural necessity" (e.g., a chastity belt) preventing her. So my graduate students wrote their dissertations on free will and determinism; the works were their own, even though at the time of writing none would want to say that they *could* have thought otherwise with a "freedom of indifference" about the subject, out of an arbitrary freedom to think as they pleased.

It never occurs to Gunther Stent to allege that science is less a human enterprise if the human mind is determined by reality as known. He does not say that he is less a free thinker if he does not simply invent theories of his own without limitation by the world known and by the community of scientific discourse across time. Morality as a rule-governed enterprise, and the community of moral discourse, also do not allow the sort of "autonomy" Stent understands unavoidably to contradict moral responsibility.

The more *in character* our choices are—the more the commitments of an earlier self (in their *kind*) are among our present moral obligations—the more they are now our own; and all the more do we "own the covenants" (those that we entered and those which provided our moral upbringing) that are *our own* present determinations to the right and the good. Jacques Maritain wrote of "the freedom of autonomy" and a "freedom of fulfillment."[4] Whether his language is acceptable or not, it does seem to me that "autonomy" is not a moral notion or the presupposition of any, nor a reason to be given entrance into serious ethical or political discussion. If instead we spoke always of "liberty," we might better be able to see that there is no inconsistency or incoherence between moral obligation and a liberty of choice genuinely our own.

(b) The foregoing does not entail the claim that the whole of morality is a rule-governed activity in the sense that the principles governing one realm or role or relationship meshes with those of any other into a seamless robe or entire, ordered system. There may be moralities (or aspects of morality) that are indeed incompatible with other moralities (or aspects of morality). Still these incompatibilities need not be frontal contradictions or para-doxes, since the incompatibles may not *meet*. This is the conclu-sion Stent should draw, for example, from Isaiah Berlin's interpretation of Machiavelli; instead he casts up a contradiction. One sort of responsibility is that of a prince in his official capacity. Another is that of a private person. Both could be correct analyses of those responsibilities; then one decides whether to remain a private person or become a public person. There need be no rule governing such a choice. Still the morali-ties of the private and the public realm are only different, sepa-rate responsibilities.

While I do not happen to agree with this Machiavellian (and some say, Lutheran) solution, I see no contradiction or paradox in adopting different moralities governing realms or activities and responsibilities that *are* separate and different. The prince does not do wrong; he exercises the right statescraft when he acts in a fashion that would be wrong for anyone in a private capacity. Likewise, it would be wrong for any private person to act as if his vocation was that of a public official. The moralities arrive at no collision; they are separate or parallel, double-moralities. Max Weber made a similar distinction between an "ethics of respon-sibility" and an "ethics of absolute ends."[5]

The same can be said about Sartre's example of the mother-loving would-be resistance fighter. If that young man had any doubt about adhering to the proposition that Gandhi was a better man than Hitler, he was wrong. Sartre may have supposed that such a judgment would have to be invented autonomously, too. But then Sartre was an irrationalist, and cannot be called to testify about the chasms in the nature of moral reason itself. Instead, we should say that the more anyone finds it morally impossible to believe that Hitler was a better man than Gandhi the more he exercises both liberty and responsibility; all the more is this "his own" moral judgment and one he did not invent by a free-wheeling autonomy.

This, however, does not prevent us from allowing that not all aspects of morality are reducible to equally clear principles. No seamless robe need be thrown over the entire arena of morality, no more than over physical and moral science together. Nothing said so far requires us to say that the choice between caring for his needy mother and joining the resistance was a moral judgment of the same order as the one commensurating Hitler and Gandhi. Again—as with the prince—there are "vocations" or ideals of life that may be incompatible, but which do not count as contradictions or paradoxes for the simple reason that separate roles or relations are served.

One could say, of course, that the prince or the private person, or Sartre's young man, *choose the choice* of the role and relationship that he deems to be more important. We could say that in these cases the actor invents his responsibility. Even so, this does not seem to me to be accurate language. True, an observer can say that the actor could have done otherwise in those instances. It seems clear that anyone who claims to be able to do otherwise than adhere to the judgment that Gandhi was a better man than Hitler, and anyone who says that this judgment is a choice that needs to be chosen, thereby displays an amoral autonomy. But there is nothing immoral about public responsibility that is different from private duty. To do both would perhaps be to choose between incompatibles, but there is no *contradiction* involved in choice of one rather than the other. A responsible prince or Sartre's young man, whichever vocation is chosen, still would say that their moral judgment *is* as *is* the last dictate of their moral understanding, *is* as *is* their strongest motive to good, *is* as *is* their apprehension of the greatest good or their greatest apprehension of the good.

These can be called indeterminate decisions[6] about vocations or ideals of life, in contrast, on the one hand, to commensurate decisions in which choice is arrived at in areas of morality that are corrigible to meshed reasoning, overriding principles, and so on, and, on the other hand, to inventing one's choice quite arbitrarily. I shall return to this view—that moral reason discovers no seamless system, nor is flawed because it does not—when I tack in the direction of agreement with Stent; but not to agree that here moral reasoning runs into irresolvable contradictions. There is no contradiction between ideals of life that are quite separate and different. Instead, the difficulty lies in understanding how we do make reasonably defensible choices among different ideals of life.

(c) Another paradox or complementarity or contradiction in the very nature of human reason itself that Stent discovers is between the outlook of a participant and an observer. Stent's overall thesis is that "the scientific approach" and "the ethical approach" are "two aspects of the global, intuitive ideology by means of which we structure our experience." Morality and science are "related via a fundamental resemblance: both are internally inconsistent (in addition to being mutually incompatible)." The cleft palate, however, that produces the family resemblance is our failed attempt "to harmonize our position as spectators and actors in the great drama of existence." This is the chief flaw in the nature of rational consciousness itself. The flaw is generic to both global approaches; Stent names the deficit "intuitional" complementarity. An irremovable conflict between subject and object arises from using reason to know either the physical universe or the moral order. I make no comment on the instrumental, metaphysical, and intuitional complementarity or contradictions which, Stent believes, contemporary science has come upon.

Still his account of the conflict in moral reason between actor and observer, subject and object, seems overdone. If Stent means to find in moral reasoning an incurable breach between the positions of spectator and actor, I judge that he has been misled. He has mistaken the appearance of twentieth-century Anglo-American philosophical ethics (which all too often seems to be, or actually is, a "spectator sport") to be the reality. Indeed, one *can* ask of much recent moral philosophy whether it does not manifest the problem ethicists have in paradoxically trying to harmonize their position as *spectators* and as *actors* in the great drama of human existence, and in the moral history of humankind.

It was not always so, nor need be so. Recently, I have been reading the ethical writings of Frances Hutcheson,[7] who flourished in the first half of the eighteenth century, and who as much as any other author in that age accepted standards of rigor in ethical analysis, and on whom several subsequent, narrower schools (including utilitarian "computation") depended. His treatises are filled with astute ethical *analysis*. Shall we call this his position as a rational spectator of moral existence? At the same time, his treatises have their "use" or "application" (the third and final part of Puritan sermon-form) for self-examination, for moral nurture, and self-improvement. Judgments of approbation or esteem or of disapprobation and dislike were directed to all reasonable actors, the author himself included. I very much doubt that Hutcheson could have believed that one can be a good moral philosopher and a bad person.

Hutcheson's moral philosophy may be criticized, amended, or rejected for various reasons today. But his treatises are an example to show that in moral philosophy itself there need be no fundamental conflict between the positions of the spectator and of the actor. In an article directed to his fellow schoolmen, a leading contemporary American ethicist, William Frankena, writes that Hutcheson was not a "naturalist," not an "intuitionist" or "cognitivist" of any other sort, not a "subjectivist," not a "utilitarian," not an "emotivist," but was a "noncognitivist"[8] [i.e., he believed that with no more information than is drawn from the presence of malevolence or maleficence "out there" in others or in oneself, our "inner sensible" disapprobations are valid]. On these grounds Frankena recommends that his colleagues could learn a great deal from reading Hutcheson—with what more profit than the wisdom to know that moral wisdom did not arise with them, I do not know.

That is rather like recommending the reading of Plato to metaethicists or logical positivists who, in their talk intervening in all talk about morality, may have imagined that they first thought of the need to define one's terms, while failing to mention the fact that Plato proves also that one can define one's terms *while* doing political philosophy, perhaps better then. In the case of Hutcheson, Frankena does not mention the fact that all his treatises were also works for edification of moral agents. This is rather like recommending the Socratic dialogues without noticing the fact that in additon to positioning himself as a spectator of the indefensible assumptions of military generals, the pious, and so on, Socrates may well—and quite consistently without paradox— have aimed at cultivating a Socratic irony in the moral actors he confronted. There is some agent-"edification" in that thought, if I may once again use that St. Paulish expression. In sum, the notion that within moral philosophy there is a necessary inconsistency or paradox (*demanding* complementarity as a solution) between speculation and action seems to me to be false.

There need not be a yawning gap between the agent and the

spectator in moral knowledge. Moral philosophy has frequently, and not superficially, provided resolutions of this dilemma. We may need to draw the opposite conclusion when we follow moral reason itself driving on to the borderline between morality and religion.

Rational consciousness appears to be, in different ways, a crucial difficulty both for Richard Alexander and Gunther Stent, and peculiarly *problematic* for both. We could readily understand, with Alexander, how rational self-consciousness evolved for the survival of human organisms if the luminosity of that consciousness straightfowardly served the business of gene-proliferation. But how or why rational consciousness evolved to *suppress* that primary function into the secondary functions of human cultural enterprises remains a great mystery, even or especially in evolutionary terms.

From his scientific approach, Gunther Stent finds rational consciousness to be no less problematic, even if his view is in no measure reductive. From the very nature of human reason arise the paradoxes and contradictions he addresses. To both Alexander and Stent, in our interface discussions, a naive humanist or a sophisticated one as well could respond as follows: Rational consciousness is something all of us know better than we know anything else. We know ourselves more certainly than the objects or laws of any science—including sciences such as sociology and psychology that have sought, after the model of the physical sciences, to make rational consciousness an object of study. Anyone who asks the meaning of rational consciousness *eo ipso* misunderstands (as Kierkegaard said of sin). Rational self-consciousness may be an inexplicable mystery, but humankind is more mysterious without than with this deep mystery (to reword Pascal on the mystery of sin). Rational consciousness is, indeed, a mystery, not a problem that can be solved (to invoke Gabriel Marcel's distinction between a "mystery" and a "problem").

Therefore, I do not understand why Alexander and Stent continue to insist from the point of view of their sciences that rational consciousness is so problematic. Since this is inevitably who they are, why do they not come over to the side of personal consciousness—the actor, not the spectator, in Stent's terms—and enjoy it? Why do both in quite different fashion insist on projecting "solutions" from the side of natural science alone, or (in the case of Stent) predominantly? Here, I know, I simply state the hard requirements of interdisciplinarity. Still it is my opinion that humanists, including ethicists, have for decades sought to learn all they could about natural and biological sciences, and I have not noted an equal intellectual reciprocity from scientists.

Indeed, more than reciprocity is required, since rational consciousness is uniquely human, and the foundation of both science and morality. For this cause Kant assigned a primacy to reason in its practical employment (morality) as against reason in its pure employment (science). Kant's dualistic philosophy (which is to be rejected) was a consequence of his sturdy effort to insure that (as Stent rightly insists) science not be contaminated by moral considerations, while yet correctly holding to the primacy of practical reason. It is from this point of view that I say—and judge any human actor should say—that all sciences and their constructs are far stranger than the rational consciousness that produces them. The problem is not rational consciousness, but how and whether and with what degree of certitude we know anything *ad extra*. In a world of constructs, the constructor is least problematic. To speak anthropomorphically, it is the physical universe or the moral order that seem to be in difficulty—in disclosing their reality to us.

(d) Stent offers one specific example of moral contradiction, namely, the task of harmonizing justice and charity into a common or coherent goal. Following Bohr, he asserts that strict application of law has no room for displays of charity; and that, conversely, benevolence and compassion may conflict with *all* ideas of justice. This collision of opposite norms singularly proves, according to Stent, that when we "pursue to the bottom of the night the moral laws that govern the good will," these will be found "to lack coherence, just as do those of science."

In our discussions I suggested that many moral philosophers would undertake to resolve the justice/charity problem instead of fleeing to paradox. Resolution of the issue could be sought in any one of several ways of reasonably sorting out values in conflict. Someone who believes that justice and charity fall within the range of a definite hierarchy of commensurable objective values, or that they come under John Rawls's "lexical" ordering, will conclude that as a rule charity overrides justice, or justice overrides charity. It matters not which is the overriding value; a resolution is found on either of these views, and no one need cry paradox. Thus, I suggested that conflict-resolution should be undertaken in the case of justice and charity in a way to be compared with, say, conflict between the requirements to save life and to keep a promise.

Stent replied that saving life and keeping a promise are not in "inherent logical conflict"; these duties conflict only in contingent cases or particular circumstances. By this response, of course, Stent simply *reasserted* his view that justice and compassion do inherently conflict logically. This seemed to me no answer. In the instance of both sets of moral norms one needs *a case*: in the first instance, a perpetrator of some injury upon whom justice is to be visited or to whom charity should be extended; in the second instance, one needs a moral agent caught between conflicting claims to save a particular life or keep a particular promise.

In either case, ordinary ethical disagreement is about which claim is overriding. Then, if an ethicist concludes that saving life as a rule overrides keeping a promise, he does not abandon that proposed coherence if later he comes upon or is reminded that there are circumstances when keeping a particular promise is more important than saving life. Instead, an ethicist would ordinarily attach one or more feature-dependent "exceptions" to the ordered principles of conduct already laid down. Thus, medieval theologians who answered in the negative the question whether in shipwreck a wise man should ever take a plank away from an ignorant sailor, usually added: *unless* the man who will otherwise drown is a king! Against Stent's assertion and reassertion that justice and charity are in "inherent logical conflict," it seemed reasonable to me to deal with conflict between these values or claims in the same way moral philosophers go about resolving other value-conflicts.

There is another possible resolution that should be mentioned here, before taking up the one I proposed in our discussions. One need not believe that the hierarchically more important value—justice or charity—overrides the other. It is also reasonable to believe that justice is a universal requirement of everyone everywhere at all times, while charity is by contrast an electable "counsel of perfection." In both Jewish ethics,[9] and perhaps more extensively in Christian ethics, there has always been a place for "works of supererogation" going beyond but never contradicting justice, or what is commanded of everyone or naturally due to everyone. In philosophical ethics Urmson's essay "Saints and Heroes" expresses a similar outlook.[10] Here is another solution to be considered before resorting to ethical incoherence.

Since I understood Gunther Stent to be searching for a symmetrical, equipoised contradiction between justice and compassion in order to find in morality a family resemblance to the head-on contradictions he discerns to be the upshot of physical science, I asked him whether he would consider the possibility that charity and justice are asymmetrically related. This was to suggest an additional resolution of his sole specific moral paradox or contradiction. On this view, charity would be in tension with justice, it is true; but this would be a vital and morally significant tension, not a nonrational dilemma. According to this view, charity or compassion need never violate justice; still charity does more than go beyond justice in works of supererogation. Charity impinges on justice dialectically to perfect justice, to keep justice *just*, to sensitize all of us to what is truly due (just) to a fellow human being. In our world of toil, finitude, bias, and sin it is no small achievement to be just. Compassion, ideally enabling us to penetrate to the other person as he is, though a malefactor, is needed to keep our actions and attitudes entirely apt to his due (just), no less than to extend exceptional mercy. This point of view entails no flat contradiction or collision between charity and justice. It happens to be one of the major points of view in traditional Christian ethics in our perennial discussions of the relation between "love" and "justice."[11]

It is not for me to say whether I am Chesterton's wit of consistency or his humorist of inconsistency. Still I now take a different tack, and shall endeavor to deepen the antinomy Bohr and Stent discover *within morality* between justice and compassion until we reach the borderline between morality and religion. At this depth I believe we do discover a contradiction produced by moral reason that moral reason itself is unable to resolve. To expose the depth at which moral judgment leads to an antinomy to which specific religions alone give adequate answer, it will also be necessary to question the resolution suggested in (c) above to the agent/spectator problem in morality.

Upon further reflection on the paradox of justice and compassion, I rather think that both Stent and I were approaching this problem *within ethics* too much from the point of view of spectators of the moral life. This is a quite proper stress for philosophers and ethicists to make; and within that approach various solutions of moral conflicts are always possible. I argued that ethical systems most to be admired do not open a grand canyon between spectators and actors of the moral life. Still I want to grant that there is an evident tension within ethics, and a polarity (not a contradiction) according as the stress is placed on exploring moral questions "out there," as it were, and exploring moral questions in such reflexive fashion that the self is always implicated. The "existential" moment has been characteristic of past ethical analysis (the Bible, St. Augustine, Royce, and N. Hartman may be instanced), just as terms were defined by Plato and Aristotle while doing ethics and politics. It is the modern period alone that has allowed self-implication and speculative clarity to split apart. Still there does seem to be this tension or polarity of emphasis within ethics. It afflicts an ethics of "the virtues of the moral agent" no less than any other: moral character can be written speculatively about others or humanity in general or it can be probed to depths that are self-consciously self-implicating.

The above is background for saying that Stent's justice/charity problem is perhaps more incorrigible than I first thought. Various solutions have been mentioned that can be proposed when we are speculatively thinking about others or about the justice/charity problem in general. These may even be edifying discourses. Nevertheless, if we reflect about the justice/charity problem with a profound degree of self-implication it turns into the justice/forgiveness problem. I mean when that moral problem becomes fully "our own."

When we think of the justice that is *our* due, a justice that is fitting to our deserts for sins of omission and commission, a noncontradictory case for forgiveness is more difficult to make than in the solutions proposed above. So I want to say that Stent's evidence on this point may have more force than I first thought. These second thoughts come from having reread N. Hartmann's great work on axiology; and from following him not into the depth of the night but rather into the religious depths to which a profound understanding of morality necessarily penetrates, if it has not ceased to be self-implicating.

N. Hartmann discovers a plethora of polarities in the realm of values:[12] between valuational height and valuational strength; between necessity and freedom; between purity of heart (to will one thing) and many-sidedness or comprehensiveness in value achievement; between universality and singularity or individuality ("So act that the maxim of thy will could never become the principle of a universal legislation without a remainder"[13]); between self and common good; between quantity and quality of goods; between activity and suffering as values; between goodness and moral efficacy; between doing wrong and suffering wrong; between pursuit of the noble or the uncommon and pursuit of intimacy; between justice (antiquity) and brotherly love (Christianity); between magnanimity and humility; between wisdom and happiness; between self-control and spontaneity; between truthfulness and love; between keeping one's distance and being a part; between love of the nearest (brotherly love) and love of the remotest and radiant virtue (Nietzsche); between equality and respect for the unequal; between retrospective, traditional ideals of life and prospective ideals; between imparting and receiving; between useless and useful virtue; between ethical and aesthetic values; etcetera, etcetera.

Many of the value-tensions can be understood in terms of "complementarity"—a word Hartmann uses in its meaning in ordinary language, i.e., the relation is one of "reciprocal conditioning, an interwoveness"[14] whether on the same plane or between different levels of value. Hartmann invokes a hierarchy of values in at least partial solution of discrepancies he observes.[15] Some of the most significant polarities he elaborates are "ideals of life" that are simply separate moralities or plans of life that are alternative vocations, as I have suggested, and not contradictions in moral reason.

Still Hartmann refuses to take any easy way out of these

antinomies. "Perhaps a solution of the discrepancy lies in a higher valuational region, of which we have no comprehension." Then "the antinomic character of opposites would be due only to consciousness (to the sensing of values), and our limitations would be the cause of our inability to reconcile them. But it is also possible that the system, pursued further, would not converge or would even diverge, and, if our vision could transcend its limits, must manifest bolder discrepancies."[16] In other words, the realm of values may not be a seamless robe; there may be metaphysical discrepancies and not an ultimate harmony unknown to us. In any case, the moral agent, with his present, actual discernment of values, must construct a moral life in the midst of intuitional antinomies. He must choose to make a whole life one way or another; and this is a far more significant and problematic task than believing one theory of physics for certain purposes on Monday, Wednesday, and Friday, and another on Tuesday, Thursday, and Saturday.

Moreover, appeal to discernible gradation of values does not always provide a lexical ordering, or a basis for saying that a higher value overrides a lower one. In the first place, heterogeneity is most evident among the higher values. ". . . In the lower values the antithetic has vanished and can be reconstructed only by analysis, while in the higher values the synthesis seems to be lacking and the antithetic alone seems to rule."[17] In the second place, the strength of lower values may prove equivalent to the supervalence of higher values in actual choices. Thus, "the unconditional preference for the higher is restricted by an equally unconditional preference for the more fundamental values."[18]

The second of the foregoing considerations brings us again to Stent's justice/charity problem. At least for Hartmann, the antinomy cannot be resolved by simply saying (as he does) that brotherly love is higher than justice, for justice is stronger. An unequivocal espousal of charity over justice (or vice versa) denies the problem more than resolving it. Similarly, Nietzsche "rightly saw that love for the far distant is the higher moral value. Yet he was at the same time wrong; for brotherly love is the 'stronger' value."[19]

So something about justice is not penetrable by human compassion. "That murder, theft and all real 'crimes' are felt to be the most grievous moral transgressions, is due to this, that the justice which they violate is based upon the most elementary of goods-values (life, property and the like). . . Hence the unique moral import of justice. This import, however, does not attach to its height, but to its strength."[20] Appeals to the higher value of brotherly love only set up the antinomy; such appeals in no way help to relieve this moral conflict. Add to this the value of personality: the self continuous over a life-span. The moral agent who made himself a murderer or a thief or did grave injury or betrayed a trust does not cease to be one who did those things. Regret or remorse that are not pathological always remain fitting and true. For charity to claim to deny or omit the justice due that personality would be a false pretense, and finally an assault on both justice and personality.

At this point one could develop a theory of just punishment. Such a view would be some version of the theory of retribution which holds that punishment, however roughly, fits the crime or the dereliction, and that other defenses of punishment treat the personality as a thing (an illness to be cured—than which there can be no more boundless incarceration or victimization—or a thing to be *used* to deter others). To go in this direction would be a proper development of a quite sensitive spectator aspect of ethical analysis. We would be talking primarily, if not only, of justice due to others, or to persons in general. Beside these claims it must be said that charity, too, penetrates to the personality and does not annul justice. Pity or sympathy would be the proper name for a disposition that would have us do less than the just.

On the other hand, we can explore the justice/charity problem with stress more and more upon self-implication, upon our own just deserts. Here I rather think that theories of just retribution go somewhat awry into sentimentality when expressed in terms of the criminal or the negligent "needing" or even "wanting" some fitting punishment or recompense—a sentimentality to be compared with an understanding of charity as pitiful relief directly contradictory to justice. Nevertheless, we need to pursue to the bottom the justice/charity problem when generalities are forgotten—even good ones—and the moral agent is wholly self-involved. The justice/charity problem turns into a guilt/forgiveness problem if the ethical analyst does not fail to remember himself in all his thought about moral responsibility and moral failure. The primary question is no longer just deserts, appropriate punishment, or recompense; or the relation of charity to that. The question now is, how can I who made myself a murderer, a rapist, a thief, a dissembler, or unfaithful to a trust be forgiven or receive forgiveness and a new moral beginning without violation of the personality I am (i.e., nonpathologically guilty)? Here, I judge, we have a polarity, an antinomy, a dialectic, and existential encounter that lends support to Stent's "intuitional" complementarity. This is how the justice/charity problem looks from in the midst of moral failure or breakdown.

Sören Kierkegaard and Fyodor Dostoevsky probed more deeply than any writers I know the antinomy or paradox or dialectic in a personality that remains itself over time (guilty) yet changes (actuated by forgiveness). Stent needs to go to this level (as N. Hartmann does in effect) to obtain his best data.

A culprit or a violator of trust makes a breach with the good. The next step, according to Kierkegaard, manifesting the continuity of such a personality, is to despair *over* sin (this means a breach with the possibility of repentance).[21] Next after that (not necessarily in temporal succession) comes despair *of* the forgiveness of sins.[22] The prepositions "over" and "of" are important because in the first instance the guilty personality maintains itself with strength, clinging to guilt by plunging into deeper or more heinous offenses. He can never forgive himself for it. In the second instance, the guilty personality out of weakness despairs of the possibility of proffered forgiveness. He directly picks a quarrel with that possibility.

All of Dostoevsky's sinners show these possible developments from an original guilt in relation to his "Christ figures" (e.g., Raskolnikov in relation to Sonia) even when the main direction of the development of their personality is in the direction of the possibility of actualizing forgiveness and being changed by forgiveness. In the enigmatic character in *The Possessed*, Stavrogin with his deeply ambivalent confession, Dostoevsky portrays a personality development both in terms of Kierkegaard's despair *over* sin and in terms of despair *of* the forgiveness of sins. Stavrogin's breach with repentance (following an original breach with the good) takes the form of sinking still deeper; he is out to prove that there can be nothing more monstrous than Stavrogin and his deeds of defiance of the wretched multitude at the cross-roads where Raskolnikov knelt and kissed the earth. At the same time, he quarrels with the possibility of an actualization of forgiveness even in his "confession." If he is a personality, he is guilty; if guilty, he can never forgive himself for it; and if guilty he can never be forgiven as who he is. "He can never forgive himself for it—but now in case God would forgive him for it, he might well have the kindness to forgive himself," Kierkegaard wrote.[23] Stavrogin defies this prospect when he refuses the priest Tihon's forgiveness (asking also himself to be forgiven by Stavrogin, both silently in their hearts). That awakened memories of "ancient monkish formulae."[24]

So I suggest that the guilt/forgiveness problem is, indeed, a deeply entrenched opposition—an opposition that may lead to personality continuous through radical change, but may equally well intensify guilt and its thralldom. Here we come upon the definitive reason the positive religions of the world cannot be simply reduced to the bearers of moral reason. For moral reason—the severity of self-judgment and the moral dereliction and paralysis it produces—brings humankind to a border-question which positive religions address. Here we come to a border where stands the God of Judaism who is both entirely just and forever faithful and merciful to his people. Here we verge on the solution of the problem of justice and mercy that Christianity addresses to the ultimate moral conflict and to the human condition in the mystery of the Atonement. Gunther Stent quite properly may not want to go that far. I have wanted simply to say that in the dialectic of guilt and forgiveness he has perhaps the best evidence drawn from human moral experience for at least intuitional complementarity; and for metaphysical complementarity, too, if there is no God who is both entirely just and surprisingly merciful in the contradiction of a cross.

NOTES

1. Jonathan Edwards, *Freedom of the Will*, ed. with introduction by Paul Ramsey. *The Works of Johathan Edwards*, (New Haven: Yale University Press, 1957).

2. Rousseau held such a notion of freedom. A person of free will cannot say today what he will do tomorrow, else his future actions will not be "his own"; he will not *then* be fully "responsible." Still, Rousseau did not hesitate to incorporate such a will into "the general will." Atomistic, contextless individualistic freedom and totalitarianism have the same source: a loss of the meaning of "one's own."

3. Edwards does not say "is *determined* by" in the foregoing statements. This "correction" of his *Freedom of the Will* was introduced into *all* editions following his original. See Ramsey, ed., Introduction, pp. 17–19.

4. Jacques Maritain, *Integral Humanism*. (Notre Dame, Ind.: University of Notre Dame Press, 1973).

5. "Politics as a Vocation," *From Max Weber: Essays in Sociology*, in H. H. Gerth and C. Wright Mills ed. (New York: Oxford University Press, 1946), pp. 77–128. In note 17 of his present chapter Stent simply cannot see the difference between a contradiction and "wholly separate" moralities pertaining to different spheres of human activity or to different vocations. Nor would I undertake to read Machiavelli's politics in terms of "solution" by feature-dependent "exceptions."

6. David K. Lewis's account of "indeterminate comparisons" is an apt description of decision one way or the other in the example above, where there is no single measure by which the options can be gauged. "Overall similarity," he writes, "consists of innumerable similarities and differences in innumerable respects of comparison, balanced against each other according to the relative importance we attach to those respects of comparison. Insofar as these relative importances differ from one another, and from one person to another, or differ from one occasion to another, or are indeterminate even for a single person or single occasion, so far is comparative similarity indeterminate." (David K. Lewis, *Counter-factuals*. [Cambridge, Mass: Harvard University Press, 1973]), chap. 4, sect. 42, pp. 91–95). In a similar vein the British moralist W. D. Ross wrote that we are "faced with great difficulties when we try to *commeasure good things of very different types*." (W.D. Ross, *The Right and the Good*. [Oxford: Clarendon Press, 1930], p. 144. Italics added). In no case of indeterminate choices, however, does the agent simply flip a metal coin; these are not matters of indifference such as whether to pick up a pin or not. One chooses for good reasons even between options that are strictly incommensurable. We will encounter other examples of "indeterminate" choice between "good things of very different types" in N. Hartmann in the final section of this chapter. For additional discussion of indeterminacy, see

my chapter "Incommensurability and Indeterminancy in Moral Choice," in *Doing Evil to Achieve Good*, ed., Richard A. McCormick and Paul Ramsey (Chicago, Ill.: Loyola University Press, 1978), pp. 69–144.

7. Frances Hutcheson, *An Inquiry into the Original of our Ideas of Beauty and Virtue* (1725) and *An Essay on the Nature and Conduct of the Passions*, with *Illustrations Upon the Moral Sense* (1728).

8. William Frankena, *Journal of the History of Ideas*, vol. 16, no. 3 (June 1955), pp. 356–75.

9. The rabbinic term is *lifnim mishurat hadin*; "inside the line of the law." As I understand it, the expression does *not* mean "within the minimum requirements." It means rather in the direction to which law also points or, we might say, the spirit of the laws. On the other hand, this is not a "supercredit" morality. The Jew is commanded to aspire to be holy. Saintliness or an ethics of *imitatio Dei* is not just a lofty ideal but a pressing obligation. The reason the Temple was destroyed—one comment has it—is that the Jewish people in that day stood upon the *din* and refused to act *lifnim mishurat hadin*. This was to teach us that a purely legalistic community observing the bottom line specific commandments (the *din*) to the neglect of holiness cannot exist—least of all the Jewish people. See Aharon Lichtenstein, "Does Jewish Tradition Recognize an Ethic Independence of Halakha?" *Modern Jewish Ethics*, ed. Marvin Fox (Columbus, Ohio: Ohio State University Press, 1975), pp. 62–88.

10. J.O. Urmson, "Saints and Heroes," in *Moral Concepts*, ed. Joel Feinberg (Oxford: Oxford University Press, 1969), pp. 60–73.

11. In his present chapter (note 16), Stent simply reasserts again his conviction that unlike other value-oppositions justice and compassion are in inherent logical conflict. He replies to my suggestion about "charity perfecting justice" by saying that even if that is the actual consequence and the consequence is morally desirable, this merely adds to rather than detracts from the "fundamentally paradoxical character" of morality. To this I respond that a desirable paradox is not an intolerable logical contradiction. We would then be driven to an examination into the meaning of the terms Stent uses and whether they mean the same. I also suggest that Stent's quest for a unitary science permits no seams in the robe of morality and no overlaps or folds in it as well.

12. Nicolai Hartmann, *Ethics*. vol. 2 *Moral Values* (New York: Macmillan Co., 1932). (German original, 1926).

13. Ibid., 2: 359. "Hence the categorical imperative has within itself its own opposite. It involves its own converse. Its limitation lies not outside of it, but in it" (2: 360).

14. Ibid., 2: 392.

15. "Thus, for example, brotherly love is evidently higher than justice, love for the remotest is higher than brotherly love, and personal love (as it appears) is higher than either. Likewise, bravery stands higher than self-control, faith and fidelity higher than bravery, radiant virtue and personality again higher than these" (2: 387).

16. Ibid., 2: 77.

17. Ibid., 2: 419.

18. Ibid., 2: 460.

19. Ibid., 2: 463. Just as Sartre is an atheist because God cannot be allowed to exist, if man is to be free, so I suggest that Hartmann was a modern Platonist who did not believe in God because of the incoherence he discerned in the moral cosmos and refused to speculate was overcome out of human sight beyond our present discernment of values. Among religious persons, Protestants (esp. Lutherans) are apt to be people who believe in God but nevertheless acknowledge that there may be irresolvable conflicts of *moral* values in this disordered eon; while Catholics tend to deny that *moral* values can ultimately conflict because they believe in God; they are convinced that *right* (even if tragic or feeble) solutions can always be determined and determinative for actual choices. By contrast Lutherans are convinced that one must "sin bravely." Are we to add Hartmann and Stent to their company? If so, we must note that Lutherans add, "and ever more bravely believe."

20. Ibid., 2: 455.

21. Sören Kierkegaard, *The Sickness Unto Death* (Princeton: Princeton University Press, 1941), pp. 178–84.

22. Ibid., pp. 185–204.

23. Ibid., p. 182.

24. See Paul Ramsey, "God's Grace and Man's Guilt" in *Nine Modern Moralists*. (Englewood Cliffs, N.J.: Prentice-Hall, Inc., 1962), pp. 35–55 for fuller exposition.

Evolution, Social Behavior, and Ethics

Richard D. Alexander

Introduction

NOTHING SEEMS LIKELY to influence analyses of the relationship between science and ethics as much as would a significant revision of our view of either science or ethics. Yet refinements of evolutionary theory within biology during the past twenty years seem to me to have provided a compelling new model of culture and human sociality which dramatically alters our interpretations of all human activities, including both science and ethics. This model has been developed elsewhere and the findings responsible for it described;[1] here I shall only summarize the attributes of the model, and the way in which it departs from earlier views, before discussing its apparent meaning for the current confrontation, or interaction, between science and ethics.

Culture theorists, philosophers, and historians have always wrestled with two related problems in their efforts to develop grand theories, the relationship between individual and group interests and the identification of function. Although various combinations of interpretations have been tried, the only one apparently consistent with modern evolutionary theory has not. Function, as *raison d'etre*, has characteristically been divided into proximate and ultimate forms. Proximate forms, such as satisfaction, pleasure, happiness, and avoidance of their alternatives, are more likely to be visualized as significant at the individual level; partly for this reason, psychology has developed with an emphasis on the individual. Some functions, such as efficiency of organization or operation, which could be regarded as either proximate or ultimate, are usually interpreted as group-level phenomena because social theorists have not commonly been concerned with genetic or physiological efficiency; this is especially true in anthropology, where explaining culture has been a principal focus; it is not so true in psychology, as Freudian theory indicates. Survival has often been regarded as the ultimate function and interpreted at either individual or group levels, although, because of frequent conflicts of interest, it obviously cannot always be interpreted at both levels.

The model recently developed within modern biology involves three assumptions: (a) proximate functions are never their own reasons for existence, but, in evolutionary terms, exist to serve ultimate function, hence, take their particular forms because of their contribution to ultimate function;[2] (b) ultimate function is invariably reproduction of the genetic materials because (i) no alternative to natural selection (differential reproduction of genetic alternatives) exists to explain the history of form and function in living things; (ii) natural selection proves both logically and empirically necessary and sufficient (in its present theoretical form); and (c) effects of natural selection on function are realized almost entirely, if not entirely, at the individual level or lower.[3]

As discussed later, and elsewhere,[4] this model returns the concept of function to survival, but to survival of genes (or polygenes, supergenes, and chromosomes[5]—not of individuals (which clearly have not evolved to survive), and not of groups (which, however, give more of an illusion than do individuals of having the function of facilitating only their own survival.)[6] Genes evidently have promoted their survival through effects leading to finiteness of individual lifetimes,[7] and, in social species, sometimes to indefinite prolongations of identifiable social groups. That this conclusion is discomforting to an organism with consciousness only at the individual level is not an appropriate reason for denying it.

The main element of the new view of sociality I have just described is clearly a return to a kind of individualistic and utilitarian view of history. It is, however, a view of individualism or utilitarianism never before held or advocated in efforts to explain human behavior and culture. Previous explanations of culture and human striving, as the outcome of individuals seeking to realize "their own best interests" or to "maximize their outcomes"[8] have never explicitly identified these "interests" and "outcomes," or else they have defined them in terms of either (a) proximate rewards, like happiness or (b) survival.[9] The view from evolutionary biology identifies "own best interest" in terms of reproductive success (or, in our current, novel, rapidly changing environment, surrogates of reproductive success), and hypothesizes that hedonistic rewards relate solely to such returns if they are interpreted in terms of the environments of history.[10] Growth, development, aid to reciprocating friends, and the acquisition of power are seen as the accumulation of resources; assistance to offspring and other relatives represents the redistribution of accumulated resources. Culture is seen as the cumulative effect of this "inclusive-fitness-maximizing" behavior[11] by all of the individuals who have lived during history. Culture, then, is the result of endless compromises, conflicts, power interactions, cooperative events, and formation and dissolution of coalitions. According to this view, there would be no single "function" of culture as a whole, as some anthropologists have supposed; nor should we expect even a few indentifiable functions.[12] Aside from those rare issues on which everyone agrees because everyone is aware (or behaves as though aware) that all of our interests are the same, I am suggesting that culture is an incidental effect of our separate, conflicting strivings in which success tends to be (in historical or evolutionary terms is invariably) measured in relative not absolute terms; that culture is the environment into which we are born and according to which we must achieve our goals; that cultural inertia, giving it the quality or appearance of being something greater than the humans responsible for it, is largely owing to the simultaneous effort of every one of us to use and manipulate it to serve our own interests, to keep everyone else from so using it when their efforts conflict with our own, and to extend (temporally and otherwise) our ability to redistribute resources according to our own interests.

At least eight major issues have clouded efforts to develop culture theory in this direction. First, reproduction involves altruism to other individuals, and in humans a bewildering array of genetic relatives of varying degree and varying needs is socially available to each individual. As a result, the altruism of nepotism gives an illusion of group function. On the other hand, the complexity and accuracy of knowledge of *differences* among kin support the idea that nepotism has been a major avenue of reproduction by *individuals*.[13]

Second, effects of the peculiarly human mode of reproductive striving, through group-living, persist as culture and technology long past individual lifetimes. This also gives an illusion of group function. As suggested earlier, much of this effect is also recognizable as a result of the striving of individuals to provide for relatives and descendants as far as possible into the future.

Third, as a part of group-living we are constantly forming and dissolving coalitions, or subgroups, of individuals who temporarily have common interests. Although this too gives an illusion of group function, the mere fact that coalitions are temporary and shifting indicates otherwise.

Fourth, we have turned our group-living and group-competitive behaviors to the development of nations within which reciprocal behaviors apparently derived historically from nepotistic interactions within clans and tribes form the social cement,[14] and within which extensive nepotism is both downplayed by law and thwarted by geographic mobility of individuals and families. This effect creates circumstances in which the altruism of nepotism is "misdirected," and others in which altruism with the function of maintaining acceptability in the group, or gaining status, and, hence, access to resources, again creates the illusion of group function.

Fifth, the accelerating rate of cultural innovation has caused massive novelty in our environment,[15] thwarting analyses based on function, except as interpreted in terms of past environments. Although this situation may lead to frequent errors, analyses of human behavior are still most likely to be accurate if they are developed from an understanding of the effects of a history of natural selection, with allowances for the particular kinds of environmental changes known or suspected to have occurred.[16]

Sixth, it has proved exceedingly difficult to trace the pathways between gene expressions and complex behaviors, so that the relationship of the latter to genetic reproduction, and therefore the importance of interactions among relatives, is still viewed with scepticism. The significance of this scepticism is much reduced by the knowledge that (a) the complete ontogeny is known for no behavior in any organism and (b) complex and accurate predictions about behavior have been made on a wide scale from a knowledge of selection alone.

Seventh, proximate mechanisms have not previously been hypothesized whereby altruistic nepotism and the altruism of reciprocity could be directed appropriately so as to maximize inclusive fitness (the reproduction of one's genes) and yet be commensurate with what is known about the plasticity of human behavior and theories of learning. At least in terms of reasonable theory I believe that this problem has been solved.[17]

Eighth, humans have found it difficult to evaluate with disinterest the suggestion that their evolutionary background has primed them to behave as the reproductive machinery of the genes. This fact seems to result in part from a tendency to self-deception which has its advantages in an extraordinary ability by humans to detect deliberate deception in others.[18]

Despite these difficulties, the theory that culture is no more or less than the outcome of inclusive-fitness-maximizing behavior by all of the individuals who have lived during history appears capable of surmounting the difficulties encountered by the older theories.[19] Although efforts have been made to describe this view of culture as "Hobbesian" or "utilitarian" in ways rendering it out of date, or as not different from other approaches that have already been tried and discarded, it is in fact distinct from any view previously generated. Although efforts have also been made to associate it with some particular ideology, such as social Darwinism, its testing is a procedure in natural history; regardless of what may be said, by either its proponents or its opponents, it is not properly ideological in nature.[20]

Science as a Social Enterprise

If my arguments to this point are acceptable, then science may be considered as a particular kind of activity of individuals, sometimes operating in groups, with certain unique characteristics and consequences. Its central attribute is its unusual degree of self-correction, induced by the criterion of repeatability of results. This aspect of scientific method, theoretically, at least, forces the practitioners of science to explain fully the methods by which they make their discoveries and reach their conclusion. The resulting tendency for scientific findings continually to approach correctness in explanation gives an illusion that scientists are devoted to a search for truth, hence, are somehow unusually humble and altruistic. Instead, the system of investigation called science, however it may have begun, *forces* its practitioners to report their methods as well as their results, or risk being exposed as unscientific and drummed out of their profession.[21] Scientists compete by striving to acquire authorship for as many of the best ideas as possible. This competition includes identifying and publishing the errors of others. As nearly all scientists are aware, the slightest taint of deliberate falsification of results or plagiarism is often enough to damage a career permanently, and may be vastly more significant than mere incompetence. I speculate that science, as a method of finding out about the universe, began as a consequence of competition among the ancients to prove their ability to comprehend cause and effect and to meet the challenges of one another for preeminence in this enterprise and the prestige and leadership that went with it. The requirement of repeatability is what distinguishes science, indeed, diametrically opposes it to dominance or prestige by virtue of claims of divine revelation or knowledge conferred by deities— although the two kinds of effort may exist for exactly the same reasons.

To understand why the public tolerates and supports scientists—even, sometimes, regarding science as the most prestigious of all enterprises—we must turn to the products or results of scientific investigation. These results are represented not only by all of the products of technology but by innumerable changes of attitude toward ourselves and our environment as a result of new knowledge. In some sense, essentially all of the reasons for societal affluence, and many of the reasons for our ability to achieve a modicum of serenity in the face of the uncertainties, complexities, and competitiveness engendered by the reasons for affluence, are seen as products of science. So, I suggest, science is supported for the same reason that copyright and patent laws are maintained to allow inventors to profit from their inventions. We evidently believe, individually and collectively (or we behave as though we believe), that the discoveries made by scientists are likely to benefit all of us sufficiently to make their support worthwhile. This view of science also contributes to the impression that scientists are humble truthseekers, in no way out to maximize personal gain. The truth, however, is something else, as is suggested by the enormous scale on which scientists are employed directly by organizations that exist for the sole purpose of making profits.

Now we can see that, so long as what scientists discover represents solutions to problems that face *all* humans, the relationship of science to any system of ethics regarded as functional and acceptable at the group level (that is, as helping everyone about equally) is clearly a harmonious one. Even a science practiced by individual scientists who are totally selfish in their reasons for doing it would tend to help the group involved, except when a discovery gave a scientist such personal power as to allow him to seek his own ends in conflict with those of everyone else or the group as a whole; or to the degree that scientists themselves form subgroups with common interests among themselves and different from those of others.

Scientists employed by subgroups, such as corporations, seeking their own profit rather than that either of the group (nation?) as a whole or of others in the society, are somewhat removed from the continual scrutiny and approval of the collective of individuals called the public. Given the view of science I have just presented, such scientists may be expected to develop and pursue lines of investigation that do not represent the interests of the group as a whole, or even of the majority of individuals within it. Technological and other products of science which create serious problems for society, I suggest, may frequently be expected to come from these kinds of scientific enterprises. Accordingly, in this particular realm, many problems in the relationship of science and ethics may be expected to occur. For example, what is the net value to society as a whole of new herbicides, insecticides, patent medicines, cosmetics, and particular trends in automobiles, farm, and industrial machinery, computers, appliances, office equipment, and so on? Trends in such products may frequently proceed in directions catering to individual needs, desires, whims, and weaknesses, such as susceptibility to novelty, desires to prolong the phenotype at whatever cost (even, in the eyes of relatives, using all of the resources one has saved during a lifetime), or desires to reserve, at great cost, the opportunity to reproduce far into the future (for example, through sperm banks). Given such propensities, and the readiness of people to accept placebos, some of the directions taken by corporation-dominated science are bound to be detrimental, not merely to most of the populace but to all users, while nevertheless profitable to their creators and manufacturers, and to the stockholders.

These assertions, of course, do not speak to the question of what proportion of the scientific discoveries useful to all members of the group are also likely to come from scientists employed by profit-seeking subgroups because of the profit incentive. Also, although government scientists, who may create weaponry raising the most serious of all ethical questions, may seem to be excluded, in the sense involved here they may also be regarded as employed by subgroups, since such weaponry is presumably developed explicitly for employment against the members of other similar groups (nations) when the interests of the different groups are sufficiently in conflict in the eyes of their leaders.

The above view of science is entirely compatible with the general theory of culture and sociality described earlier. It does not appear to me to be counterintuitive, though it is surely not the most widely held view of science.[22] I believe that it tends to resolve certain paradoxes in generally held views of science.

The next question is: What does the new view of human sociality mean for our understanding of ethics, and, in turn, what does the view of ethics so generated mean for the relationship of science and ethics?

The Biological Basis of Ethics

Consistent with the above arguments I hypothesize that ethical questions, and the study of morality or concepts of justice and right and wrong, derive solely from the existence of conflicts of interest. In social terms there are three categories of such conflict: (a) individual versus individual, (b) group versus group, and (c) individual versus group. In biological terms two kinds of returns are involved in judging conflicts of interest: (a) those coming to Ego's phenotype and (b) those coming to Ego's genotype, through the success of various kinds of relatives including offspring, and representing reproductive success. In evolutionary terms, all returns are of the second kind, and, as theories of senescence and reproductive effort indicate,[23] our efforts to garner the first kind of returns are expected to be shaped so as to maximize the second kind; there is no other reason for lifetimes having evolved to be finite.

The recent exacerbation of ethical questions has been caused by an accelerating tendency for discoveries from science to cause new kinds of conflict and to cause conflict in new contexts. This situation has caused us to reexamine the basis for ethical norms, seeking generalizations which may assist us in extrapolating to solve the new problems. The effort is actually urgent, since the difference between the processes of organic and cultural evolution are such that the latter continues to accelerate in relation to the former, so that we may be assured that new ethical questions will be generated at ever-increasing rates in the future.[24]

The two major contributions that evolutionary biology may be able to make to this problem are, first, to justify and promote the conscious realization that it is conflicts of interest concentrated at the individual level which lead to ethical questions, and, second, to help identify the nature and intensity of the conflicts of interest involved in specific cases. Undoubtedly the most dramatic and unnerving aspect of these contributions is the argument, or realization, that all conflicts of interest among individuals, in historical (evolutionary) terms, resolve to conflicts over the differential reproduction of genetic units, hence, that conflicts of interest exist solely because of genetic differences among individuals, or histories of genetic differences among individuals interacting in particular fashions. I emphasize that the major barrier to acceptance of this argument—absence of theories about proximate (physiological and ontogenetic) mechanisms acceptable in light of learning theory and the modifiability of human behavior—has been at least partly eliminated.[25]

The above arguments indicate that analyses of ethics, either from a descriptive approach or as an interpretation of the sources of normative ethics in the past, must be phrased from the individual's viewpoint and must bear on the problem of how the individual is most likely to maximize its inclusive fitness. This is true even if most concepts of right and wrong, most laws, norms, traditions, and reasons for courses of action, were established in generations past and are resistant to change. The inertia of culture does not remove the individual's historical reasons and tendencies to strive, it only restricts or alters the manner of striving and the degree to which the ends involved are likely to be achieved.

In the individual's terms, then, a statement by a biologically knowledgeable investigator about the normative ethics *of yesterday*, applicable in any cultural situation, might come out as follows[26]: I "should" treat others so as to maximize my inclusive fitness. My treatment of relatives "should" be more altruistic than my treatment of nonrelatives (that is, altruism to kin should be more likely than altruism to nonkin in situations in which phenotypic returns are unlikely). My treatment of both relatives and nonrelatives "should" be developed in terms of (a) effects of my actions on the reproduction of relatives (including offspring), hence, the reproduction of my genes; (b) effects of my actions on how I will be treated by those directly affected by my actions (how will interactants treat me subsequent to my actions toward them?); (c) effects of my actions on how my relatives will be treated by those affected by my actions; and (d) effects of my actions on how I will be treated by those only observing my actions, and either (i) likely to be interacting with me subsequently or (ii) likely to be affected by the success or failure of my actions because of the observation, and, hence, acceptance or rejection of them by still others. It is particularly perplexing that we must investigate the extent to which our behavior supports this hypothesis under the realization that, if such goals do guide our behavior, they are nevertheless not consciously perceived, and, if the hypothesis is correct, this means, paradoxically, that we are evolved to reject these goals whenever we are asked to evaluate them consciously. This does not mean that we *must* reject them, but that individuals not aware of all this are expected to behave as if these were their goals even if denying it is so, and that to convince them of self-deception may be difficult, and will be most difficult for the precise activities about which they deceive themselves, for the same reason that they do so. The question is testable: Do we or do we not behave as predicted, whether we think so or not, when we are not yet aware of the predictions? It is the same kind of question anthropologists always must ask when they undertake to analyze the structure of a culture alien to their own.

By these arguments the complexity of ethical issues derives not from their general basis but from the diversity and complexity of sources of conflict, and of the means by which they are altered.

We are led to a division of normative ethics into those of the past—before development of the realization that genetic interests underlie conflicts of interest—and those of the future, following conscious understanding of such arguments. It is crucial that this distinction be recognized; otherwise, what I have said above will be interpreted erroneously as naively deterministic, with new knowledge of the significance of history not acknowledged as having effects on the future of human sociality or the determination of ethical procedures.[27] I appreciate the way Albert Rosenfeld put this particular point:

> . . the individual who militantly seeks to have the quest for knowledge brought to a halt is often the same individual who is outraged by the sociobiological suggestion that we are more controlled by our genes than we realize. We *are* more controlled by our genes than we have realized [This is a reasonable assertion, since not too many years ago we hadn't even heard about their existence]; therefore, the more we discover about the mechanisms of genetic control, the better equipped we will be to escape these controls, through our enhanced awareness, to transcend them so that we may, for the first time in our history, work for ourselves, instead of for our genes, exercise truly free will and free choice, give free reign to our minds and spirits, attain something close to our full humanhood.[28]

Why should biologists, social scientists, philosophers, and historians find it so difficult, or distasteful, to accept what Rosenfeld has grasped so well? I am inclined to suggest that what is involved are the reasons for cultural inertia and the nature of science, already mentioned here. Leaving aside the obvious virtue of some conservatism about novelty, the emotionality of responses to this issue suggests to me that those of us who make our living in this subcultural arena are reluctant to accept new paradigms, which, if they succeed, represent someone else changing the rules in the middle of our game; we have learned how to use the system—in our own subarenas of science and humanism—to meet our own ends, and we resent the suggestion that we must in any sense start all over again.

Perhaps as well it has not for a long time been profitable for social scientists to entertain truly novel theories, partly because of the supposed relationship between new ways of viewing human activities and the potential for misusing them. Thus, someone has said that a natural scientist is remembered for his best ideas, a social scientist for his worst. Perhaps the new paradigm in evolutionary biology will be first absorbed into fields like economics, and by laymen, who are curious but lack the vested interests and other inhibitory baggage of much of academia.[29]

Justice, Happiness, and Keeping Up with the Joneses

Rawls developed the idea that justice correlates with happiness, and that happiness may be identified as follows: "A person is happy when he is in the way of a successful execution (more or less) of a rational plan of life drawn up under (more or less) favorable conditions, and he is reasonably confident that his intentions can be carried through . . . adding the rider that if he is mistaken or deluded, then by contingency and coincidence nothing transpires to disabuse him of his misconceptions."[30]

But Rawls fails to consider fully how individuals decide upon particular courses of action, thus, why there is any likelihood at all of selecting a plan of life that is *not* likely to be carried through, particularly in an affluent society where scarcely anyone is actually in danger of starving, freezing, or otherwise dying prematurely because of inability to secure necessary resources. In others words, he has failed to explain why people strive, and what he has left out seems to be the crux of the problem, and the source of the conflicts of interest that lead to ethical questions. I think we can be certain that, even in affluent societies—and, I would venture, *especially* in some such societies—there will be much evidence of unhappiness. Why should this be so?

It should be so because, again in historical terms, success is only measurable in relative terms. We set our goals and determine our plans of life in terms of what we observe others about us achieving; such goals are irrational, or likely to be inaccessible and thus to lead to unhappiness, when different individuals (a) strive from different resource bases, and fail to take this into account; (b) fail to consider the different sorts of obstacles placed in their ways (because of race, sex, physical or mental handicaps, or other bases for discrimination); (c) fail to consider trends in society that may eliminate possibilities open to others; or (d) fail to consider the extent to which achievements of others have required use of excessive power, influence, chicanery, or injustice against others (and the attendant risks). I think we can predict that unhappiness as a consequence of unlikely or irrational personal goals is likely to be most prevalent in societies that are hierarchically structured, so that lofty goals may be developed from observations of the success of others, and yet so constituted as to generate severe inequalities of opportunity so that the perceived goals are inaccessible for what are logically interpreted as unjust reasons.

In natural selection the likelihood of a genetic element persisting depends entirely on its rate of change in frequency *in relation* to its alternative; changes in absolute numbers are irrelevant. Among the attributes of living creatures, whatever can be shown to have resulted from the action of natural selection may be expected to bear this same relationship to its alternatives. This means that we should not be surprised to discover that the behavioral striving of individual humans during history has been explicitly formed in terms of relative success in reproductive competition. As I have noted elsewhere[31] this is the reason why justice is necessarily incomplete, why happiness is not a commodity easy to make universal, and why ethical questions continue to plague us, and can even become more severe when everything else seems to be going well.

Right and Wrong

Interpreting the concepts of right and wrong in terms of conflicts of interest is a difficult task. First, there is an implication of absoluteness about right and wrong which gives an illusion of group function to their invocation. This flavor is promoted by legislative bodies and law; by authority in the form of parents, organized religion, and other sources of power, influence, and leadership; by persistence of meanings across generations; and even by our use of the terms right and wrong in the context of correctness and incorrectness about decisions or answers, or understanding of factual matters (e.g., the *right* or *wrong* distance, direction, number, or answer; a *right* line is a straight line; the *right* hand is the correct one; *right* now means precisely at this time; and so on).

Yet all of the arguments I have presented so far suggest that this implication of absoluteness and group function has some significance other than actual unanimity of opinion or equality of return to all individuals. What is this significance?

Parents begin instilling the ideas of right and wrong in their children, and this is probably the normal origin of the concepts for most individuals. Initially, at least, right and wrong are for children whatever their parents say is right and wrong. What, though, are usual concepts of right and wrong in parents' views of their children's behavior? One might suppose that children are simply taught by their parents never to deceive, always to tell the truth, the whole truth, and nothing but the truth; therefore, that children are taught always to be altruistic toward others, to be certain that justice is afforded all those with whom they interact, and that their own interests are secondary to those of others or of the members of the group to which they belong.

Alas, it cannot be true. As we all know very well, children so taught, who also obeyed their parents' teaching faithfully, could not be successful, at least in this society; whatever they gained personally would immediately be lost. They would be the rubes of society, of whom advantage would be taken at every turn.[32]

I suggest something so different that it may at first sound pernicious: that parents actually teach their children how to "cheat" without getting caught. That is, that parents teach their children what is "right" and "wrong" behavior in the eyes of others, and what truth-telling and forthright behavior actually are, so that from this base of understanding children will know how to function successfully in a world in which some deceptions are sometimes profitable, some unforgivable, and hence expensive, and some are difficult to detect, others easy. I suggest that parents are more likely to punish children for (a) cheating close relatives, (b) cheating friends with much to offer the family in a continuing reciprocal interaction, or (c) cheating in an obvious, bungling fashion, sure to be detected, than they are to punish them for simply cheating (I am using the word "cheating" here in a very general way, referring to any kind of social deception or taking of advantage). In other words, I suggest that the concepts of right and wrong are instilled into children in such fashion as to guide them toward inclusive-fitness-maximizing behavior in the particular societies and sub-societies within which they are growing up and are likely to live out their lives; that they are taught by parents accustomed to living by these rules; and that the courts and prisons are filled with individuals whose teachers failed, for one reason or another, to impart just these concepts of right and wrong.[33]

The reason that the concepts of right and wrong assume an appearance of absoluteness and group-level uniformity of application, then, are that (a) on some issues there actually is virtual unanimity of opinion, especially when dire external threats exist, as during wartime, and (b) it is a major social strategy to assemble as a coalition those who agree, or who can be persuaded to behave as though they agree, and then promote the apparent agreement of the subgroup as gospel. On these accounts relatively few ethical questions actually *seem* to involve disagreements between *individuals*: In one fashion or another one or both individuals is likely to have made his grievance appear to be that of a group. This is relatively easy to accomplish if the presumed offender constitutes a potential threat to others not directly involved. We subscribe to laws against acts like murder, rape, robbery, and usury not so much because strangers are victims as because we have assessed, consciously or unconsciously, the probability that we or those on whom we depend, from whom we expect to receive assistance or resources, or through whom we expect to achieve reproductive success, may sometimes be in a position similar to that of the victim.

In this light one may ask about the source of the apparent recent rise of attention to issues like child abuse, rape, and the rights of minorities, women, and the mentally and physically handicapped. I suggest that, as individuals, we regard ourselves as more vulnerable in the modern, urban, technological, socially impersonal environment, in which we are increasingly surrounded by strangers, and which bureaucracy, weaponry, and medical knowledge of new gadgetry and substances affecting the functioning of the human body and mind seem to place us increasingly at the mercy of others. I speculate that the recent rise of interest in the rights of even nonhuman organisms represents an extension of the same trend—an effort to preserve our own rights, before they are directly threatened, by singling out others whose rights are directly threatened and using their situation to develop the social machinery to protect ourselves.[34]

A Concluding Remark

I have been asked by the editor to discuss briefly the limitations of the approach I have attempted here. First, I would reiterate my opinion that evolutionary understanding (therefore, science) has little to contribute to the *identification* of goals in systems of ethics and morality.[35] Second, in regard to the analysis of human sociality—the "natural history" of activities like science and the formation and maintenance of systems of human behavior—I am willing to risk seeming unduly optimistic in supposing that evolutionary understanding represents *the central key*. Beyond this, I am impressed with the degree to which the conclusions of authors totally outside evolution seem to converge on those derived from modern evolutionary approaches. Thus, I agree with Friedmann that "The only general conclusion to be drawn is that, in any society that preserves a modicum of individual responsibility, there is a tension between individual ethics and social morality on the one part, and social morality and the legal order on the other part. How much these three spheres of normative order influence and modify each other is a question that cannot be answered in absolute terms."[36]

I believe that an evolutionary approach leads us to the same conclusion, but I also believe that it tells us, better than any other approach, why Friedmann's conclusion is reasonable and what are the likely degrees and patterns of expression of the interactions he discusses.

Mankind's self-interpretation, its conception of itself, its essence, and its destiny, is not without influence on what it then is.[37]

NOTES

1. See R. D. Alexander, "Natural Selection and the Analysis of Human Sociality," in *The Changing Scenes in the Natural Sciences, 1776-1976*, ed. C. E. Goulden, Philadelphia Academy of Natural Sciences Special Publication 12 (1977):283–337. In this paper I made a special effort to trace the sequence of changes in thinking responsible for the current model, because it seemed to me that much of the existing confusion about "sociobiology" stems from a failure by the authors of books in this area to identify and trace what has actually happened since 1957. For example, E. O. Wilson, in his massive and influential 1975 volume, *Sociobiology: The New Synthesis* (Cambridge, Mass.: Harvard University Press, 1975) defines sociobiology as "the systematic study of the biological basis of all social behavior." But this is not a new kind of study in biology. Moreover, the adjective "biological" when applied to behavior by social scientists all too often means "genetic," and it often is used explicitly to mean "other than social" in efforts to account for the ontogeny of behavior. Further, although Wilson says that "the organism is only DNA's way of making more DNA" and gives credit to W. D. Hamilton's (1964) theory of inclusive-fitness-maximizing (kin selection) (i.e., that *genetic reproduction can be enhanced by helping nondescendant as well as descendant relatives*) in explaining altruism, in my opinion he muddles the question of group selection which is crucial to understanding altruism. To make matters worse he refers to the seminal arguments of George C. Williams in *Adaptation and Natural Selection* (Princeton, N.J.: Princeton University Press, 1966) that *selection is highly unlikely to be effective above the level of the parent and its offspring* (regarded by many as responsible for the entire revolution) as Williams' "fallacy"! In effect, Wilson reintroduced genes into the formula, Genes plus Environment Yield Phenotype (including behavior), without clearly telling the reader why this can now be done satisfactorily; he persists in using the phrase "genetically determined" when referring to human behavior (even, sometimes, without specifying that he is referring to *differences* in behavior); and he gives the impression that the main change is simply a massive accumulation of very relevant data from field studies (later, in "Animal and Human Sociobiology," in *The Changing Scenes in the Natural Sciences 1776–1976*, pp. 273–81, he actually says this). But it is

not true: A massive *refinement of theory* reoriented the study of behavior. It may be difficult for outsiders to understand from accounts like Wilson's what is really new in evolutionary biology, and why it is important. The revolution was caused by the arguments of Williams and Hamilton, italicized above.

2. Gunther Stent, in a critical review of Richard Dawkin's *The Selfish Gene* (Oxford: Oxford University Press, 1976) recently published in the Hastings Center Report, has missed the point, in his distinction between deliberate and nondeliberate altruism, that "intent" is a proximate mechanism; a paradoxical aspect of its molding to contribute to ultimate function is that not all goals are conscious. This is not to suggest that "intent" is a trivial aspect of behavior or that it is not important to distinguish intentional and unintentional altruism and selfishness or kindness and cruelty. After all, intent is a central aspect of the definition of such terms, demonstrating its importance. It is crucial to ask *why* intent is so important to us, when it would seem that *consequences* are what count. The reason, I believe, is that intent has consequences outside the immediate circumstances. I think we *use* intent to enable us to predict about events additional to the ones in which we are immediately involved, just as we use information about whether associates follow the rules or play fair in trivial circumstances, or in games, to determine whether we should interact with them in more serious matters. We actually believe that he who is cruel or kind to others—or to animals, children, and other vulnerable beings—is likely to be cruel or kind to us as well. We are positive toward someone who *intends* to be altruistic for the same reason that we are negative toward someone who *intends* to be cruel: He may do it to us.

Stent also fails to grasp the all-important distinction, in evolutionary arguments, between incidental effects and evolved functions (well explained by Williams in *Adaptation and Natural Selection*). Stent's contention that evolutionary theory is not predictive is serious, not because it is true, but because he echoes a misconception prevalent among those accustomed to determining the nature of scientific predictiveness from theories dealing with nonliving phenomena. Stent, like some others, regards "the concept of 'fitness' [as] the Achilles' heel of Darwinism, for which a substitute has to be found if natural selection is to be upgraded from the status of a retrodictive historical theory to that of a predictive scientific theory." He acknowledges that "fully predictive evolutionary analyses are available" for "bounded situations in which the context can be completely specified," such as "the development of a drug-resistant bacterial strain from a drug-sensitive strain in a culture medium containing that drug." But he does not regard such predictions as adequate to give evolution "full standing as a theory in the natural sciences." He believes that what is needed is "some concept formally equivalent to fitness, but descriptive of an intrinsic quality." He remarks that "Dawkins evidently hit upon selfishness as a substitute for fitness." Maybe he did. But I would recommend to anyone interested in these questions (including both Dawkins and Stent) that they begin with Darwin, not Dawkins. The following is only one of his several grand challenges to falsification (C. Darwin, *On the Origin of Species. A Fascimile of the First Edition with an Introduction by Ernst Mayr.* (Cambridge, Mass.: Harvard University Press, 1967), p. 201, 1st ed., 1859.

> If it could be proved that any part of the structure of any one species has been formed for the exclusive good of another species, it would annihilate my theory, for such could not have been produced through natural selection.

Fitness is a *relative* concept, and it has no significance except in the environment of the organism. There is no such thing as absolute fitness, except in some trivial formulations of population genetics. Unlike non-living materials, living organisms actively compete, and their phenotypes, by definition, represent evolved capabilities to adjust in the face of particular kinds of competition. This does not mean that some kind of conceptual barrier to predictiveness is inherent in either an evolutionary theory based on fitness or the nature of living organisms. It only means that predictions about the evolution of life will be more difficult than predictions about nonliving phenomena, and that Stent's notion of an intrinsic quality equivalent to fitness and independent of immediate circumstances is irrelevant. There are no surprises in this for anyone who has truly considered the relative complexities of the aspects of the living and nonliving universe so far available to us.

One invariably predicts in what Stent calls "bounded situations." There are no theories which predict in the absence of assumptions. The only question is whether or not the predictions are useful in analyzing the phenomena under study. Stent may have developed his notion that evolution is not predictive partly from remarks by prominent evolutionists like Ernst Mayr and George G. Simpson to that effect; I have heard their statements cited to support such arguments. But Mayr and Simpson meant to refer to macroevolution, or the long-term patterning of life forms across geological time, which is essentially nonpredictive because we cannot reconstruct extinct enviroments in sufficient detail to understand the precise nature of adaptive change by natural selection that occurred prehistorically. This does not mean, however, that we cannot predict very extensively and with great accuracy about life from the assumption that the traits of extant organisms are the *cumulative results* of the microevolutionary process, guided chiefly by natural selection. The philosopher who wishes to understand how this is done ought to go to the current literature of evolutionary biology and not run the risk of generalizing from what he gratuitously refers to as a "vulgar popularization" by a mere "thirty-six-year-old student of animal behavior, [who] teaches at Oxford, and . . . seems to have published only one sociobiological paper . . ."

3. The reader should beware that, from this point on, when I use the term "function" I mean it in the sense of (b) above—as *evolved* or *adaptive* function, as distinguished from either "incidental effect" (see G.C. Williams, *Adaptation and Natural Selection*) or some assumption of physiological or other function in the individual that is not at least visualized as part of, or a contribution to, the ultimate function of reproductive maximization.

4. R. C. Lewontin, "The Units of Selection," *Annual Review of Ecology and Systematics* 1 (1970): 1–18; G. C. Williams, *Adaptation and Natural Selection*; E. C. Leigh, "How Does Selection Reconcile Individual Advantage with the Good of The Group?" *Proceedings of the National Academy of Sciences* 74 (1977): 4542–546; R. D. Alexander and G. Borgia, "Group Selection, Altruism, and the Hierarchical Organization of Life," *Annual Review of Ecology and Systematics* 9 (1978): 449–74.

5. There appears to be a feeling in some circles that a failure exists to define gene adequately for its use in discussions of behavioral evolution. The impression one gets is that if definitions were sharpened then implications of unacceptable determinism would disappear (or, alternatively, that evolutionary analyses of behavior would be shown to be inappropriate). Partly this feeling seems to derive from the error of supposing that such definition-sharpening would principally involve precision in describing gene function in terms of physiology or ontogeny— of generalizing about the connections between gene effects and behavior. But the generalization for this direction of definition, adequate for use of the concept of gene or genetic unit in evolutionary analyses, even of behavior, already exists: It is that genes always realize their effects in environments, and their effects change in different environments. I do not imply that all self-proclaimed evolutionists so use it, or use it appropriately or properly. Because the use of gene by evolutionary biologists actually refers principally to heritable or recombining units— or alternatives (and assumes the above physiological-ontogenetic-functional generalization or definition)—to refine the evolutionists' definitions (usages) would chiefly be a matter of describing the sizes and

divisibility of genetic units; this activity would not bear on the question of genetic determinism, as may be supposed. Genetic determinism, in its unacceptable forms, implies that only *some* behaviors are "genetically determined" (E. O. Wilson, "Human Decency is Animal," *New York Times Magazine*, October 12, 1975, pp. 38–50); that there are reasons for believing that some human social behavior is not learned (E. O. Wilson, "The Social Instinct," *Bulletin of the American Academy of Arts and Sciences* 30 (1976): 11–25); or that human behavioral variations like homosexual tendencies depend upon genetic variations which exist because of their contribution to homosexual behavior (thus, that the "capacity" for homosexuality exists only in "moderate frequencies" in the human population—E. O. Wilson, "Animal and Human Sociobiology"). In fact, either all human behavior is "genetically determined" or none of it is; unless learning is defined in a fashion dramatically more restrictive than its current usage in the social sciences there is no reasonable alternative to the hypothesis that all human social behaviors are learned; and even if some human behavioral *variations* are genetically determined (i.e., environmental variations are not involved in their expressions), there is, for example, no evidence that the capacity to behave either homosexually or heterosexually, even in rather ordinary environments, is absent in any human.

Biologists who develop general theories about behavior seem vulnerable to becoming the caricatures their adversaries initially make of them. Thus, many ethologists, originally interested in distinguishing behaviors with cryptic ontogenies from behaviors dependent upon obvious learning contingencies also were led eventually to defend them (as "innate" and "instinctive") as if they had virtually no ontogenies at all. The same thing need not have happened in the current circumstance, and this explains why some of us resent being called sociobiologists as long as to most nonbiologists the term expressly means acceptance of particular views about the ontogeny of behavior (see *Addendum 1*, pp. 150–52). It is surprising to me that Wilson, who has spent his life working on the social insects, in which the strikingly different castes are almost invariably determined by environmental variations, should seem so determined that such a vaguely defined behavioral variation as homosexuality in humans must depend upon a genetic polymorphism. Such causes were postulated for social insect castes, but they turned out to be wrong, at least in nearly every case.

6. Stent (Hastings Center Report) confuses the issue by referring to the efforts of molecular biologists to define genes in molecular terms as if theirs were the first efforts at useful definition of genetic units, with definitions functional in evolutionary analyses only coming along later

to "denature" the "meaningful and well-established central concept of genetics into a fuzzy and heuristically useless notion." This is nonsense. The gene concept was functional as a recombining unit, and highly useful as such, a half century before knowledge of DNA as its molecular basis; it has not ceased to be such a concept in evolutionary genetics, population genetics, and Mendelian genetics, despite Stent's assertion that for "all working geneticists" the concept is restricted to the unit of genetic material in which the amino acid sequence of a particular protein is encoded. Stent says that genes were "previously conceptualizable by classical genetics only in terms of differences or alleles." True enough, and they are still so conceptualized in studies outside molecular biology. The reason is that this is a very useful concept. We are back to the fact that fitness is only a matter of better versus worse in the immediate environment (Williams, *Adaptation and Natural Selection*). The important thing about genes is not what they are but what they do, and the most important thing they do is work together to produce organisms; we know very little yet about how they do that, and except for very few simple cases involving simple organisms what we know about it was not learned by studying either DNA or amino acid sequences. To behave as though all such things have to wait until we work up from the molecular level is to fail to comprehend that the secret of life is not DNA after all, but natural selection; the structure and integrity of the DNA molecule, as well as its relationship to the identity of the recombining units, are all products of natural selection. Satisfactory understanding of genetic units ultimately will involve connecting molecular-level structure and function with complex phenotypic effects, like behavior, the genetic basis of which will continue to be studied chiefly through recombination; such understanding is unlikely to be accomplished by either of these approaches alone.

7. G. C. Williams, "Pleiotropy, Natural Selection, and the Evolution of Senescence," *Evolution* 11 (1957): 398–411; W. D. Hamilton, "The Moulding of Senescence by Natural Selection," *Journal of Theoretical Biology*, 12 (1966): 12–45.

8. E. Walster and G. W. Walster. "Equity and Social Justice," *Journal of Social Issues* 31 (1975): 21–43.

9. A particularly good example is Jeremy Boissevain's approach in *Friends of Friends* (New York: St. Martin's Press, 1974). Another is B. F. Skinner, *Beyond Freedom and Dignity* (New York: Alfred A. Knopf, 1971), in which the author discusses positive and negative reinforcement in terms of *individuals* but skips to the group or species level to discuss cultural change (even though, curiously, moving back to the individual level to discuss *objections* to deliberate designing of culture through

conscious control of behavior). Never does Skinner hit upon the obvious: that *individuals* are evolved to *reproduce*: and this flaw, it seems to me, causes his entire theme (of behavioral control, design of culture, or search for "an optimal state of equilibrium in which everyone is maximally reinforced") to collapse.

10. For discussion of how the consideration of nepotism alters analyses of networks and systems of social exchange, see R. D. Alexander, "Natural Selection and Social Exchange," in *Social Exchange in Developing Relationships,*, ed. R. L. Burgess and T. L. Huston (New York: Academic Press, in press); "The Search for a General Theory of Behavior," *Behavioral Science* 20 (1975): 77–100; "Natural Selection and the Analysis of Human Sociality."

11. W. D. Hamilton, "The genetical evolution of social behaviour, I, II," *Journal of Theoretical Biology* 7 (1964): 1–52.

12. I am not suggesting that culture has no significance or value, but hypothesizing that the only *singular* thing about its significance, in historical terms, is that it derives incidentally from inclusive-fitness-maximizing behavior by individuals acting separately and in common-interest groups, and that its value—say, in terms of the present and future—will probably also be interpreted by individuals and common-interest groups on the basis of its ability to contribute to inclusive-fitness-maximizing and the surrogates of inclusive-fitness-maximizing in modern environments. This hypothesis, of course, remains to be tested.

13. To identify kin individually is to specify them as avenues of potential inclusive-fitness-maximizing by individuals. See R. D. Alexander, "Natural Selection and the Analysis of Human Sociality."

14. R. D. Alexander, "Natural Selection and Societal Laws," in *The Foundations of Ethics and Its Relationship to Science* vol. 3: *Morals, Science and Sociality* ed. H. Tristram Engelhardt and Daniel Callahan (Hastings-on-Hudson, New York: The Hastings Center, 1978).

15. For a discussion of the reasons why cultural evolution continues to accelerate in relation to organic evolution, and for other references, see R. D. Alexander, "Evolution and Culture," in *Evolutionary Biology and Human Social Behavior: An Anthropological Perspective*, ed. N. A. Chagonon and W. G. Irons (North Scituate, Mass. Duxbury Press 1979)

16. Thus, tendencies to become deleteriously obese or to seek "excessively" immediate pleasures, such as overconsuming sugar when it is abundant, are most likely to be understood by considering the kind of environment in which these propensities evolved.

17. See note 15 and references therein; also see R. D. Alexander, "Evolution, Human Behavior, and Determinism," *Proceedings of the Biennial Meeting of the Philosophy of Science Association* 2 (1976):

3–21; R. D. Alexander and G. Borgia, "Group selection, Altruism, and Levels of Organization of Life." *Annual Review of Ecology and Systematics* 9 (1978):449–74.

18. See R. D. Alexander, "The Search for a General Theory of Behavior," *Behavioral Science* 20 (1975):77–100; R. D. Alexander, "Evolution Human Behavior and Determinism,"; also R. D. Alexander and K. M. Noonan, "Concealed Ovulation and the Evolution of Human Sociality," In: *Evolutionary Biology and Human Social Behavior*.

19. See R. D. Alexander, *Darwinism and Human Affairs*. (Seattle; University of Washington Press [in press].

20. An evolutionary model does not deny that events contrary to inclusive-fitness-maximizing occur, only that when present they are most likely to be interpretable in terms of the history of environments in which they and their ontogenetic-physiological backgrounds were selected.

21. This does not exclude the possibility that some or even many scientists are, in fact, at least to the best of their ability to describe their motivations, devoted to a search for the truth. Repeated and sufficient positive social reinforcement for approaching this condition, and negative reinforcement for diverging from it, can surely bring it about.

22. Neither is it new. P. W. Bridgman, for example, expressed essentially this idea in *Reflections of a Physicist*, (New York: Philosophical Library, p. 227), in these words ". . . in scientific activity the necessity for continual checking against the inexorable facts of experience is so insistent, and the penalties for allowing the slightest element of rationalizing to creep in are so immediate, that it is obvious to the dullest that a high degree of intellectual honesty is the price of even a mediocre degree of success."

23. G. C. Williams, "Pleiotropy, Natural Selection, and the Evolution of Senescence: *Evolution* 11 (1957): 398–411; W. D. Hamilton, "The Moulding of Senescence by Natural Selection," *Journal of Theoretical Biology*, 12 (1966), 12–45.

24. R. D. Alexander, *Darwinism and Human Affairs*.

25. R. D. Alexander, *Darwinism and Human Affairs*.

26. Exactly the same set of statements could be developed into a set of *predictions* about the behavior of individuals in any extant society in which knowledge of the predictions does not exist.

27. Anyone incredulous about my acceptance of Rosenfeld's interpretation, or who fails to appreciate its extent (perhaps because of his own inability to visualize a compatibility between natural selection as a causal agent in human behavior and the kind of freedom of decision or will implied by Rosenfeld), will regard the inevitable paradox of more

and more profound self-analysis as something other than a problem for all analysts and observers; he may even see it as a special problem for the evolutionist. To the contrary, the problem will lie in the particular form of the bogey man of determinism seen in the mind's eye of such a critic, and will only disappear when his biological sophistication has exceeded the level indicated by his incredulity. A commentator on this paper, for example, suggested that I am guilty of the fallacy of self-referential inconsistency. An evolutionary view, however, may instead resolve this philosophical paradox. Thus, to say that humans have *evolved* to be nothing but inclusive-fitness-maximizing systems is not to say that in all environments they can *only* be such. Who can say what humans so evolved may do in an environment of both self-reference *and* knowledge of their evolutionary background?

28. Albert Rosenfeld, *Saturday Review*, December 10, 1977, pp. 19–20.

29. I am not arguing here that all cultural inertia has such causes, or that all cultural inertia is retrogressive; rather, only the obvious point that part of cultural inertia results from individuals and groups acting in their own personal interests, and that these interests may be realized by conserving essentially any aspect of culture, including demonstrably false ideas and interpretations.

30. John Rawls, *A Theory of Justice* (Cambridge, Mass.: Harvard University Press, 1971), pp. 548–49.

31. R. D. Alexander, "Natural Selection and Societal Laws."

32. It is worth considering in what kind of society this would not be so. I suggest that the criteria are not complex. A certain minimum contribution of each member to the common good must be specified. All material benefits and reproductive outlets (or their surrogates) above this minimum must be equalized among societal members, with graded rewards existing only in the form of differing degrees of social approval (indicated by entirely symbolic awards such as nontransferable and otherwise valueless medals, or by titles such as various orders of heroism). It would be a necessary concomitant that societal members not meeting the minimum contribution and otherwise accepting these criteria either be exiled to a less desirable circumstance or otherwise eliminated from society.

33. I allow for the essential certainty that in some circumstances, and perhaps for certain offspring more than others, parents actually manipulate offspring to maximize the parent's inclusive fitness rather than the offspring's own (See R. D. Alexander, "Evolution of Social Behavior," *Annual Review of Ecology and Systematics* 5 (1974):325–83. J. E. Blick, "Selection for Traits which Lower Individual Reproduc-

tion," *Journal of Theoretical Biology* 67 (1977):597–601, has noted that one part of my 1974 argument was wrong; this does not detract from the general asymmetry of the parent-offspring interaction, resulting from the phenotypic power difference and the facts that offspring depend on parents and parental care evolves to maximize the parent's reproductive success.

34. The advent of socialized medicine, at least in a society like our own, may actually exacerbate this problem in some respects, because it has the interesting consequence of causing medical care to become a burden on *society as a whole* which may sometimes lead to its validity or feasibility being judged in cost-benefit terms less directly relating to the welfare of the individual patients involved. Since none of us is likely to favor classes of discrimination likely to affect ourselves detrimentally, one might expect that common afflictions will sometimes be compensated when rare ones are not, or that medical compensation could become excessive in circumstances in which all in society feel threatened by the system.

35. See also R. D. Alexander, "Natural Selection and Societal Laws."

36. W. Friedmann, *Legal Theory*, 5th Edition, (London: Stevens and Sons, 1967), p. 47.

37. Michael Landman, *Philosophical Anthropology* (Philadelphia: The Westminster Press 1974), p. 22.

Addendum 1

DESPITE WILSON'S APPARENTLY erudite discussions in some parts of his 1975 book with respect to genetic and behavioral variations (e.g., pp. 26–27), several facts suggest a deficiency in his view of the relationship between genes and behavior which, although not unique to Wilson or even unusual among scientists, may underlie what I regard as a poor and confusing response to the critics of his book. Thus, although he carefully defines "instinct" (p. 587) and "innate behavior" (pp. 26–27), no definition or clear conception of the nature and limits of learning, which is treated as some kind of opposite, occurs in the book. Early in the book (p. 26) he notes that ". . . it is meaningless to ask whether blue eye color alone is determined by heredity or environment . . . . [because] Obviously both the genes for blue eye color and the environment contributed to the final product." Nevertheless, on p. 237, he asserts, with respect to birds, that "In some the male song is transmitted from generation to generation entirely by heredity, with no learning required." (He probably *means* learning by listening to bird songs but that is not what he said; hence, he is implying that *songs* not *genes* are actually inherited and require no *ontogenies*, hence, no consistency in the developmental *environment*. The only way that I can imagine this argument to be defensible—and I doubt that it was Wilson's meaning—is through genes in the somatic cells being used as the *environment* of *development* for the behavior in question. Elsewhere *(Darwinism and Human Affairs)* I have postulated this selective background for the ontogeny of some insect sexual signals, in which there is no opportunity for the male to learn how to make the

150

signals from hearing them, or for the female to learn which ones to respond to. Similarly, on p. 151, Wilson contrasts with "directed" and "generalized" learners something called "the complete instinct-reflex machine." On p. 563, he speaks of "genetically-programmed sexual and parent-offspring conflict." Nowhere does he detail the proximate developmental or experiential mechanisms—even in the most general theoretical sense—by which behaviors appropriate to inclusive-fitness-maximizing by nepotism could evolve or be expressed in plastic organisms like humans. Of course, no one else had yet done so either (though I call attention to passages in my 1971 and 1975 papers discussing this problem (R. D. Alexander, "The Search for an Evolutionary Philosophy of Man," *Proceedings of the Royal Society of Victoria,* Melbourne 84 (1971):99–120; "The Search for a General Theory of Behavior"). Few others had encountered this problem, because few others were claiming that human behavior was evolutionarily adaptive (but see R. D. Alexander, "The Search for an Evolutionary Philosophy of Man," "The Evolution of Social Behavior," *Annual Review of Ecology and Systematics* 5 (1974):325–83; "The Search for a General Theory of Behavior"; R. L. Trivers, The Evolution of Reciprocal Altruism," *Quarterly Review of Biology* (1971), 46:35–57; "Parent-Offspring Conflict," *American Zoologist* 14 (1971):249–64).

These different statements and omissions by Wilson, taken together, may in retrospect have presaged the type of defense he would develop in response to the charge of genetic determinism leveled by his critics. In fact, in parallel with other biologists before him who had experienced the same predicament, he seems to have *become* a genetic determinist, by defending the phrase and the kind of meaning his 1975 statement about blue eyes denies. In the *New York Times Magazine* of October 12, 1975 ("Human Decency is Animal"), pp. 39–50 (and elsewhere) he suggests that some of human social behavior may be genetically determined, without specifying explicitly, even in the emotion-charged atmosphere in which he was writing, that he meant some of the *variations* in human social behavior. Even that assertion is at least premature and misleading and probably indefensible—for example, it is entirely likely that even the differences between males and females that occur during their normal development because of their initial genetic differences can all (except for production of sperm and eggs) be reversed by changing their hormonal and social environments (e.g., see John Money and Anke A. Ehrhardt, *Man and Woman: Boy and Girl*, [Baltimore: The Johns Hopkins University Press, 1972].) Those of us sympathetic to Wilson's general situation of defending himself may want to give him credit for the meanings he should have specified. Others, however, did not, and on their side, unfortunately, are his various suggestions which support less acceptable meanings (Wilson, 1976, 1977, cited above).

Wilson, like everyone before him, evidently fails to understand how organisms like humans, who can learn by sitting alone and motionless and merely reflecting on their social circumstances, and whose learned behavior can itself be transmitted by learning, could possibly be expected consistently to develop and learn along lines that would maximize their individual inclusive fitnesses or genetic success. Of course they can do so only if their *environments of development* (ontogeny) and learning are consistent over long periods. This may seem to increase the importance of the genetic element. Perhaps it does so, in some sense, for explaining the past and present, but for modifying the future it does the opposite, by emphasizing the environment.

Only as a result of the discussions at these conferences has it become clear to me that the very general and widespread failure of understanding about the bases for the actual evolution of all ontogenies and learning ability is the crux of the problem faced by evolutionists in their efforts to develop and explain legitimate hypotheses about the evolution of all behavior, including and especially that of humans. Understanding this aspect of evolution, I believe, is also a problem for any other persons who wish to participate in the development of a human understanding of human behavior, and I mean explicitly to include philosophers and humanists as well as social scientists.

Addendum 2

AT THE LAST CONFERENCE someone remarked that science cannot contribute to the problem of understanding free will. Because of my impression that this kind of assumption underlies much of the resistance to biological-evolutionary interpretations of human tendencies, and because I regard it as an unwarranted assumption, I am appending this essay (expanded in *Darwinism and Human Affairs*) which I believe shows that reasonable and testable hypotheses can be generated about the biological nature and function of what we call "free will."

An integral aspect of consciousness is the phenomenon of self-awareness, and self-awareness, in turn, at least partly involves what Robert Burns called seeing ourselves as others see us. To a biologist—probably to almost anyone at all—this aspect of self-awareness is easily seen as crucial to success in social matters; in turn, biological (reproductive) success—the focus of the evolutionary biologist's interest—depends upon social success.

In some large part our conscious awareness of ourselves and our social circumstances is taken up with what might be called social "scenario-building." Almost continually we play out in our minds the possible and probable moves in the game of social living, which of course is not a game at all but the real thing. How can I write this paper (deliver this lecture, study for this examination, approach this policeman or judge or merchant or bully or friend) so as to achieve this or that personal goal? What will he or she do if I do this or that? What action by me will most likely cause my desired ends to be achieved? If I do this, and he does that, and then I do something else, then what?—and so on.

In such scenario-building we seem to see before us alternatives. We actually perceive beforehand—through, I believe, a marshalling of all the information available to us from the past and present—possible choices that we can make. We assume that we can take any one of those choices that we wish to take. We evaluate them, and we apparently take whichever one we decide is best (or preferred or whatever). We cherish the right to make the decision ourselves, on our own bases, and the additional right to keep the reasons private, and not even to review them consciously if we do not wish to.

This projecting and weighing of possibilities, it seems to me, has the obvious correlate that the most unpredictable aspect of our environment is the sets of other social individuals and collectives with which we must interact. They too are building scenarios, and, as in a game of chess, we will be best prepared to accomplish our purposes—whatever they may be—by knowing how to respond after *different* possible responses by our interactants to given events or circumstances.

I suggest that the essence of free will is the right to build our own scenarios and act on them for our own reasons without having to justify them—in other words, that free will involves nothing in particular about the causes of our behavior except our right to determine them—to weigh costs and benefits in our own terms.

To the extent that this is a correct interpretation, the problem of understanding free will resolves to that of understanding the bases on which we make our judgments of possible alternatives and why we cherish the right to be personal, private, and individual about such judgments.

The only background I can imagine for a compulsive adherence to such a privilege by every different individual—and at the same time an eminently reasonable one in biological terms—is that the reproductive interests of every individual are unique. Only monozygotic twins, among humans, share identical sets of relatives, and even they are unlikely to share identical sets of friends. Moreover, monozygotic twins likely have no significant social history in humans because of the evidence of prevalent infanticide of twins (R. D. Alexander, "The Evolution of Social Behavior").

This means that, in biological terms, the right to make our own personal decisions about our own futures is the ultimately precious possession of individual humans. Even if societal rules and obligations actually place enormous restrictions on this privilege, we strive for the right to apply and interpret these restrictions, as they affect us, by and for ourselves.

So we are brought to the question of how we actually make our cost-benefit assessments and arrive at decisions of the sort we term exercise of free will. Only if we know ahead of time that no sense can be made of this question would the assertion mentioned at the outset of this essay be appropriate. I do not think that we know this. Instead, I offer the hypothesis that these decisions— judged in terms of the environments of history—will tend to be those which maximize our inclusive fitnesses, that we have evolved to be exceptionally good at such decisions, and that this is the precise reason for the existence and nature of consciousness and self-awareness. I have offered elsewhere the further hypothesis that it is from just this kind of individual decision-making with respect to inclusive-fitness-maximizing, by the aggregate of all humans who have ever lived, that the phenomenon we call culture has generated. I am satisfied that this hypothesis is testable, and that such testing is already underway (e.g., Alexander, "Natural Selection and the Analysis of Human Sociality").

Thus, there is no reason to regard culture, consciousness, and free will as either outside or contrary to efforts to understand humans in evolutionary terms; instead, there appear to be good reasons for believing that our understanding of these attributes— uniquely expressed in humans, though in all likelihood shared by at least chimpanzees—will best be furthered by analyzing them in evolutionary biological terms.

Reasons Alexander's View Cannot Be Proved: Response to Richard D. Alexander

Paul Ramsey

ONE QUESTION HAS PUZZLED ME since I was a precocious schoolboy. Are some babies predetermined to become Latin schoolteachers, I asked; or, alternatively, are Latin schoolteachers organisms whose ultimate function is to influence children so that some of them (as many as possible) become Latin schoolteachers? When I became a man, I put away such childish formulations of the question. Richard Alexander has provided me with a far more sophisticated way to put the question and—what is more important—a way to answer it grounded solely in biological evolution.

The question can now be (too simply) stated: are some babies genetically encoded to become Latin schoolteachers in certain operant environments, or does the phenotypical behavior of Latin schoolteachers serve exclusively to insure that their genes survive? When I fully understand and correctly explain their behavior, I should now know that "the ultimate function" of these organisms "is *invariably* reproduction of the genetic materials" (italics added). He puts the reader on notice (note 3) that whenever the word "function" is used later in this chapter, it has the meaning just stated.

156

To grasp this, I must first learn to distinguish between proximate and ultimate functions; in any environment proximate functions "exist to serve ultimate function." If my teachers were happy in their work and gained satisfaction from it—or even if they were grouchy and seemed or were actually made unhappy by their tasks but remained devoted to them—this is an appearance of things. Their happiness or devotion was only a proximate form of what they were doing. All their striving was a peculiarly human mode of reproductive striving and not ultimately the love of classical learning and culture. If there was altruism in the school system, it was "altruistic nepotism"; if there was reciprocity or a common professional ethics among them, it was the "altruism of reciprocity"—where the word "altruism" means ultimately an extended striving to maximize inclusive fitness (reproduction of one's genes). The only "returns" a teacher ever got were some "coming to Ego's phe-
. notype" and others "coming to Ego's genotype, through the success of various kinds of relatives including offspring, and representing reproductive success. *In evolutionary terms, all returns are of the second kind*" (italics added). Just as, according to Alexander, "there is no other reason for lifetimes having evolved to be finite," there can be no other reason for Latin-teaching phenotypes to have evolved nor any "function" in them beyond maximizing genetic survival. We pupils were surrogates for kin. A neat explanation of my schoolmarms, the schoolboy impishly interjects.

Alexander's Explanation of Altruism

Forms of sociality tending to manifest what we commonly call altruism can "exist only as a result of accidents, or sudden environmental changes rendering an organism temporarily maladapted or incompletely adapted; whenever present, such altruism should be tending to disappear."[1] This is the one place I have found where Alexander uses the term "altruism" as a "moral notion" inclusive of benevolent intention.

In our discussions I suggested that Alexander use "beneficial," or some such expression, for his meaning. This he does in other articles. Instead of the "altruism of nepotism" he frequently says simply "nepotism," or "altruists of a *very special sort*, whose *benefit-giving* is . . . directly or indirectly aimed at genetic relatives."[2] Instead of the "altruism of reciprocity," he frequently says "social reciprocity" in "dispensing benefits" to nonrelatives. He describes our evolved "very special sort" of altruism as "phenotypically (or self-)sacrificing but *genotypically selfish.*"[3] If "altruism" is an appropriate word for Alexander's meanings, then we can label his own position "gene-selfishness." Both are misuses of the moral notions of benevolence and of selfishness. Thus, taking my cue from the author, I urged him to use the word "beneficence" for the forms of sociality he undertakes to explain in terms of inclusive-fitness-maximizing behavior.

Instead of following my helpful suggestion, Alexander moved in the opposite direction. He added a note (2) stressing the importance of *intent*. He asks "*why* intent is so important to us, when it would seem that *consequences* are what count." The reason, he believes, is that

> . . . intent has consequences outside the immediate circumstances, I think we *use* intent to enable us to predict about events additional to the ones in which we are immediately involved, just as we use information about whether associates follow the rules or play fair in trivial circumstances, or in games, to determine whether we should interact with them in more serious matters. We actually believe that he who is cruel or kind to others—or to animals, children, and other vulnerable beings—is likely to be cruel or kind to us as well. We are positive toward someone who *intends* to be altruistic for the same reason that we are negative toward someone who *intends* to be cruel: He may do it to us.

In this explanation, it is still gene-benefits alone that count. Moreover, it is only beneficence or maleficence in some immediate circumstances (not benevolence or altruism) that insure long term beneficence in consequences of the sort Alexander values most—or has room for in his system.

Let us see how this works out. Because the conservation and proliferation of one's own genes is each actor's ultimate concern, each gives nontrivial approval to what he deems to *manifest* benevolent intentions in others. The next actor does the same, and so on. *Everyone* does so, with the result that in the aggregate a general approbation of beneficence, *miscalled* benevolence, characterizes any group we may have in mind. What others are liable to do to us is the sole issue, and so we watch carefully to see what are their characteristic actions. The same is the case in the games we play; we watch carefully to see whether an opponent *plays* fairly. No doubt reciprocity is a consequence, but not the reciprocity of *fairness* or of *altruism*.

At most, it could be said that we need others who have these dispositions. *Everyone* needs that, but no one has it. No one has it, because the approbation bestowed on kindness by each of the primary actors is entirely a matter of "preemptive defense," the defense of all that is ultimately precious, or at least operative, in their natures: the preservation and proliferation of their genes.[4] No account is given of how generous intentions in any primary actor could supervene upon the primary function of genetic maximization, except as a short-lived aberration in some environments.

The paradoxical aspect of the molding of "intent" as a proximate mechanism to contribute to ultimate function is increased when Alexander tell us that not all goals are conscious. Benevolent intentions are devoted to conscious goals, but these are proximate. Now suppose Alexander succeeds in showing all primary actors how everyone's intent is molded to contribute to ultimate function. Primary function raised to consciousness would displace those benevolent intentions. Will not everyone then act as he is expected to act, and expects to be expected to act as a reproductive predator? No one will manifest the kindness each primary actor in turn needs and approbates *in others*. Indeed, genuine generosity can only occur in others so long as they are ignorant of the ultimate function such generosity serves in the eyes of the beholder who needs it for his own reproductive maximization.

My view, therefore, remains that Alexander has given an account of certain circumstances under which interchanges of a special sort of *beneficence* may come to play a role in human evolution (and elsewhere in evolution). He has not legitimated his use of moral notions such as benevolence or altruism, which require sometimes intending the good of others for their own sake.

Alexander's Specific Interpretation of Scientists

In the section on "Science as a Social Enterprise," Alexander adduces much unquestionable evidence to prick the bubble of scientific pride. Still I find his account of the morality of the scientific enterprise too jaundiced, as surely as his account of benevolence, and of morality in general, is flawed. Doubtless not many scientists (and not many human beings) are *humble* truth-seekers. The question is whether they are at all seekers for truth, or only inclusive reproductive maximizers in their work as scientists.

To this section Alexander adds a note (21) which reads: "This does not exclude the possibility that some or even many scientists are, at least to the best of their ability to describe their motivations, in fact devoted to a search for the truth. Repeated and sufficient positive social enforcements for approaching this condition, and negative reinforcement for diverging from it, can surely bring it about." The operant environment alone produces truth-seekers scientists.

This minimal tribute is set within the general framework of inclusive-fitness-maximizing, on the one hand, and the history of environments on the other. Therefore, I must ask: What if anything is the dissimilarity between this account of a scientist's pursuit of truth and the account given of another (in this case, counterevolutionary) phenomenon? This note (16) reads: ". . . Tendencies to become deleteriously obese or to seek 'excessively' immediate pleasures, such as overconsuming sugar when it is abundant, are most likely to be understood by considering the kind of environment in which these propensities evolved." The difference, if any, is that our present tolerance or adulation of scientists flows from a belief that the benefits delivered are "helping everyone about equally" in our ultimate function, while in the long run obesity does not. Still it is difficult to understand why Alexander rejects seizing "the opportunity to reproduce far into the future (for example, through sperm banks)." This would be a desire "to prolong the phenotype at whatever cost." Any cost to be rejected, so far as I can see, must be shown to be counterproductive in our environment, or that there are better ways to attain the same end.

A brief comparison with J. Bronowski's account of *the ethics of science* should make clear the sweeping challenge and threat to the very foundations of science itself (not simply to its necessarily presupposed standards of morality, and not only to a more general humanistic ethics) that is directly entailed by Alexander's *philosophy* (for such it is). In his *Science and Human Values*,[5] Bronowski showed the logically necessary placement of certain canons of conduct in the history of science as a cultural enterprise; or, as he preferred to put the point, "the place of science in the canons of conduct which it has still to perfect." He brought up to view "the [moral] conditions for the success of science and [found] in them the values of man which science would have had to invent if man had not otherwise known them."[6] (The word "known" sets the ethics of science properly in the context of a broader humanistic ethics, of which the former is only a special case.) These canons of conduct are the necessary presupposition of there being any place whereon science, with its truth-claims, can stand. Chief among these is "the habit of truth," which has made our society and upon which the making of science depends as surely as the enterprise of science made the linotype machine or Darwin's *Origin of Species*. Another canon of conduct is the knowing-community that science presupposes, and the fact that verification has no meaning if it is assumed to be carried out by one person without reference to a community of discourse held together by moral bonds.[7] Thus, truth depends on "truthfulness"—"a principle which binds society together, because without it the individual would be helpless to tell the true from the false." Bronowski formulates a categorical imperative that is a necessary presupposition, or condition, of the possibility of scientific knowledge: "We *ought* to act in such a way that what *is* true can be verified as such."[8]

The virtues and moral standards of science are not an alien code imposed on its activity. The values of science derive neither from the personal superiority of its participants nor from "finger-wagging codes." Instead, they "spring from the pith and sap of the work they regulate"; "they have grown out of the practice of science, because they are the inescapable condition for its practice." "An ethics of science . . . derives directly from its own practice." This ethics includes the values of tolerance and democracy, since "science cannot survive without justice and honor and respect between man and man." Finally, by this essentially presuppositional method of justification, Bronowski affirms the unique value of the individual: science "must prize the search above the discovery and the thinking (and with it the thinker) above the thought. In the society of scientists each man, by the process of exploring for the truth, has earned a dignity more profound than his doctrine. A true society is sustained by the sense of human dignity."[9] Thus, for the enterprise of science man's whole dignity consists in thought (as Pascal said), no matter what the *contents* of a particular science—bent on self-destruction—may say that seems to be *reductive* of human stature generally. Man is a truth-seeking, truth-finding, and truth-using animal. A science that denies this cannot claim to be true. Bronowski goes so far as to suggest that "in societies where these values do not exist, science has had to create them."[10] If there is a culture that does not acknowledge the universal canons of conduct which are the conditions of the very possibility of science, we would have replicate a set of the values and (if this were possible) transfer it to such a prescientific precivilization. Bronowski's view may be deemed excessive and parochial if and only if "science" is construed too narrowly.

Still I would have no decisive objection to raise if Alexander was only throwing buckets of cold water on Bronowski's "idealism." Then we could try to find a *via media* between the idealism and Alexander's greater "realism" and scepticism. So radically does Alexander undercut, however, the conditions of the possibility of the pursuit of truth in science that it would be fruitless to search for a more balanced view between these two accounts of science, or these two accounts of the mind's orientation upon truth. Is it not clear that for Alexander the quest for truth is a propensity arising in some environments likely to last as long as there are positive and negative operant conditioning for this particular manifestation on the part of certain persons, and a consequent community and tradition of persons, who in this fashion engage in genes-survival?

I belong to a Club of One—myself. It is a nonprofit organization named Gloomier than Thou, Inc. Indeed, in some circles I am known as the Happy Prophet of Doom—happy because I enjoy talking about the human condition and the dim prospects for humankind in the present day, and relish seeing my contemporaries—liberals, all—trying to squirm out of the obvious. Two persons in our interdisciplinary discussions seem to me to be gloomier than I, and I'm unhappy about that threat to my cozy Club. At least their expressed views seem essentially gloomier than mine, until one or the other participant snaps to the opposite extreme of an unearthly optimism. Since my critical category for illuminating the human condition is "original sin," I ask myself: What outlook could possibly produce anyone gloomier than I? Since I never pass up an opportunity to explain a little bit of the meaning of that concept or other biblical or Christian perspectives to contemporary intellectuals who are culturally deprived of the ability even to comprehend such notions,[11] I will pursue my question briefly.

Alexander's and every other naturalistic reductionism seems to me to be both a false and a gloomier view of the human condition and of our prospects than was ever produced by any variant on the theme "original sin." A Reinhold Niebuhr, for example, would certainly have said than man's capacity and quest for truth makes science possible, while man's propensity for self-aggrandizement, deception, and self-deception makes all sorts of cautions and precautions necessary, and warrants deep suspicion of the quest.[12] He often pointed out how the "hard sciences" have certain built-in constraints upon a scientist's egoism, forcing the mind to conform itself to reality, while bias and prejudice and one's location in culture and class are the more released as one moves along the spectrum to the "soft sciences." No one is a pure seeker for truth. Niebuhr could certainly have written Alexander's sentences: ". . . The system of investigation called science . . . *forces* its practitioners to report their methods as well as their results, at risk of being exposed as unscientific and drummed out of the profession"; "this competition includes identifying and publishing the errors of others. As nearly as scientists are aware, the slightest taint of deliberate falsification of results or plagiarism is often enough to damage a career permanently, and may be vastly more significant than mere incompetence." This seems to me to be the proper "realism" to set alongside Bronowski's idealism. The context in Alexander, however, is one in which he seems to me to have dehumanized the scientist and the scientific enterprise far more than Niebuhr's critical category of "original sin" ever entailed. There is a vast difference between "reductionism" and "sin." So I read Alexander to be gloomier than I about the human condition.

So also is Alasdair MacIntyre, with whom I have far more agreement. From his present chapter and other writings brilliantly analyzing the moral fragmentation of all modern societies, one gets the impression that there is nothing to be done to put the pieces together again, no fragment or tradition worth joining with any hope that life may again be breathed into these bones. I rather wish I could say to MacIntyre, I am *as* gloomy as thou. Then we would have a Club of Two. But I cannot. The reason, I think, is because from the perspectives I bring to his data and bring to bear upon the modern condition and the human condition generally, I never had good religious reason to expect anything other than fragmentation in humankind's knowledge of good and evil—not since God's verdict at Babel when he confused human tongues lest we succeed in our human pretense to build a tower to high heaven. But this does not mean that there is no building to be done on the human city, or nothing to be gained from ethical inquiry as an ongoing enterprise.

MacIntyre looks—with realistic, unexpectant eyes—for a new unity of the moral ethos as a happening to come; and, as we shall see, Alexander flips over to an unearthly optimism.

Circularity

Alexander describes his new view of sociality as "clearly a return to a kind of individualistic and utilitarian view of history"—even as a "Hobbesian" or "utilitarian" view of culture that may be thought "out of date." He claims, however, that his is "a view of individualism and utilitarianism never before held or advocated in efforts to explain human behavior and culture," one that is "distinct from any view previously generated." This claim is no doubt true.

Nevertheless, Alexander's account—however novel—manifests some of the characteristics of classical utilitarianism and is open to the objections that have often been brought against this school of ethics. One of these common characteristics is worth noticing here.

All forms of utilitarianism are forced to explain aspects of moral experience and common moral judgments that apparently do not fit the theory. The British utilitarians believed that judgments about right and wrong actions were judgments concerning their usefulness to the end of the greatest happiness altogether. (Other values can be substituted for happiness, including genetic survival.) Yet they could not deny that ordinary moral discourse contained many seeming *terminal* appeals besides happiness—to justice, for example, to fairness, and to virtues such as courage or temperance. The utilitarians needed to show that these apparently terminal norms or virtues were not truly final (cf. not the ultimate function of the human organism). To accomplish this task a theory of "lapsed links" was devised,[13] a psychosocial history of morality.

According to this account, mankind once abundantly experienced the conduciveness of justice, fairness, courage, temperance, etc., to the end of greater happiness. This was to say, teleology justified and established the respect we have for these virtues, moral roles, and relationships. There was moral experience of the connection. It was imprinted on our consciousness. Then mankind forgot about the connection of virtue with happiness. The linkage lapsed from vivid memory, and so moral language came to be filled with deontological, justice, and virtue terminology (which are only seemingly independent of happiness). For purpose of social reform in nineteenth-century England, it was necessary to couple the links again with the greatest happiness in order to dispel the false limits to be found in traditional morals, law, and social structures. Thus the claim was that sound reasoning about good consequences is quite sufficient to sustain and account for the moral substance of the intermediary terms that falsely were believed by many to have an independent meaning and normative weight. The theory of "lapsed links" explained the "false consciousness" of the independence of some aspects of ethics from ends.

Alexander's explanation goes deeper than that, even if he does not go quite to the bottom of the night. Indeed, everything is clear where he bottoms. The most important thing genes do is work together to produce organisms; the most important thing organisms do is to produce and conserve genes, not what human organisms *think* they do or *intend* to do. The process of genetic survival has forged a "link" between itself and consciously entertained goals. It also "lapsed" those links, suppressing the ultimate function of altruism or justice to below the level of every conscious human enterprise, encoding us even to reject Alexander's explanation of our virtues. I judge that my comparison of the utilitarian psychosocial lapsed-link theory with Alexander's "sociobiological" lapsed-link theory is an apt one. If this is so, we must say of both resorts to such explanations that they reveal nothing so much as that the school of thought or the theorist in question has pressed a univocal account of human behavior too far, and that they secretly suspect that there are some aspects of morality that are not entirely corrigible to the explanation proffered.

It was quite necessary for Alexander to propose a novel form of the "lapsed-link" theory—one never before held or advocated in efforts to explain human behavior, culture, and morality. Once he identified "best interests," "maximizing outcomes," "happiness" and "survival" (of individual or group) with "reproductive success" or "surrogates of reproductive success," it remained necessary for him to explain why human consciousness and moral experience are apparently not aware of this primal striving. Hence he asserts a "lapsed-link" theory distinct from any previously generated.

We are first placed on notice of the need for some theory to explain (or explain away) contrary data by Alexander's puzzlement over (or is it relish for?) an upsurge of rejection of his theory. His conclusions will be "*discomforting* to an organism with consciousness only[14] at the individual level," but this is no reason for denying it (italics added). His views must face widespread "scepticism"; this requires explanation. The truth, however, is something else than the claim that scientists are hearty pursuers of truth. His account of science as a proximate function is not for Alexander "counterintuitive," but he grants that it is not the mostly widely held view. To resolve all conflicts of interests into "conflicts over the differential reproduction of genetic units" is not only "dramatic" but "unnerving." "Alas, it cannot be true" that parents provide any moral nurture for their children except that which will ultimately serve their own gene-proliferation. His own view will "at first sound *pernicious*" (italics added). Thus, it seems that actual human consciousness is peculiarly problematic, and ordinarily accepted moral judgments as well. We could even say that we human beings are afflicted with false consciousness. Just so, the British utilitarians had to explain (or explain away) many immediate elements of moral consciousness in order to reduce ethics and public policy to happy consequences alone.

The "lapsed-link" theory was an elaborate way of begging the question in favor of happy consequences as the only norm. It assumed what had to be proved, and, moreover, contrary to the testimony of moral experience. A similar circularity afflicts Alexander's attempt to explain human sociality and culture exclusively in terms of gene proliferation (his ultimate end, "interest" or "function"). Personal consciousness and its recoils must be explained in terms of the theory itself, incorporated into the "general theory" to prop it up. Contrary data in moral experience are subsumed into Alexander's single explanatory model.

On the face of it, the author assumes what has to be proved. Not, I emphasize, his refinements of the scientific theory of evolution; Gunther Stent and other scientists can argue with the author over the science. I mean rather to say, that as an inclusive interpretation of human culture, law, politics, ethics, and even science itself, Alexander assumes what has to be proved. This comes to focus in the fact that consciousness and all its forms must be given gene-proliferation explanation. Goals consciously entertained are largely if not entirely illusory, arising from self-deception, which in turn can only be explained by virtue of a returning recoil or impact of the ultimate function suppressing from consciousness the true explanation of human behavior: maximizing gene survival.

In the list of eight major reasons that "have *clouded* efforts to develop culture theory in this direction" (italics added), I read "illusion"—functional illusion—in every one of them. In short, acceptance of the theory is clouded because our consciousness is clouded to the real truth about human behavior, moral institutions, and so on. The confusion and misdirection of conscious striving itself is an evolutionary strategy. This surely begs the question that has to be proved about the conscious goals of Latin schoolteachers and more serious matters as well, namely, the thesis that the organism in all its human flourishing is only the gene's way of making more genes—in given operant environments, of course.

The circularity becomes patent when Alexander writes that

> It is particularly perplexing that we must investigate the extent to which our behavior supports this hypothesis under the realization that, if such goals do guide our behavior, they are nevertheless not consciously perceived, and, if the hypothesis is correct, this means, paradoxically, that we are evolved to reject these goals whenever we are asked to evaluate them consciously. [Here is the lapsed-link theory never before generated.] This does not mean that we *must* reject them, but that individuals not aware of all this are expected to behave as if these were their goals even if denying it is so, and that to convince them of self-deception may be difficult, and will be most difficult for the precise activities about which they deceive themselves, for the same reason they do so.[15]

Thus, Alexander has prepared for himself in advance not only a gene-proliferation explanation of consciousness and all its fruits, perplexities and recoils, but also an impregnable (because circular) defense against any and all reasons hitherto offered, or that may be advanced in the future, for believing that an adequate understanding of human sociality and ethics needs some different analysis, or even a supplementary analysis[16] or foundation in addition to the one he provides. All our conscious goals and cultural achievements are "noble lies," or at least the illusions, that our genes teach us in given environments.

Self-Referential Contradiction

As I read Alexander, science itself is located among human cultural achievements that are epiphenomenal to the human organisms's invariable enterprise of maximizing inclusive fitness (the reproduction of one's genes). That includes in particular Alexander's own science of evolutionary biology (and not only his overextensions of this into an allegedly complete interpretation of human affairs—which was at the center of my foregoing responses).

Here I must judge that Alexander's entire scheme collapses. He refutes himself. He is entrapped in what philosophers call the "fallacy of self-referential contradiction."[17] Some philosophers, I grant, have *stipulated* that this logical contradiction is to be resolved by *stipulating* that their theories are exempted from the requirements placed by them upon all other interpretations. By *declaring* that other viewpoints are on a second-order level below one's own interpretation, one could escape the fallacy of self-referential contradiction. That seems to me to be fudging.[18] Alexander must submit his own particular biological science (and, of course, also his far reaching extrapolation from it) to the test of his own theory of all theories. His own view *as a scientist* can be no more than an organism's "inclusive-benefit-maximizing" genetic behavior. If his theory is correct in *what* it says about science among our conscious enterprises, there is no ground in it upon which to rest a truth-claim in its behalf. Alas, it cannot be so. It can only be the author's preferred gene strategy.[19] This means logically that no one even among the science-prone elite— such as we are—need pay any more attention to Alexander's genetic science (leave aside his extrapolations to culture and ethics) than we should pay attention to someone who says that "angels are blue."

Further to illustrate the fallacy of self-referential contradiction fatal to Alexander's view of *science*, consider the dictum of Nietzsche, that "I am not much more than an animal taught to dance by blows and scant fare."[20] The words "not much more" admit, of course, a softer claim like a few of Alexander's lapses from his stronger claim. Without that opening to a broader view, this statement of Zarasthustra's (considered alone) can be excluded from the realm of truth, scientific or otherwise, because it excludes itself from claiming to be true by alleging that it is in some important sense inclusively the case. The statement is a self-referential contradiction. The speaker is either (a) much more than an animal stricken and starved if such a statement is to be entered into intelligible discourse about who or what man is (in which case the statement is false) or else the speaker is (b) only an animal taught to dance, also in that particular statement, by blows and scant fare (in which case no one can claim to know the statement to be true; it can exert no claim upon the assent of another human intellect). Blows and starvation that produced the proposition that "angels are blue" would have equal (i.e., no) claim to truth, or to represent the nature of things as they are.

A science that cannot account for its own truth-claims as such cannot be science. In particular, the view that all human thought solely serves genetic survival cannot claim to be true. To claim this contradicts the alleged science itself; it is footless; it has no leg upon which to stand except reproductive survival. Who then can say, another "science" might work as well or proximately function better toward that success?

At one, somewhat obscure, point in his paper Alexander seems to concede that this is the case. Claiming that his position is "distinct from any view previously generated" and from particular ideologies such as social Darwinism, he states that "its *testing* is a procedure of natural history" (italics added). If a meaning is to be assigned to such a testing, what can this be if it is not that we shall have to wait to see whether those who espouse this particular science are more successful than others in spreading and conserving their genes—and, in turn, the genes for such espousal? In which case, the science cannot claim to be true now or later, but only to be more than any other science conducive to reproductive survival (and so the science survives) as, it predicts, "angels are blue" will not.

As long as Alexander refuses to come out of the closet, however, he remains secure. It is always open to him to affirm and reaffirm that the most important thing going on in these discussions of ours is environmentally adaptive. Hence, he writes at one point, "We may expect that merely reading these words could represent a significant alteration of the adaptive environment of some readers." Upon being told that "he is compelled to do in any situation what will be for him most reproductive," someone may propose to lay a wager with Alexander that he can do the unexpected. To win the bet, he alters his behavior. But then the size of the bet was his unwitting cost-benefit decision having reproductive advantage, and he neglected to consider "what it means that the intensity of our argument, or the number and significance of the persons observing our disagreement, might also influence his decision about which course of action to take . . . . A history of differential genetic reproduction is thus most deterministic for the human still unaware of it."[21] The same thing can be said if I now lapse into silence, and of a reader's reasonable conviction that I should have done so long ago.

Apart, therefore, from Alexander's account of ethics, altruism, justice, right and wrong, culture, and human striving in general, his view of genetic survival seems to me to pull the foundation from under the very possibility of science itself. By "science" I here mean no highfalutin view of science as knowledge of Truth, but only apprehension of the natural facts of the case. This *particular* view of the science of evolution contradicts itself whenever, if ever, it claims to be a true account of all things that are. It has no room for its own validity. It can only claim (if we pay attention to its contents) to be a viewpoint we are evolved to reject.

I add—though it needs no saying—that there may be "naturalisms" or viewpoints built upon evolution as a science that have sufficient amplitude to make room for assertions of their own validity without self-referential contradiction.[22] I am not here arguing for the autonomy of the moral point of view, much less for theological ethics. Alexander's understanding of genetic survival, however, seems to me to be self-refuting in the way I have explained.

The author's central question is: "What does the new view of human sociality mean for our understanding of ethics, and, in turn, what does the view of ethics *so generated* mean for the relationship of science and ethics?" (italics added). That would seem to be at most a filial incestuous relationship; indeed, not a relationship between two terms. But let us not pause on this point. Instead, I ask: What is an appropriate response—from the other side of interdisciplinarity on the subject of the foundations of ethics in relation to science—to the central question just quoted? At the heart of the matter: How shall we respond to an ethics so generated? Simply by pointing out that a science so generated and an ethics so generated are in precisely the same predicament. Beyond that, nothing more. Silence, at last. For *any* positive counterproposal concerning a moral point of view is bound to be consumed by a science that has already consumed itself in self-referential contradiction. Meantime, an ethicist is entirely free to pursue his organism's gene-proliferating phenotypical tasks in his own fashion. This the ethicist can do, secure in the knowledge that no objections or reductive interpretations from evolutionary science (as Alexander understands it) can touch him. For that science tripped over its own feet. The conditions of the possibility of scientific truth-claims went bottoms up. This particular general theory of mankind's cultural enterprises self-destructed the science on which it was built.[23] It therefore has no power to criticize negatively the claimed independence or quasi-independence of a moral point of view based on reason or on revelation.

Alexander's Utopian Vision of One Possible Future

I confess that when I first read Alexander on the normative ethics of yesterday and those of the future, I thought he was using the word "normative" as I am accustomed to use it as an ethicist; and that the quotation marks around the word "should" only indicated a scientist's reluctance to speak "normatively," i.e., imperatively. I now see that the word "should" was only *predictive* of what, on the hypothesis of inclusive reproductive maximization, we would find to be descriptively the case about a society's actual norms or moral teachings. The "norms" of past and extant moralities (mores) confirm, as expected or "predicted," the ultimate evolutionary function (another and more basic state of affairs). "I 'should' treat others so as to maximize my inclusive fitness. My treatment of relatives 'should' be more altruistic than my treatment of nonrelatives," since "altruism to kin should be more likely than altruism to nonkin in situations in which phenotypic returns are unlikely."

Leave aside the world of difference between a scientist's use of "normative" and "should" for descriptions or predictions of states of affairs and the meaning with which any ethicist uses such moral terms. Alexander's meaning only strengthens the incredulity I expressed concerning Rosenfeld's hope that genetic truth shall make us free "for the first time in our history" to "work for ourselves, instead of our genes, exercising truly free will and free choice, give free reign to our minds and spirits, attain something close to our full humanhood";[24] and strengthens the incredulity I expressed concerning Alexander's statement that consciousness of inclusive reproductive maximization can enable us "to cancel, literally to *cancel*, any behavioral traits identified to [us] as typically or uniquely human, which [we] then decide [we] do not like."[25] Why must not any "statement by a biologically knowledgeable investigator" about the normative ethics of tomorrow "applicable to any cultural situation" be the same as his predictive statements about past moralities? Why should not the concepts of right and wrong continuous across generations be the same? Is it only in this society that children are taught to be truthful or to deceive with cleverness to guide them toward inclusive-fitness-maximizing behavior, or else lose out? I do not myself subscribe to Alexander's cynical view of the moral education that has characterized past and present societies. But if true, he has given us no good reason for believing that any futures hold forth significant change.

Alexander does draw a speculative picture of an environment in which parents could teach their children (without making them "rubes of society, to whom advantage would be taken at every turn," not to deceive, to tell the truth, to be just and even altruistic in their dealings with others. In note 32, he considers what kind of society would have to exist in which it would *not* be true that children must be taught no more than the outer limits of nepotism and reciprocity soundly grounded in inclusive-fitness-maximization. This would be an environment in which all things are guaranteed to work together noncompetitively for good to all those who serve reproductive proliferation. (I am confident that the scriptural allusion back of that sentence will be plain to everyone.) The environment can be easily construed:

> A certain minimum contribution of each member to the common good must be specified. All material benefits and reproductive outlets (or their surrogates) above this minimum must be equalized among societal members, with graded rewards only in the form of differing degrees of social approval (indicated by entirely symbolic awards such as nontransferable and otherwise valueless medals, or by titles such as various orders of heroism). It would

be a necessary concomitant that societal members not meeting the minimum contribution and otherwise accepting these criteria either be exiled to a less desirable circumstance or otherwise eliminated from society. (n. 32.)

This is a picture—like many others—of an ideal utopian environment in which the lion of genetic survival shall lie down with the lamb of righteousness; and a child shall play at the hole of an asp without being stung for its own innocent kindness. History to date has been prehuman; now the age of the human spirit and righteousness can begin. The picture is also one of an *enforced* equality of access to reproductive outlets and an *enforced* alignment of every individual's relentless striving to proliferate his genes with the common good.

Moreover, what is the *use* of a useless award or medal? Has not Alexander explained to us that the ultimate function at work in all proximate human behaviors is not only that they actually maximize the individual's genes-survival but also may only be *believed* to do so? Why will prizes cease to be prized for that ultimate function? Has not Alexander forgotten the stringent genetic account he has given of all *heroism* and of self-sacrifice? From that account I extrapolate that Jesus from the cross commended his mother to the care of his beloved disciple John, not knowing she would remain perpetually virgin (that dogma came later); that the ultimate function behind his proximate behavior could be predicted to lead to greater esteem for everyone of the brothers (or cousins) mentioned in the Gospel accounts, or was believed by him to redound to the credit of surrogates for kin having like-minded genes! It may be expected that any prizes offered to heroes of the common good will disturb or be believed to disturb the equality of reproductive access or its surrogates in the new aeon. Either human biological and cultural evolution will have suddenly stopped, or else the prizes will have the uses with which we are familiar. In any case the morality of yesterday will resume among those who are "exiled to less desirable circumstance." Therefore, the remedy must be to "otherwise" eliminate them from society; and this will require a purge without end in the age of the new freedom and the new humanity.

And who will be the Enforcers? At first I thought to say that they must be an oligarchy of properly instructed evolutionary biologists. From time to time there will arise a Wilt Chamberlain who dearly loves to play basketball for the esteem it gets him. This will have to be suppressed if a counterrevolution to unequal access to gene proliferation is to be prevented. In the age to come the task of rulership will not be simply to beguile or direct ultimate function into the service of the common good in an environment in which children can be educated in benevolence as the regnant moral point of view. Instead, ultimate function must constantly be forced to these ends. If genes are kings, only geneticists with that knowledge can be fit rulers. Or so I first thought.

Then it dawned on me that evolutionary biologists cannot constitute a suitable oligarchy of Enforcers. For they are bound to be persons from all our yesterdays. Even animated discussions[26] among them of divergent interpretations of evolutionary theory or someone offering to wager that Alexander is wrong, alters the environment, proximately advantaging phenotypes, ultimately advantaging genotypes, one way or another. If genetic knowledge is to work for ourselves, instead of our genes; and if we are to exercise truly free will and free choice and attain something close to full humanhood, that knowledge must be supposed possessed by rulers who are from outside biological evolution. Fortunately, such rational being exist: *angels* will be Enforcers. With angels to guard them, children can be taught to be benevolent without becoming rubes. Then too, scientists can pursue truth with equal dispassion, since their own inclusive-fitness-survival is already forcibly assured and always maintained *equal* by rulers who do not belong to humankind.

NOTES

1. R. D. Alexander, "Evolution, Human Behavior and Determinism," *Proceedings of the Biennial Meeting of the Philosophy of Science Association*, 2 (1976): 3–21.
2. Ibid., p. 7 (italics added).
3. R. D. Alexander, "Natural Selection and the Analysis of Human Sociality," in *The Changing Scenes in the Natural Sciences, 1776–1976*, C. E. Goulden, ed., *Philadelphia Academy of Natural Sciences Special Publication* 12 (1977), pp. 283–337 (italics added).

4. The author's explanation (Addendum 2) of "free will" in a self-conscious organism is that each of us engages in "scenario-building" in an environment that is quite unpredictable because other individuals and collectives are also building their own scenarios. Every one of these decisions are cost-benefit assessments "of the sort we term exercise of free will." Our "compulsive adherence" to personal privacy manifests the fact each scenario-builder is a unique maximizer of inclusive fitness in cooperative competition to gain benefits from every exchange.

5. J. Bronowski, *Science and Human Values* (New York: Harper Torchbook, 1959). (First published 1956).

6. Ibid., p. 13.

7. Ibid., pp. 61, 72–73

8. Ibid., p. 74. "All scholars in their work are . . . oddly virtuous. They do not make wild claims, they do not cheat, they do not try to persuade at any cost, they appeal neither to prejudice nor to authority, they are often frank about their ignorances, their disputes are fairly decorous, they do not confuse what is being argued with race, politics, sex or age, they listen patiently to the young and the old who both know everything" (p. 75).

9. Ibid., pp. 77, 80, 81, 83.

10. Ibid., p. 81

11. Anyone who needs it can reflect that there are great cultural myths other than the two biblical stories I invoke here that contain much the same wisdom—in contrast to the rationalism of the present age.

12. Compare the topic sentence concerning man's capacity for justice and inclination to injustice in Reinhold Niebuhr's *The Children of Light and the Children of Darkness: A vindication of Democracy and a Critique of Its Traditional Defense* (New York: Charles Scribner's Sons, 1944), p. xiii.

13. John Gay, *Concerning the Fundamental Principle of Virtue or Morality* (1731), in *The English Philosophers from Bacon to Mill*, ed. Edwin A. Burtt (New York: Modern Library, 1939), pp. 769–85.

14. Does the word "only" suggest that if the mechanism of genetic evolution itself, and not individual organisms, was the residence of consciousness, there would be no discomfort?

15. Also, cf.: "For no more complex task can be imagined than that of an organism, complex enough to analyse itself, undertaking the analysis by means of the very attribute to be analysed, when one of those attributes is a resistance to all such analyses." Alexander, "Natural Selection and the Analysis of Human Sociality."

16. In the main Alexander presses hard his single-factor explanation against, for. example, cultural anthropology. There are only a few

instances of a softer claim. He explains "the avunculate" or "mother's brother" lineage in some societies in terms of genetic adaptation to environmental situations in which the husband lived away in another village. This lowers confidence in paternity, and geneotypical selfishness directs itself into the formation of "mother's brother" system. But why cannot "mutual aid" explain the same data, whether as an alternative or supplementary theory? In Alexander's own words, "It is difficult to see how a woman could gain from her spouse having a low confidence in paternity, but she is not as constrained to provide for him confidence of paternity if she can depend upon her brothers and other relatives for child support and other assistance." Indeed, here Alexander presses only a far softer claim against anthropologists, namely that the "patterns are *entirely consistent* with a Darwinian model of human sociality." ("Human Selection and the Analysis of Human Sociality," italics added). Either account seems to me to be equally "predictive"; and both may be confirmed as against the stronger claims of either to be the sole and exhaustive account. A and B may be compatible accounts of X; this latitude is generally admitted in historical interpretation.

But usually not by Alexander. Nepotistic benefit-giving to one's kin enables Alexander to explain kinship systems, the outer limits of the extension of such benefit-giving, together with incest avoidance and out-marrying, while also explaining any seeming *prima facie* exception or variation from his gene-survival explanation. Faced with the prohibitions of marriage within forbidden degrees of consanguinity (and affinity, both as developed in Western church tradition), Thomas Aquinas (or whoever was the author of *Summa Theologicae*, Part III Supplement, QQ. 50 and 54) affirmed that the clues to the meaning of all those detailed prohibitions were two: (a) to restrain carnal concupiscence, even perhaps preventing wife-murder (by, for example, the prohibition against marrying one's deceased wife's sister. [That sensible interpretation in an extended or nonnuclear family environment would today require a prohibition against marrying the woman or man living next door or the spouse of one's professional colleagues!] (b) To *extend friendship*, since socially one already has sufficient reason for friendship with one's close kin. I understand Alexander to say that these or any other explanations can only be proximate reasons beneath which the hidden ultimate reason is gene conservation. Generally he admits no *supplementary* explanations that may also be operative, let alone alternative ones.

17. The best article I know on this fallacy is Richard M. Rorty's "The Limits of Reductionism" in *Experience, Existence and the Good*, ed. I. C. Lieb (Carbondale, Ill.: Southern Illinois University Press,

1961), pp. 100–16. The following statements of the argument are sufficient for our purposes: "All rational inquiry is reductionistic; all abstract
thought selects aspects of a subject matter as paradigmatic and ignores
other aspects. Thought is reductionistic or nothing, and the criticism
only makes sense if it is narrowed down. When it *is* narrowed down, it
usually turns out to be the claim that a reduction of X to Y is
illegitimate because the very process of reducing presupposes some X
that is not reduced. This claim . . . we shall call 'the appeal to self-
referential consistency'." "In its narrower form, the antireductionist
criticism is one of three great patterns of argument which philosophers
often use. The other two are the appeal to fact, and the appeal to
simplicity (crystallized in the phrase 'Occam's Razor')" (p. 100). Alexander scores A on facts and simplicity (so far as I am competent to
determine; scientists may grade him A or otherwise). Humanists like me
should be able to say, however, that he flunks the test of self-referential
consistency. His is what Rorty call an "overstringent reductionism" (p.
110). Rorty's further words are not insignificant, even if unlikely to
deflect Alexander from his course: ". . . It is precisely when the gambit
[the argument against self-referential inconsistency] is *refused*, and the
reductionist replies that his concern is with certain delimited subject
matter which does not include his *own* activity of inquiry, that a given
type of inquiry is liable to separate itself from philosophy and to set up
shop as a science" (p. 102). In any case, "even if all other appearances
can be saved by the reductionist theory under attack, the appearance of
saving them [e.g., by an overstringent reductionist science] can't be"
(p. 103).

18. Initially Rorty, too, deems this ploy to be *as hoc*ism (I prefer the
more exact rhetorical term "*ad hoc*ery"). He does not dismiss the ploy
as readily as I (a simpleton in philosophy) do. Nevertheless, in the final
analysis Rorty probes behind *levels* of discourse to distinctions of *kinds*.
(Perhaps for "kinds" we could substitute "*sciences*.") The latter entail
rules of discourse, which (strangely enough, for anyone who thinks
rules must be claimed absolutes) means a sense of the *fallibility* of one's
own science or interpretation. "When we bring such a charge [of self-
referential inconsistency], we're saying that this reductionist has somehow excluded himself from the universe he's analyzing or describing,
while yet maintaining that this universe is in some important sense all-
inclusive, And when we say *this*, we're saying . . . that he can't
account for the fact that his analysis or description is one among
many—that his activity of inquiry is *fallible*" (p. 112). "A distinction of
kind which includes a notion of a rule can, so to speak, turn around and
look at itself as a rule, as offering a chance to see the subject matter in

a new way. A distinction of kind which does not include this notion cannot consistently look at itself at all, because it cannot be conscious of itself as a distinction" (p. 113). "But as soon as one see one's self as *making* rather than *finding*—as a proposer of rules [a science?] rather than a discoverer of facts—one realizes the possibility of alternative rules [alternative science? such as anthropology or moral science?]" (p. 114). Coming back from these depths, the upshot is, at the least, that "the point of diminishing returns for reductionism comes when it can no longer construct a metaphilosophical account of itself" (p. 111).

19. As of every lifetime (which, I insist, must encompass the author's own, and his thoughts at this very moment), the science itself can be no more or no less than a strategy for reproduction of a group of genes (the genotype). Or, as Alexander prefers sometimes to say, in order to take account of environment, "every individual's lifetime is a series of *unwitting* cost-benefit decisions, leading to a maximization of reproduction" (italics added). Rephrasing Malinowski's statement that a culture is a "gigantic metaphorical extension of the physiological processes of digestion," Alexander writes that if the word "reproduction" is substituted for "digestion" and "culture" is replaced by "phenotype," then "the basic theory on which all biology operates is correctly stated" (Alexander, "Natural Selection and the Analysis of Human Sociality)." If that is all of biology, and if biology is all there is to human reality, the question arises, whereon do the truth-claims of biology have room to stand? Is there any *reason* we should live by this metaphorical extension instead of any other?

20. Friedrich Nietzche, *Thus Spoke Zarasthustra*, Prologue 6.

21. Alexander, "Natural Selection and the Analysis of Human Sociality."

22. Suppose an anthropologist hypothesizes that "man is what he eats." That proposition is a truth-claim that is self-referentially inconsistent. By contrast, the hypothesis that "Man is 99 44/100% what he eats" may ascribe too large a role to the economic factor, modes of production, etc., in human history. It may be incorrect, even stupid, in so far downgrading the role of human intentionality, art, morality, law, and religion in human affairs. Still it is *not* self-referentially contradictory to hold this proposition to be true, and to continue to accumulate evidence to support it. My argument was, and is, that Alexander apparently holds a viewpoint that is self-referentially inconsistent. For his basic proposition to be true there must be some X that is not reducible to Y, to gene-survival. Man and his communities may be 99 44/100% *that* (if only Alexander would settle for his few softer claims). But no accumulated evidence can prove his stronger claim to be true,

since that would undermine also the truth claims for the science on which he bases his strong assertions.

The fallacy of self-referential inconsistency takes aim at the over-stringency and all-encompassing character of the philosophy of biology (or of economics) espoused, not at the stringency or anything else about the manner in which it is held. One may possess these views lightly or hypothetically or with any degree of modesty or tentativeness, or he may hold onto them tenaciously and be strenuous or adamant about his espousal. It is *the view possessed*, its contents and excessive stringency, not *how* it is held or advocated, this is at issue. To say that one is only advancing a hypothesis is about as irrelevant as the fact that Alexander is a very likeable fellow, modest and open-hearted in interdisciplinary discussion. Still the viewpoint put into the discussion cannot be shown to be true, since there must be some X in Alexander and the rest of us that is not reducible to Y at the moment we are exploring the truth of Y. His theory may save all appearances save one, namely, the truth claims of the science itself.

23. In his chapter, in note 27, Alexander completely misses the point of self-referential *inconsistency*. He mistakenly believes that I brought into view only self-reference, i.e., self-awareness, self-analysis. Then he averts to his utopian speculations about an environment in which an organism has achieved both self-reference and knowledge of its ultimate function. A reader of this footnote—together with Alexander's Addenda—might mistakenly suppose that I raised the "bogey man of determinism" vs. free will. I have said enough about that issue in my response to Gunther Stent. Reductionism, not determinism, is the objection I bring against Alexander. Not for a moment do I believe that he "autonomously" chose his choice of the scientific position he holds; yet it is truly "his own," the last conclusion of his understanding. My point is simply that his theory of theories is omnivorous; it consumes itself and cannot consistently claim to be a truth known. Even if an ideal nonhuman observer knows Alexander's account to be the absolute truth, Alexander cannot know this, or successfully claim to know this, without contradicting his own account of the human mind, and his own science.

24. Albert Rosenfeld, *Saturday Review*, December 10, 1977, pp. 19–20.

25. Alexander, "Evolution, Human Behavior, and Determinism," p. 7. This statement is followed on the same page by: "According to this theory, we should have evolved to be exceedingly clever nepotists, and we should have *evolved* to be nothing else at all." Also see my text above at n. 1, on the disappearance of altruism, if this should emerge temporarily because of some sudden environmental change.

26. See my text above, at n. 21.

5

Theology and Ethics: An Interpretation of the Agenda

James M. Gustafson

"THAT THE CONTEMPORARY THEOLOGICAL SCENE has become chaotic is evident to everyone who attempts to work in theology. There appears to be no consensus on what the task of theology is or how theology is to be pursued. Some see it as the 'science of religion'; others as exposition of the Christian faith; still others as prophetic pronouncement on the conditions of, for example, contemporary American culture (or Western cultural [sic] generally). There are those who are attempting to develop a 'non-sectarian' theology which will not be restricted in meaningfulness to any of the great historic religious traditions; others are attempting to exploit theological insights for developing a more profound understanding of human nature; yet others still see theology as primarily a work of the church attempting to come to better understanding of itself."[1]

Gordon Kaufman's statement is accurate. Whether theology has become more chaotic than some other disciplines is not a matter to be judged here; surely the absence of consensus occurs in some other classic humanistic studies and in some social scientific studies as well. To prepare a paper for nontheologians in the face of this description presents an almost insuperable obstacle; if there is confusion within the discipline it is necessary to locate one's own efforts within some clear margins to make them intelligible to readers who are not very interested in, not to mention impressed by, contemporary theology. Even intelligibly to account for all of one's assumptions, not to mention defending them is a much larger assignment than can be accomplished in a paper.[2]

Assumptions

Just as individual philosophers have distinctive ways of organizing and defending their views, so do theologians. Just as philosophers share certain common grounds, at least within general "schools" of philosophy, so do theologians. I shall begin by stating and briefly expounding eight assumptions that I make. The first six, I believe, are generally shared by theologians in the Christian tradition. All of them, with appropriate qualifications, can be used in Jewish theology as well. The last two are not so widely shared.

1. To work as a Christian theologian is to work within a historic tradition which is grounded in the rich and diverse collection of texts that form the Bible. Rich and diverse must be emphasized, for not only does the Bible contain a variety of types of literature, but also these texts were given their present form over extended periods of time and are related to the historical experiences and individual concerns of their authors.

2. The historical character of the Bible is accepted. By "historical character" I wish to suggest the following. The texts were written under particular historical conditions, and thus to understand them requires that they be related to those conditions insofar as scholarship makes this possible. The subject matter of the texts is frequently historical events or historical persons; little or no "speculative reasoning" in the classic Thomistic sense can be found in the Bible. Even within the biblical books the significance of certain historical events and persons is used to interpret the significance of contemporary events and persons, and also to suggest the significance of the future.

For the theologian this means that from its beginning his enterprise has been grounded in historical and social experience and for many theologians (not only modern ones) it means that efforts to ossify particular interpretations of biblical persons and events violates both the actuality and the value of this historical character of the Bible.

3. The tradition of thought and life of the community of Christians obviously continues to have historical character, and thus provides rich and diverse resources. For example, Augustine's theology developed in relation to events in his life, events in Roman history, events in the life of the Catholic Church, and in relation to religious and philosophical ideas that prevailed in his time. Certain events and persons in the history of the community become more decisive than others in formulating the significance of the religion, both intellectually and in practical activities. Contemporary theology, as part of the tradition, is shaped and reshaped in relation to knowledge and concepts from philosophy and other fields, and in relation to political and other events.

4. Every effort to formulate a coherent theological perspective must be selective from the richness and diversity of the Bible and the tradition, in relation to the events and ideas of the time and place in which the theologian and the community are living and thinking. This "historical" character of theological work is assumed and accepted. When the religious communities are in unusual flux, as Kaufman's statement suggests they are today, the criteria to be used to evaluate theological perspectives and statements are less clear.

5. There is a "faith" aspect to all genuine *theo*logy. (I stress *theo*logy since much of the activity of theologians today simply uses religious symbols to disclose some dimensions of human experience while remaining agnostic about whether there is any meaningful reference to a deity.) This faith aspect is not, in my conception of theology, a blind acceptance of ecclesiastical or doctrinal authority. Rather it is a confidence, sometimes painfully weak, in an ultimate power that has brought the "worlds" into being, sustains them, and determines their destinies. It is a confidence, sometimes an even weaker one and sometimes a confidence that is lost, in the goodness of this power. I call it a "faith aspect" because its claims are never fully demonstrable in rationalistic or scientific terms. It is a faith aspect for which reasons can be given, but such confirmation as it has is also affective. The evidences that are drawn upon to explain and

defend it are taken from the experience of communities and individuals recorded in the documents of the tradition and confirmed in contemporary life.

6. Traditional and contemporary theologians are correct when they affirm the mystery of God, not only for epistemological reasons, but also on experiential grounds. The awe experienced in religious life stems not only from the limitations of our knowledge of the ultimate power, but also from our sense of dependence on powers we did not create, the determination (acknowledgedly a very strong term) of the worlds by powers and events humans cannot fully control. Two comments on this assumption are required. First, theological statements are never literal, they are always tentative. Second, theological statements are abstractions from more primary religious language.

7. Theological language has primarily a practical function (which is not to deny it has other functions); it provides the symbols and concepts that interpret life in the world (not merely individual human life) so as to sustain and give direction to a way of human life. I stress the "primarily," for there are apologetic functions of theology, functions of elucidation of its plausibility, and so forth, directed to persons both within and outside the religious community.

8. Theology provides a way of construing the world. I follow, here, with a slight emendation, a construction by Julian N. Hartt. Hartt indicates that to construe, in a religious context, "is more than a linguistic-intellectual activity." His more substantive affirmation is: *"it means an intention to relate all things in ways appropriate to their belonging to God."* [3] My alteration would be: "an intention to relate to all things in ways appropriate to their *relations* to God," though I share with Hartt in that part of the classic theological tradition that stresses the sovereignty of the ultimate power at least in the sense that the destiny of the worlds is not in control of a biological species recently evolved on one planet. The formulation, "an intention to relate to all things in ways appropriate to their relations to God," clearly includes an ethical imperative, and within the necessary modesty of theological knowledge, a grounding of right relations and proper ends of human conduct. The moral question for humans within the context of a theological construing of the world becomes "What is

God, the ultimate power, enabling and requiring humans to be and to do?" The affirmation that we are to relate to *all things* in ways appropriate to their relations to God is very significant; it extends the scope of activity and of ends beyond the confinements of the "moral" as this is often articulated by theologians and philosophers alike; it provides a basis for some critical judgment of the anthropocentrism that has characterized western religion and ethics. (In the theologies based on the Bible the "doctrine of creation" is the backing for such a view; Christian theologians have, since early times, in their speculative theologies appealed to New Testament texts that stress that "all things" are created in and through Christ [as the second person of the Trinity] for a Christological authorization of this point.)

These eight assumptions are quite general in character; no single precise way to develop the relations of theology and ethics is necessitated by them. Certain ways, however, in which theology and ethics have been related are excluded by them. One is the use of the Bible as verbally inspired in such a way that the theology and the morality present in it have a dogmatic authority. The ethical teachings of the Bible in this literalistic view have the authority of a literal inspiration, as do the theological teachings; the task of theological ethics is then to apply these teachings to present occasions. Protestant fundamentalism and certain Jewish orthodox views of the revelation of Torah cannot be developed from my assumptions.

A second excluded way of relating theology and ethics is that of a purely rational philosophical theology which establishes the metaphysical principles grounded in the being of God from which ethical principles are derived by deduction or by inference. While the assumptions do not exclude the use of reason and common human experience in the authorization and development of theology and ethics, the Bible and the historic tradition carry weight as a source for understanding the relations of all things to God.

The assumptions do permit a *development* of both theological and ethical thought. The historical character of both the Bible and the tradition is stressed, and the recognition is made that religious communities as historical entities change and develop as they relate their traditional sources to contemporary events and knowledge. To indicate the possibilities for development does not mean that there are no presumptions in favor of the tradition, nor does it indicate that there is no significant continuity in theological and ethical thought. Thus, while development is permitted, attention to the tradition is required. My assumptions are the ground for a direction of theological ethical thought that is too "relativistic" for many religious persons and thinkers, and too "conservative" or "traditionalistic" for others.

The last two assumptions are the basis for the development of the rest of this chapter.

Construing of the World Theologically

Particular historical communities can be identified in part by the ways in which they construe the world. Particular individuals who have relatively coherent life plans and outlooks on the world are likely to have tacit if not articulated centers of meaning and value from which they construe the world. Theology involves construing the world from a position of believing in and beliefs about the ultimate power.[4]

In this section I shall focus on "construing the world" in order to illustrate the aspects of ethical thought that are affected by a theological viewpoint. In the next section I shall indicate what is involved in relating to all things in ways appropriate to their relations to God.

What are the sources of a theological perspective and construing of the world? My conviction, only asserted and not defended here, is that all the sources are grounded in the experience of human beings as they reflect upon and articulate the significance of historical events, the natural world, and individual occasions in the light of their (affective and also conceptualized) sense of the reality of an ultimate power. The presence of the Deity is always a mediated presence; it is mediated through the experiences of humans in their relations to the natural world, to other individuals, and to historical events. Without a sense of the presence of the Deity in these experiences they cannot yield a theological perspective. (It can be noted that here I am rejecting those views of theology and of religion that call any concern that is "ultimate," any symbols that represent a hierarchy of significance, any attitude of reverence, or any dominant interest, theological or religious. Such things do function to construe the world, and in this sense they function like a theology functions.)

There is a variety of forms of expression of the reflections on human experiences in the light of the sense of the presence of the Deity. The theologically significant forms of discourse even within the Bible are many; most of them are in primary religious language. For example, one has the mythic accounts of the creation in the book of Genesis; one way to interpret these is as efforts to express the significance of the origins of the world and of human life in the world in the light of the presence of an ultimate power. Historical narratives are the basis of interpreting the significance of historical and political events under the conviction of the presence of Yahweh; the exodus narratives and even the accounts of it given in the books of Kings and Chronicles are of this sort. The poetic discourse not only of the Psalms, but also of the Song of Deborah, early hymns as in Paul's letter to the Philippians, and others, express the religious significance of human experiences. Prophetic discourse, a kind of literature of moral and religious indictment, has a distinctively evocative way of bringing human conditions under the light of beliefs about God. There are symbols, what some New Testament scholars (following literary critics such as Wheelwright) call tensive symbols, such as the kingdom of God. Metaphors, analogies, and parables abound, pointing, often cryptically, to the religious significance of natural, social, and interpersonal events. And, particularly in the Christian scriptures, there are concepts such as sin and righteousness which have been shaped to express somewhat more precisely those meanings of human experience in relation to God that are expressed in other linguistic patterns in other places.

The point of stating this partial list is to indicate that in the Bible (and one could also indicate similar things in the postbiblical tradition) there are many literary devices by which the world is construed theologically; also many aspects of human experience—experience of the natural world as well as history—are construed theologically.

For the purposes of this chapter I shall indicate three aspects of the "moral world" that have been, and continue to be construed theologically. To these shall be added a more inclusive theme. The circumstances in which action takes place, the agents and their acts, and the ends and consequences of action can all be construed theologically. Finally, the meaning and significance of the whole, of all things related to each other, is construed theologically. Such is the audacity of theology, responding as theologians must do to the conviction that the ultimate power is related to the whole, to all things in their interrelatedness. I shall develop each of these with a selected illustration; I am not prepared to defend the adequacy of the theology of each illustration I use, but I am prepared to defend the intention they illustrate as part of the theological task.

First, the circumstances of action. Contemporary liberation theologians present rather vivid examples of how historical circumstances are construed theologically in such a way that religious and moral significance is disclosed. Characteristic of most, but not all, of this literature is the isolation of the exodus of the Hebrew people from bondage in Egypt as a paradigmatic event, an event that discloses the divine intentionality for humanity. The Hebrew people were oppressed in Egypt; Yahweh, their God, not only desired their liberation, but was present in the historical events that led them out of the house of bondage. Exodus takes on a symbolic significance; it discloses not only what the God of the biblical tradition desires for humans, but also how he "acts" in and through historical events to achieve his intention. The observation is made that the circumstances of large portions of humanity in our present time are those of oppression. The sequence of events symbolized by exodus is used to interpret the plight of present humanity, the purposes of God for humanity under these conditions of oppression, and the direction of the course of events that reasonably follows from this interpretation of the circumstances, namely, movements for liberation. Put in the current religious vernacular, where there is oppression God wills liberation; where there are movements for liberation, there is the presence of God; persons who conscientiously desire to act consonant with the will of God under these circumstances are engaged in the political and other struggles for liberation. The general point is that circumstances are construed by the use of a historical religious symbol in such a way that their theological and moral significance is disclosed; a course of action seems to follow reasonably from this construal of the circumstances.[5]

Second, moral agents and their acts are construed theologically. Reinhold Niebuhr's theology and the ways in which he used it in his ethical writings provides a good illustration of this. Niebuhr, particularly in *The Nature and Destiny of Man*, formulated a theological interpretation of the human condition that is deeply informed by the theologies of Paul, Augustine, the sixteenth-century reformers, and Kierkegaard.[6] Briefly summarized, humans have "spirits," which is a way to indicate that they have capacities for "free self-determination."[7] To have this freedom is to be anxious, and out of this anxiety persons act in such ways as to refuse to acknowledge their finitude, their creatureliness. Presumably, if they were rightly related to the Creator they would properly acknowledge their limits, and if they shared in the Christian "myth" they would have a ground of confidence that the destiny of the worlds is finally to be in the control of an almighty power who will fulfill it in accord with his redemptive and loving purposes. The persistent character of the human condition, however, is that in our loyalties and in our actions we wrongly use our freedom. This is the case even for those who share Niebuhr's religious views. Human beings seek to overcome their anxiety by fixing upon objects of confidence and loyalty that provide security, but essentially a false security. They develop false senses of confidence about their own motives and about their own moral capacities. Their sin is their wrong use of freedom. This is not only a moral indictment; it is also a religious indictment, for while lack of trust in God is "inevitable" it is not "necessary."[8]

Niebuhr's doctrine of sin is not the whole of his theology, but it is an important aspect of it. A theological concept, sin, for which he finds backing in the biblical accounts, in traditional theological reflections, and in general human experience, becomes a basis for construing moral agents and their acts. His intention is to disclose some things about humans, universally, or at least almost without exception, which have to be taken into account in the assessment of their conduct both as individuals and in social collectivities. The theological construing of human agents provides not only an interpretation of the significance of their actions (even, for example, the most altruistic actions are corrupted by the desire to secure the agents' own sense of righteousness), but in his case also an explanation of their actions. Given this theological account of human agents, certain attitudes follow, certain ways of critically assessing particular agents and their actions follow. To say the least, an attitude of a wariness is grounded; a self-criticism and a suspicion of others is supported pertaining to their moral claims and their moral intentions. Human agency is theologically construed so that one aspect of it is brought to rather vivid consciousness. Practically, during the years of Niebuhr's development, this view functioned to disclose the moral pretensions of "liberal" Christians and of nonreligious thinkers and leaders.

The ends and consequences of action are construed theologically. The *telos* of human action has been construed theologically throughout the tradition, and particular consequences of human activity have been assessed in relation to whether they contribute to, or deflect from the fulfillment of that *telos*. Systematic developments of this task have absorbed constructions by philosophers or philosophical theologians who are not primarily identified with the religious tradition. The theology and ethics of Thomas Aquinas present themselves as obvious candidates to illustrate this point. The grand, cosmic pattern is clear: all things come from God and return to God. The neo-Platonic sources for this have always been evident. Human action, and human life more inclusively, are part of the "all things" that are oriented toward God. The "supernatural" end of human life is communion with God, friendship with God, the vision of God. The natural end of human life is the fulfillment of its natural goodness. The dependence on Aristotle for the development of the "morphology" of the human has always been clear and acknowledged. While there is no unbroken continuity between the fulfillment of the natural end and the supernatural end (the grace of Christ which is in part dependent on the assent of faith is required), human actions and their consequences are judged to contribute to or deter from the fulfillment of the supernatural end. Actions, including moral actions, that are in accord with human nature contribute to the fulfillment of the natural good, and since the natural end is directed toward the supernatural end they also contribute to the fulfillment of the supernatural end. The ends of life, both "supernatural" and "natural" are construed theologically. Even the natural is construed theologically in such a way that assessments of the consequences of human action can be made in the light of judgments of what constitutes the flourishing of human nature, the fulfillment of the human both temporally and eternally. The development of the ethics of natural law occurs within this interpretation of the ends of human life; the consequences of human action are judged, to be sure, by moral norms, but these moral norms have theological backing; they are part of a theological ethical construing of life.

Finally, many theologians have been concerned to construe "the whole" theologically. Already we have noted this in the *exitus et reditus* pattern of Thomistic theology (Augustinian and other theologies also share in it). That such attempts are audacious is very clear; that there is legitimacy to them in the theological enterprise, especially for theologians who are disposed to strong views about the sovereignty of the Deity, is also clear. My illustration of a construing of "the whole" is Jonathan Edwards' *Dissertation Concerning the End for which God Created the World*, which like his more widely known *Dissertation Concerning True Virtue*, was published after his death.[9] The essay is vintage Edwards, and in a sense vintage eighteenth-century Christian theology. It consists of three parts: an introduction which carefully explains his use of terms (a virtue in Edwards not always present in the history of theology), a chapter "Wherein is considered, what reason teaches concerning this affair," and a chapter "Wherein it is inquired, what is to be learned from Holy Scriptures, concerning God's last end in the creation of the world." My judgment is that the first chapter determines the second, that his speculative philosophical argument provides the principles by which he selects his biblical materials and interprets them. (Indeed, one section of the second chapter is largely the stating of proof-texts with exposition of them in terms of the first chapter).[10] A critical Pauline text indicates the flavor of the enterprise, "For from him and through him and to him are all things. To him be glory forever" (Rom. 11:36, RSV). The most succinct summary sentence is as follows: "Therefore . . . we may suppose, *that a disposition in God, as an original property of his nature, to an emanation of his own infinite fullness, was what excited him to create the world; and so, that the emanation itself was aimed at him as the last end of creation.*[11] God makes himself his own end. The creation in generally neo-Platonic terms is an emanation of the fullness of the being of God; there is a properly proportionate relation of all things to each other in the creation; the interests of all creatures (who participate in this emanation) is God's own interest; their value is their value to God; and ultimately God's end is his own glorification. It is not important here to elaborate the argument, or to review Edwards' own answers to objections to his argument. My intention is only to illustrate briefly that a theologian attempts to construe the significance of the "whole" and how he does it. Classic doctrines of divine providence, with all their variations, are a part of this purpose. Given certain views about the nature of the Deity it is reasonable for theologians to construe in meaningful (granted speculative) terms the significance of the "whole."

In this section I have attempted to indicate what is involved in a theological construing of the world, and particularly the "moral world." As was indicated in the first paragraph, theologians are not the only persons engaged in such an enterprise. The conditions *sine qua non* for a theological construing of the world are "believing in" and "beliefs about" the reality of an ultimate power. Not all persons who call themselves theologians in our time would agree with the necessity of these conditions; any story, for example, that provides an orientation of the agent or the community toward the world is judged by some to be at least religious, if not theological. One can be a thoroughgoing Feuerbachian and still claim to be a theologian (not merely as a scholar working in theological texts, but also as a constructive theologian) in our present times. The root objection to this on my part is that while the traditional claim adhered to here creates its grave difficulties, any other approach surrenders what has made theology a distinctive field and endeavor.

Relating to All Things Appropriate to Their Relations to God

That persons do construe the world theologically, I take it, is indisputable. That it is a reasonable thing to do, even when claims to plausibility and not to truth in a traditional narrow sense are made, is questionable from many perspectives, and not merely contemporary ones, but historical ones as well. To assume that anyone cares about such an enterprise outside of the communities of those who are disposed to believe in the reality of an ultimate power and those who judge it to be false and pernicious enough to require elimination is in error. (My observation is that much of the concern by contemporary theologians for "method," while important to the clarification of theological work, is largely an effort to justify its legitimacy to a population that does not take it seriously enough even to care whether it is legitimate. At the same time participants in religious communities are getting little critical and sophisticated interpretation and understanding of the faith that lies within them from theologians.)

That the intellectual agenda required to make a case for relating to all things appropriate to their relations to God is too vast to be developed thoroughly here, not to mention defending how the agenda might be fulfilled, must be admitted. I indicated in my seventh assumption that theological language has primarily a practical function; it provides a way of construing the world that sustains and gives direction to a way of life. A religious perspective is self-involving; it includes a basic intentionality of the "will" as well as "linguistic-intellectual activity." Religion is a matter of the affections in a rich Edwardsian use of that term as well as a matter of the "intellect."[12] To make a case for relating all things appropriate to their relations to God requires that the readers entertain at least hypothetically the possibility that there is an ultimate power related to all things, and that persons can have a sufficient conviction of this reality to orient their individual and communal lives toward and by it.

I propose here only an outline of the task of theological ethics, that is, of the choices that are involved in the intention to relate to all things in ways appropriate to their relations to God. I shall indicate what I believe to be the most crucial problems, and therefore the critical judgments that the theologian must make. I shall also indicate the significance and the limits of this enterprise for moral life.[13]

The most obvious problematic area is to discern with some certitude how all things are related to God. Speculative philosophical theologians such as the "process theologians" and "transcendental Thomists" and Tillichians among contemporary theologians are better able than I to develop theories about the relations of all things to God. Clearly there are significant differences between these three groups, and one can add the followers of Teilhard de Chardin, theologians who choose to remain silent on these philosophical-theological issues, and others to the options that are discussed. In addition to the problems of how all things are related to God is the problem of *what* one judges the divine ends and purposes to be, and on what basis one comes to such a judgment.

As regards the matter of the theories of the relations of all things to God, I take it that there are two important ways of thinking. One, which is clearly dominant in the biblical tradition and which continues in theologies through the centuries that are strongly oriented by the Bible, is to use analogies of the person and of roles (or perhaps they are only metaphors) to speak of how God is related to all things, and particularly to persons. The second, which involves a judgment that personal terms are too misleading, is to use more abstract language such as "the ground of being," or "being."

From the biblical tradition I select two sorts of language that have been used. One, which is based strongly in the Torah tradition, is the language of God as a power and authority who determines the course of events, and who exercises his moral authority through commands. The analogy (or metaphor) is drawn, I believe, for social experiences of a certain sort; human societies were organized under the authority of a leader, part of whose role it was to issue commands. Yahweh was judged to have this sort of "social role." The relations of the people to Yahweh are those of subjects to an authority, and the proper language for understanding their actions is that of obedience or disobedience to his commands. To be sure, on other grounds, namely, his covenant with his people (also a social analogy or metaphor), they were persuaded that his intentions were for their benefit, but the condition for receiving the benefits was obedience to his commands. The development of moral and religious rules took place in the context of believing in and beliefs about Yahweh; he had the power to determine the consequences of the historical course of events of his people, and he had the power and authority to issue (as a result of his covenant with them) commands.

The second sort of language from the biblical tradition that has been used is that of "God acting." Some such notion is present in the idea of covenant and the idea that the consequences of obedience or disobedience to the commands were "in the hands" of God the determiner of the historical destiny of his people. What I wish to indicate here is that the notion of "God acting" has been developed somewhat independently of the notion of commands, and that it is drawn from reflections upon the nature of human action. God is understood to be an "agent" just as persons are agents. Like persons he is understood to have intentions which are fulfilled or not in part through human action and in history. Like persons, he has a volitional capacity, not only in the sense of stating what is desirable, but also in the sense of exercising power in such ways that his actions can be fulfilled. "Knowledge" of his intentions is gained through his "revelation" of himself. Many different views of how God reveals himself, of course, have been used to back this kind of assertion. My own view, acknowledgedly weak from the perspectives of those more orthodox than I, is that interpretations of God's intentions are developed and discerned through events of human history and human experience, as communities who live in the sense of the presence of an ultimate power reflect on these events and experiences in the light of that sense.

The ongoing task of theology becomes one of seeking to interpret God's action in all events and relations in which humans participate—interpersonal, political and historical, and natural. One biblical tradition in which this is done is that of the eighth-century prophets, the literature of moral indictments based not only on infractions of the law (which the prophets assume that the people know and believe themselves obligated to obey), but also on the conviction that God is speaking by the voice of the prophet (a very personal metaphor) to the people through the consequences of the historical and personal events in which they participate.

Whereas the dominant moral language of the commander-subject pattern is obedience and disobedience, in modern times the dominant language of the language of God acting is appropriate responsiveness to the action (intentions and activities) of God in the events in which humans are participants. God is related to all things as the ultimate agent whose intentions and purposes are to be discerned in all events. (Whether God is an omnipotent agent who absolutely determines each event in detail, or a limited agent, is, like the view of revelation, a matter on which there is dispute, though "hard determinists" are hard to come by in recent theology.) As some recent Protestant theologians have stated the matter, the morally appropriate response in a religious context requires that persons discern God's action, or discern the intention of God's activity in the circumstances in which human action is required. The processes recommended for doing this vary from complex procedures of interpretation to an almost purely intuitive sense on the part of members of the religious community. Human actions are to "respond" to God's action, or are to "endorse" God's action, or to be "consonant with" God's action, and so forth.

(I wish to indicate that even within the biblical, more social and personal language, the language a theologian chooses to use for the analogy or the metaphor predisposes him or her to a particular way of describing moral experience, and in turn to particular ways of prescribing how moral actions should be guided and judged.)

The second way of thinking about the relations of all things to God, as indicated above, attempts to use more abstract language such as "ground of being" partly because theologians judge the use of personal terms to be excessively anthropocentric and misleading. For some theologians the effort stands quite independent from the historic distinctiveness of the Christian religious tradition. It is a matter of ontology and metaphysics, and the adequacy of a delineated position is to be judged by evidences and argumentation appropriate to those fields. The philosophical theological argument is not deemed by some theologians to be stating explicitly what is implicit in the religious tradition; what the historic religious traditions add is an account of the human condition in relation to the Deity whose nature is expounded philosophically. Others believe that in their more abstract language they are expounding a philosophical theology that, if it is not implicit in the historic religious language, is at least a rational interpretation that is coherent with the more primary religious language. The philosophical theology is an exposition of the faith, or apologetically an interpretation of the meaning of the faith in language that presumably has wider public accessibility. In this approach the anticipated result is not so much rational "proofs" for the existence of the Deity and the ways in which the Deity is related to all things, so much as an illumination or expository analysis of the primary religious language in language that is less personal and less determined by religious historical particularity.

One example of this which shows its importance to ethics can be drawn from the Thomistic interpretation of law. In this work, as in many others in the Christian tradition, the concept of participation plays a crucial role. Put briefly, the pattern is that the moral law of nature participates in the mind of God; it participates in the divine intentionality of and for all things. While it is argued on exegetical grounds that there is a biblical acknowledgment of a natural moral law (using the first two chapters of Paul's letter to the Romans, and the concept of man being made in the image and likeness of God and the "high Christologies" of the New Testament as principal bases), there is no *theory* of natural law developed in the biblical texts. The more speculative doctrine of the natural law is to be defended on purely philosophical grounds, including the concept of the participation of the natural in the divine purpose, but it is also an exposition of what is implicit in (a stronger claim) or of what is authorized by (a weaker claim) certain biblical themes, texts, and concepts. One consequence of this view is that the biblical moral teachings are deemed to be expressions of this natural moral law, for like it they are also expressions of the divine intentionality in which human life participates. The historical biblical teachings are justifiable on the basis of the more speculative philosophical theology and ethics (with three principal exceptions in Thomas's writings: the command to Abraham to slay Isaac, the "suicide" of Samson, and Hosea's marriage to Gomer).

The advantage that is presumably gained by such an enterprise (and many other examples of the same intention on the part of theologians could be given) is that the relations between God and the moral, between theology and ethics, are established on rational principles on which all rational persons might agree, and thus the historical particularity of the biblical tradition is not an obstacle to making universal claims for the moral principles and moral values that are stated. An example of this is the claim that Roman Catholics make, a correct one in principle, that their teaching on abortion is not a Catholic or Christian teaching, but is based upon human reason, on the natural moral law.

I have attempted to indicate that there have been two general ways used to delineate how God is related to all things, and particularly to persons. The first was using the more personal and social role language of the biblical tradition, and the second the more abstract and impersonal language of various metaphysical theories. The second large issue, alluded to previously but not lifted out clearly, is how the theologian can claim knowledge about God's relations to all things. "Revelation," conceptualized in a variety of ways and with various justifications of the ways in which it is conceptualized, is one claim. The other general claim is that reason exercised in relation to human experience, or in relation to human knowledge of the natural world, is a basis for knowing how God is related to all things. That there are mixed claims is also the case: what one finds in the biblical and ongoing tradition is itself a process of human reflection on the nature and purposes of the ultimate power (a weak view of revelation), or there is a basic coherence between speculative thinking about the nature of ultimate reality and what is known through the particular historic tradition in which that reality has revealed itself. I shall illustrate how a strong doctrine of revelation works.

The modern classic of this approach is the work of Karl Barth. Faced with what were to Barth insuperable obstacles for claiming natural knowledge of God, and yet deeply convinced of the reality and presence of God (who is a God for man), he opts for the fundamental principle that knowledge of God can come only through God's revealing of himself. God, who is free, chose freely to reveal himself through the history of the Jewish people, and ultimately through the person and events of Jesus. With joyous confidence and with brilliance, Barth then can expound the theological themes he finds central to the biblical tradition. The fundamental knowledge of God that he discerns is that God is gracious, that he intends the good of man. While there is a historic particularity to the locus of the revelation of God, what is revealed there is of universal significance; the sovereign power who is gracious intends the salvation, the fulfillment of all humans. Indeed, the prime reality is that all humans *de jure* do participate in the goodness of the divine reality and the divine intention.

Without appropriate attention to how this is worked out in relation to ethics in the pattern of the relation of the divine reality and intention to the proper human response to it, one point nonetheless needs to be made clear. One moral consequence of this view of God's revelation is that the primary command is "Thou *mayest* . . . " and not "Thou shalt not . . . " This does not rule out certain almost absolute prohibitions of conduct in certain circumstances, but it does ground a basic affirmation of the goodness of the creation, and a basic openness (a word Barth uses) to new possibilities of human well-being in the world. Not only is the way of construing the world grounded in his exceedingly strong view of revelation, but what he finds revealed (a gracious God) grounds an orientation toward life in the world.[14]

That Barth's confidence in revelation in the Bible is excessive to many other theologians is indeed clear. That theologians, such as myself, who choose not to accept his certitude, but nonetheless do not relinquish a claim of some biblical authorization for their work, must find some "mixed" view is also clear. Indeed, both classic Catholic theology and all "liberal theology" since the Enlightenment have been engaged in establishing some reliable knowledge of God drawn from biblical sources and from common human experience and reason. No matter how much "knowledge" is justified, *what* is claimed to be known is crucial to how a theologian or a community construes the world both religiously and morally.

What is claimed about God and his intentionality is patently related to the sources used. Both the more philosophically developed aspects of the tradition and those that are developed more biblically offer various delineations of the significant characteristics of the ultimate power and its purposes. Different delineations become the bases for different inferences of a generally moral sort. Different degrees of certitude claimed for what is known also affect what moral inferences can be drawn from theological statements. I shall illustrate these matters from current discussions in Roman Catholic theology and ethics.

The neo-Thomist manuals of moral theology that dominated the latter part of the nineteenth century and the first six decades of the present century are not known for carefully relating the moral prescriptions to basic theological principles, though it is clear that they assumed certain principles that were articulated in the neo-Thomist theological tracts. Put oversimply, the theological principle that governed the moral theologians was that of a divine law in which the natural law participates. What was crucial was the opinion that the Deity had an almost absolutely fixed, immutable and eternal moral law from which prescriptions could be deduced or inferred and applied to changing historical and natural conditions with the greatest of certitude. The point made in polemical writings against these manuals is that God's moral order was "static," and that it was assumed to be known with certitude. Certain polemical attacks on it distinguish between the "classical" tradition and the modern "historical" ways of thinking.

The point of significance for our discussion is that for many reasons both Roman Catholic theology and moral theology began to reconceptualize the knowledge of God, and that the new concepts are correlated with changes in both the procedures of moral theology and in some of the particular moral judgments that are made. (One significant factor was the increasing use of the more personal language and the more historically oriented ways of thinking that have dominated most of Protestant theology in recent decades.) As against the "neo-Thomists," who construed the relation of all things to God in terms of the requirement that all things conform to God's law conceived in "static" terms, the revisionists have conceptualized God as (in part) creating the conditions of possibility for some novelty in human life and in the relations of humans to each other in society and in relation to the natural world. When the Deity is conceptualized more as a "dynamic" presence than as a "static" order, there is a basis for some significant changes in ethical thought. The way is opened for continuing revision of the moral tradition and even for discovery of new possibilities of human action that might sustain

human well-being. When the Deity is conceived in more "personal" terms, and correlatively humans are conceived more "personally" (in contrast to "physically"), the considerations that
have to be taken into account in the domain of the ethical
become increased in number and complexity. I forego here the
opportunity to develop this with a more specific illustration, but
the controversy over *Humanae Vitae* by Pope Paul VI provides
material by which this can readily be done. Not only is there a
change in what is believed about God, but correlated with certain
changes is a qualification of the traditional certitude about the
wrongness and rightness of certain human actions. The relations
of all things to God are conceptualized differently, in part because God is thought about differently; how the world is then
construed is different and a difference in both procedures of
ethical reflection and of particular judgments in some cases reasonably follows.[15]

I have by no means indicated all the crucial points at which
judgments are made by theologians both about how the ultimate
power is known and what is claimed to be known about the
ultimate power. Also I have not indicated at all how different
judgments about humans and their capacities affect the development of theological ethics. I have attempted only to indicate
something of what is required if one is to fulfill a project based
on the last two assumptions stated in the early part of this
chapter.

Finally, what contributions theology makes to ethics clearly
depend upon the choices and specifications of theological points
by particular religious communities or individual theologians.[16]

NOTES

1. Gordon D. Kaufman, *An Essay on Theological Method* (Missoula,
Mont.: Scholars Press, 1975) p. ix.
2. I have given my own views about theological ethics in Gustafson,
Can Ethics Be Christian? (Chicago: University of Chicago Press, 1975).
3. Julian N. Hartt, "Encounter and Inference in Our Awareness of
God," in *The God Experience,* ed. Joseph P. Whalen, S.J. (New York:
Newman Press, 1971), p. 52. This theme is elaborated in Hartt, *The-
ological Method and Imagination* (New York: Seabury Press, 1976).

4. I cannot undertake here to discuss the crucial matter of whether and how such believing and beliefs might be justified. My own views are most fully expressed in *Can Ethics Be Christian?*, pp. 82–116.

5. I have critically assessed this use of historical analogies, in ibid., pp. 117–44.

6. Reinhold Niebuhr, *The Nature and Destiny of Man,* 2 vols. (New York: Charles Scribners Sons, 1941, 1943).

7. Ibid., vol. 1, p. 16.

8. Ibid., vol. 1, p. 251–60.

9. Jonathan Edwards, *The Works of Jonathan Edwards,* 2 vols. (Edinburgh: Banner of Truth Trust, 1974; reprint of 1834 ed.), vol. I, pp. 95–121, 122–42.

10. This judgment is not concurred in by Paul Ramsey, who is editing these texts for the Yale edition of *The Works of Jonathan Edwards.* Oral communication, January, 1978.

11. Edwards, *Works,* vol. I, p. 100, col. 1.

12. See Jonathan Edwards, *Religious Affections* (New Haven: Yale University Press, 1959), pp. 93–124.

13. I have developed this with more specific relation to medical ethics in *The Contributions of Theology to Medical Ethics* (Milwaukee: Marquette University Press, 1975).

14. For Barth's views on some medical moral problems, see Karl Barth, *Church Dogmatics* III:4 (Edinburgh: T. and T. Clark, 1961), pp. 397 ff.

15. For further development see Gustafson, *Protestant and Roman Catholic Ethics* (Chicago: University of Chicago Press, 1978), pp. 80–94.

16. See, Gustafson, *Contributions of Theology,* for further development.

Response to James M. Gustafson

Hans Jonas

A DIFFICULTY IN COMMENTING on Gustafson's chapter lies in its more interpretative than positional stance, which allows few clues as to where the author himself stands—what he wishes to be identified with in the theological spectrum he so skillfully and impartially spreads out before us. The choice to interpret the agenda rather than enact it for us is, of course, entirely legitimate, but it leaves the commentator somewhat short on issues to come to grips with. Conceivably, the choice itself, perhaps less than free, might be a matter for comment if it could be taken to reflect the troubled state of theology in our time: its loss of self-confidence and its infection by the prevailing scepticism, historicism, cultural relativism, and so on. Some of Gustafson's own stated "assumptions" seem to point in that direction. However that may be (and such a reading of his reticence may be quite mistaken), the nontheologian and secularist would for argument's sake have welcomed something more assertive to envy and feel challenged by, something more positive to salute and get his teeth into. Especially, the philosopher wishes for a hard line in his counterpart across the fence, to bring him face to face with the—either conflicting or complementing—*excess* of faith and revelation over reason and what its stringent charter lets it do. The charter of creedal theology, after all, is allowed to be different at the outset of the encounter. Admittedly, it is easy for the outsider to be hypothetically radical in behalf of a cause he has not to live with afterward. But the itch is irresistible, and this is not the first time that I feel driven—I don't know whether by the whisperings of a theologian manqué in myself or from the philosopher's need to confront a challenge at its strongest—to put myself in the theologian's place and by proxy to attempt to draw some lines of what "we others" could expect from him in answer to the riddles we share, if he but dares to use the powers of his mandate. The impudence of thus appropriating his part is excused only by my deep respect for his very mandate, whose voice indeed I deem indispensable in the concert of men's groping for ultimate directions. It is in this spirit that I offer running comments on a number of points in Gustafson's chapter and then don his garb for an experiment of my own, along the way also occasionally trying to focus the discourse somewhat more than he has done on the particular issues to which this Institute is dedicated.

I take note of the *eight assumptions* stated on pp. 182–85. *Assumptions 1–4* deal with the *historicity* of the theological endeavor: the historical character of the Bible itself, of the Christian tradition grounded in it and successively reinterpreting its message in the light of changing times, and the historical character of any present theological work in relation to the conditions of our own time. My only comment here is that I would have expected a Christian theologian to insert a word on the transhistorical status of Jesus Christ the Savior, or at least on the very peculiar "historical" character of the "Christ event" in its claimed redemptional significance for all subsequent time. However, this is no concern of mine.

Assumption 5 states the "'faith' aspect" belonging to all genuine theology. Most fundamentally put, that aspect is "a confidence . . . in an ultimate power" as the creative, sustaining, and determining cause of the world, and (less certain) in the goodness of this power. "Power" is an impersonal term, "goodness" has at least personal connotations. In most of Gustafson's discourse, the term "ultimate power" (for God) notably dominates. It is a matter of faith because not rationally demonstrable, though rationally defensible.

Accordingly (*assumption 6*), we must acknowledge the "mystery" of God, with the consequence that theological statements are never literal and always tentative.

Assumption 7 holds that theological language has primarily a practical function, i.e., to sustain and give direction to a way of life. With this I would take serious issue (as a reduction of theology to homiletics) were it not corrected by *assumption 8*, the most important, which states that "theology provides a way of *construing the world*" (p. 184), which is surely a theoretical undertaking, even if on fideistic premises. The construing is guided by "an intention to relate to all things in ways appropriate to their relations to God," and this indeed has its practical, ethical implications as "a grounding of right relations and proper ends of human conduct." The expression "to *all* things" places a potential qualification on the "anthropocentrism" of Western religion and ethics. Here we come close to the particular interest of our circle and to Gustafson's declared topic, "Theology and Ethics." With this I shall now deal in keeping with the paper itself, which is henceforth devoted to developing the implications of assumption 8.

The major theme (p. 184 ff.) is "construing the world theologically" and how it affects ethical thought. Of the *sources* for such a construing, Gustafson says that it is human *experience* reflecting on historical events, on the natural world, and on individual occasions "in the light of a sense of the reality of an ultimate power" (p. 186). I take it that this "sense" is itself an experience, viz., "of the presence of the Deity in these experiences" (p. 186), and furthermore—though Gustafson does not clearly say so—that it means a presence not only in my experiencing but also, or primarily, in the objects thereof, the events and facts I reflect upon. But in either case—whether it is my reflective experience or its objects that I invest with a sense of divine presence—the question arises whether this is to be understood in terms of the general presence of an ultimate power in all things, or in terms of a special presence in particular things, events or experiences (a difference analogous to that between *providentia generalis* and *providentia specialis* in classical Christian theology). In the first case, that of an equal ubiquity, the "sense" in question may amount to no more than the subsumption of the particular under the universal rule of God's immanence in the world—a kind of Spinozist view which does not differentiate between a more or less of such a presence and surely cannot think of his absence from anything. Considered as sources for construing the world theologically, the nondifferentiating and the differentiating views, i.e., that of a constant omnipresence and that of chosen revelations of the divine, will produce quite different theologies, nay religions, e.g., pantheism and theism, with possibly quite different *ethical* conclusions ("sin," e.g., has no place in the pantheistic variety). Knowing Gustafson to be a Christian, I guess his to be the second of the two options. But then, "presence" is too calm, too intransitive a term. The exodus narrative, e.g., which Gustafson adduces as an example of how a historical event can be interpreted "under the conviction of the presence of Yahweh," speaks to Jews of more than a "presence." When on Passover night we chant from the Bible, "With a strong hand and outstretched arm" he led us out of Egypt, we have not mysterious presence but manifest action in mind. The distinction would be a quibble if it would not carry over into the subsequent deliberations of Gustafson under the heading of the *circumstances* of human action that can be construed theologically (pp. 188–89). There, the exodus story is used as a paradigmatic event that discloses a divine intention for humanity, and thus, since the circumstances were those of oppression, and oppression exists for large portions of humanity today, its theological construing has vast contemporary applications. Namely, "where there is oppression God wills liberation; where there are movements for liberation, there is the presence of God" (p. 188). As a moving expression of this transference from the Bible to the Now, I am reminded of the famous Negro spiritual, "When Israel was in Egyptland/ Let my people go/ Oppressed so hard they could not stand/ Let my people go." Morally and emotionally compelling by any humanist standards. But immediately we must ask: go *where*? if we do not wish to let the "theology" of that appeal simply blend into the general, secular sympathy today with liberation movements of all kinds. And here, the difference between the intransitive presence of an endorsing principle and the transitive thrust of an ulterior divine purpose can be quite consequential ethically. For instance, the plausible conclusion "where there are movements for liberation, there is the presence of God" may become a non sequitur when the premise is made to read thus: Where there is oppression, God wills liberation—*on condition* of a "covenant," i.e., on the condition that the liberated will henceforth serve him, i.e., that liberation is charged with a new obligation, is indeed a new appropriation and willed by God on that condition only. From the premise thus enlarged, it follows by no means that liberation movements per se have the automatic blessing of God (which his "presence" in them must mean)—not, e.g., if their aim or result is a rampage of licence, self-gratification, or cruelty. In the language of the scriptural archetypes: Mount Sinai, not the Golden Calf, was the divine interest in the liberation. In that archetype, by the way, a liberation movement was conspicuous by its absence: Moses was resented by his oppressed brethren, they had almost to be forced into the unwelcome freedom; and the terrible price of it for the next 3,000 years almost justifies that initial shrinking from it. I bring all this up merely to indicate that a "theological construing," especially for drawing ethical conclusions, must beware of simplistic uses of the powerful symbols of the sources, and that in the Jewish-Christian context it must go beyond sensed presence to articulate divine will, command, and action. (Note that I distinguish between loosely homiletic and strictly theological use of a biblical passage.)

As circumstances, so can *ends and consequences* of action be construed theologically, namely in relation to whether they contribute to or deflect from the fulfillment of a *divine goal* (p. 190). To the alternative of contributing or deflecting one must, I think, add obstructing, defacing, even destroying divine ends, i.e., positive counteraction to them. Now, for becoming relevant to human conduct, those ends must be known. *Discernible* divine purpose clearly would provide a norm for ethics. On its utter unknowability, let us remember, Descartes specifically based his exclusion of *causae finales,* i.e. of teleology, from a science of nature. But to the theologian it may be knowable, albeit nonscientifically, or (with Gustafson) "construable," either from the clues of nature (including man's) in the context of a "natural theology," or from the pronouncements of revelation in the context of a fideistic theology. The one would be more philosophical, the other more "theological" in the strict sense. A classic combination of the two is Thomas Aquinas's theology and ethics. If, as in that case, not only particular divine ends are disclosed in creation but an overall end of the whole, then we get those grand theological construings of the world with which, as underpinnings of an ethics, Gustafson deals on pp. 184 ff. It is here where I wish to comment somewhat more thoroughly.

Obviously, to construe "the whole" theologically, something like a cosmic teleology must be conceived. But then, it makes a great difference whether it is conceived in Aristotelian terms (as Aquinas did) or, let us say, in Whiteheadian terms. In the first case, the creation is complete in itself, a hierarchy of generic ends to be reactualized from individual to individual in their genera; in the Whiteheadian case, it is an unfinished business of ever-new ends, with creative novelty itself the overall end of creation as a whole. Surely, the ethical implications of the two views are vastly different, as man's task in "fulfillment" of the divine intent might look quite different in their light. In the Aristotelian case, it would be not to go beyond but to stay within the created order, not to complete the incomplete works of God but to preserve the *integrity* of his creation—in man himself: the integrity of the "image of God"; in the world: the plenitude of earthly life; in sum, biblically: the works of the fifth and sixth days. Being the notorious and increasingly dangerous violator of both, not to spoil them rather than to improve on them would be man's prime duty toward God. The created order (*ordo creationis*), especially where it is vulnerable—and it is that within the reach of human freedom—would set the norm: to guard it against distortion, but also from frustration; that is, not only refrain from causing the one, but also remove obstacles to its fulfilling itself. This cherishing of the given is, in goal-setting, a relatively humble ethical scheme, though in execution anything but easy, considering the terrible power—man's own—with which it has to cope (let alone any native "sinfulness"). What the more ambitious teleology of endless creative novelty, with which Whiteheadian process philosophy invests the universe, enjoins in the way of ethical norms for humans is not so clear, and our Christian theologian's comment on its compatibility with his faith would interest me.[1] But of Teilhard de Chardin's "point Omega," toward which the universe moves as its final consummation (to take another example of philosophical or speculative theology), I can say with confidence that such placing of the true end of things at the distant cosmic *future*, making their original creation a mere incipient stage for a perfection that is yet to come as the terminus of a gradually transforming ascent—thus robbing any *present* along the way of its "immediacy to God," is entirely un-Jewish; and my guess is: also un-Christian. *Historical* (as distinct from cosmic) eschatology, understood in some terms of imma- nent "gradualism" ("progress"), is a more complex question in the Jewish-Christian context, on which I will touch later.

Having at last cited by name the tradition in which Gustafson's effort stands—viz., the Judaeo-Christian tradition—and with it the common ground on which he and I can meet, I shall now make true my threat to don the theologian's robe for a while and tell how I would go about "construing the whole theologically" if I were a theologian. The basis for my attempt must needs be confined to the biblical source we two have in common, the Old Testament alone.

First, one word more about the "ultimate power," belief in and beliefs about whose reality Gustafson rightly calls "the con- ditions *sine qua non* for a theological construing of the world" (p. 192). Surely with his consent, I enlarge the *sine qua non* thus: for a biblicist theology, beliefs about this "power" must include, beyond its "ultimacy," that it is in some sense "spiritual," therefore also a seat of "interest" or "concern," and not indif- ferent. Else, some basic force of physics which theory may one day identify as the unitary root of all the diverse forces of nature (the search for such a unified force theory is on) would qualify for the title "ultimate power," the power that, from the big bang on, drives and rules the career of the universe. In the *religious* concept of an ultimate power, mentality and interest are neces- sary ingredients; and the interest is affirmative of the world and discriminating of what goes on in it, according to *Jewish* reli- gion. Taking this from now on as a basis, I find two statements in the Bible which can serve as the cornerstones for the whole edifice of a theology that leads to an ethics for man, without the help of a speculative or philosophical *theologia naturalis*. Both are from the first chapter of Genesis, the creation story: one the very first sentence of the Bible, "In the beginning God created the heavens and the earth," the other, "And God created man in his own image" (Gen. 1:27). The first conditions the relation of all things, the second the special relation of man to God; or ethically turned: the first sets a norm for man's relation to all things, i.e., the universe, the second for his relation to himself and his fellowmen. Let me, very briefly, develop at least the beginnings of theologico-ethical inferences from those two fundamental sentences.[2]

"God created heaven and earth" and then everything in them, including the multitude of life. Two related statements contribute to the meaning of this createdness of the world: the repeated one on each day's work, "And God saw that it was good," culminating in the final, "And God saw everything that he had made, and behold it was very good"; the other, "On the seventh day, God finished his work and rested from all his work which he had done" (Gen. 2:2). What have they to tell us about our relation to the world? Surely, the world's being willed by God and judged good in its creator's eyes endows it with a claim to affirmation by man. For this affirmation, the being created, i.e., willed, by God would suffice alone. But the being "good" adds to the extrinsic title an intrinsic property of its being: that such as it is, this is neither an absurd nor an indifferent universe, neutral as to value, but harbors value, and man with his value-feeling is not lost in it in cosmic solitude and arbitrary subjectivity. In this spirit, the Psalmist could aver that "The heavens tell the glory of God." And even the God of Job—by no means pure loving-kindness— could rest his case on the wonders of his creation. Belittling them as meaningless sports of mere necessity and chance would be impious under that comprehensive divine sanction of the created order. Toward the macrocosm, about which we can do little, this amounts in its ethical aspect mostly to a matter of *attitude* (such as arrogant or despairing "existentialism"); but toward the microcosm of life inhabiting this creation it also involves human *action*. Its existence in all its feeling kinds (i.e., animal species) receives a more emphatic endorsement by the creator than all the rest. While on everything else (including plants) he puts each time the summary seal that "it is good," it is at the first creation of *nefesh chaiah,* i.e., animated beings, that "he blessed them" and empowers them to be fruitful and multiply and fill the waters, etc. Stressed is the multitude of *kinds,* and although the blessing is given to their own power of filling their respective habitats, it binds man in relation to them as he is given shortly thereafter *dominion* over them. This dominion, given and thus legitimized, surely means exploitation, but also trusteeship. Exploitation without dominion is, by the universal law of life's feeding on life, the rule in interspecies relations and involves individual annihilation habitually, but not, on the whole, wiping out of kinds. Exploitation coupled with dominion poses precisely that danger, and as man's dominion has lately grown immeasurably, and with his own numbers also his needs and demands (not to speak of the gratuitous greeds of his civilization), the protective blessing of life's manifoldness at its creation is exceedingly topical today as a point of theological ethics. For the first time, one creature has become, through his power and freedom, responsible for all the others. And though perhaps not every extinction of species can be avoided in the impact of dominant man on his environment (as it surely was not avoided in past evolution), he is by the doctrine of creation clearly enjoined from wantonly impoverishing the diversity of life on this earth, which on the creator's testimony is a good in itself. Let me observe here that it is very difficult, if not impossible, from the premises of a purely secular ethics to derive something like a respect for extrahuman life, or obligations toward nature in general. What it can argue is the *unwisdom* of wanton destruction with its eventual, quite natural retribution on man's own life; or, more humanistically, the aesthetic loss suffered with the reduction of nature's magnificent wealth of forms, and thus the immorality of our robbing later generations of beauty and objects of wonder by leaving them a poorer estate. Since every secular ethics, rationalistic or other, individualist or collectivist, eudaemonistic or idealist, is necessarily *anthropocentric,* binding the title of "end-in-itself" to personhood, it cannot offer more than such cost-benefit considerations with regard to nonhuman things. A theological ethics, serious about the teaching of creation, can offer more: the element of reverence, the claim of all life to the dignity of end-in-itself, the divine will for its generic abundance, the stewardship of man for its continued presence. I need not spell out how this bears on concerns of ours.

Let me now pass to the second of the two Genesis pronouncements, the other cornerstone for a theological construing of ethics: the creation of man. Even in the sparse language of the Bible, it is clothed in emphatic, repetitive solemnity. "Let us make man in our image, after our likeness"; "So God created man in his own image, in the image of God he created him." His uniqueness is proclaimed but left mysterious. I will not try to plumb the depths of the "image" predicate. That it signifies an awesome charge is evident. In its name, humans could be exhorted "Be ye holy, *because* I am holy, the Lord, your God." This is a command, not a description, and the "because" expresses the logic of the "likeness": that it is a capacity, not a possession, and that the capacity sets our duty. While in all other cases, the "goodness" of creation rests securely in the creature and its acting by nature, in man it rests in the endowment with and for a *potentiality* which has been delivered into his hands. While all other life is innocent, he can be guilty of betraying the image. How he can do so is illustrated by what, to my knowledge, is the only later reference in the Bible to the image title of man, with the only direct practical conclusion ever explicitly drawn from it. It occurs in the so-called Noachitic law, given to Noah after the flood for all mankind until the Torah of Moses. It reads: "Of every man's brother I will require the life of man. Whosoever sheds the blood of man, by man shall his blood be shed; *for God made man in his own image*" (Gen. 9.5–6). God's argument here for capital punishment from precisely the sacredness of human life in his eyes ought surely to get a hearing in the contemporary debate, in which a nontheological, secular understanding of some such "sacredness" is often invoked to opposite effect. The measure of the sacredness, here absolute, is made the measure of the atonement, equally absolute, for the destruction of its bearer.

But as to "natural goodness" by creation, the theologian will hardly find in the Bible that the "image" distinction assures it to man as a presence that needs only be freed from the obstruction of circumstances, external and internal, to shine forth in its native purity. Much modern political ideology, as also of education, psychotherapy, and so on, is predicated on precisely this assumption. Conditions are the problem: improve them, and ethics will take care of itself. Listen to Bert Brecht in his *Threepenny Opera* (my translation):

"Who would not like to be a kind, good soul?/ Give to the poor one's own—why not? I ask./ When all are good, *His* kingdom is not far./ Who in His light would not with pleasure bask?/ Be a good person? Sure, who wouldn't rather be!/ But it so happens that on this our earth/ People are coarse and means are scarce./ To live in peace with all—who might not love that much?/ Alas! The circumstances aren't such." (*"Doch die Verhältnisse, sie sind nicht so"*: a refrain.)

Some truth in there, for sure, and at certain moments perhaps *the* truth that needs saying. But still a half-truth, as also in the more succinct and most quoted line from the same play (also a refrain) "First comes the feed, and then morality" (*"Erst kommt das Fressen und dann die Moral"*). Indeed, those denied the first may be excused from the second (especially by the luckier ones), but supplying the one does not of itself bring on the other, no more than liberation brings with it the use that liberty is for. Yet, even if these are no more than *opportunities* for meeting the real challenge of the image of God, helping to provide them and other necessary preconditions is itself a first duty toward that image. Especially to foster—beyond the palliatives of charity—freedom from oppression is bidden theologically, because it is better to serve God than men; and oppressing fellow humans is condemned as committing an insult to the mortal image of God, equally imparted to all. On all counts, religious and secular, oppression has to be done away with, and physical deprivation as much as possible. But the theologian will not fall prey to the progressivist illusion that such removals of obstacles, degradations, and privations will usher in a Golden Age. All modern utopianism—political, social, economic, technological, even psychological—is prone to that optimistic expectation. The theologians of the past, conversant with the fact of sin and the pitfalls of human freedom, knew better, or worse. "The inclination of man's heart is evil from his youth," said God after the flood, vowing to himself not to desolate the earth again because of man. Yet it was he who had created him in his own image! The seeming paradox points to the riddle that is man, which Pascal so eloquently dwelt on: poised between the infinite and the finite, between angel and beast, greatness and wretchedness, good and evil, partaking of both sides of these contraries. He can rise highest and fall lowest. The evil of the heart—of which indolence is one—will be different on a full stomach than an empty, with a commodious life than a pinched one, in security than in insecurity; but it will still be there to contend with. Neither Scripture nor experience tells otherwise. There is not the least ground for thinking that the image of God will ever be safe, certainly not by virtue of circumstances, be they the best that man can devise. They still should be striven after in a nonutopian, sober spirit. A theological ethics, therefore, when it comes to changing the world, i.e., the circumstances of men's life, will be neither pessimistic nor optimistic, but realistic. That gives ample scope to working for improvements, as justice, reason, and decency command, with no excessive expectations and at no excessive price, which any secular chiliasm is willing to pay at the cost of those living in the shadow of its supposed advent.

As always in ethical matters, the negative directives of the image attribute are easier to define than the positive—the bewareing easier than the fulfilling. The most pervasive *positive* inference from it is that every person is an end in himself and must be treated as such. This, as we know, is the supreme principle of Kant's ethics, but not really derivable from his rational premises, nor (I tend to believe) from *any* purely secular basis. From the doctrine of creation it follows naturally, and we do no injustice to Kant when we say that through his own, ostensibly immanent reasoning, there speaks the theological tradition to which he was heir.

However, with knowing *that* man is an end in himself, we do not know yet *what* that end may be, i.e., how the fulfilled image may look. But even with uncertainty about the positive "what," we can be certain about *negative* inferences from the "that," so Kant's own inference never to use persons as mere means. An even more elementary command of the image attribute, not mentioned by Kant, follows straight and uniquely from the fiat of its creation: that man must not be allowed to disappear from the earth. His presence in the world, if willed by the creator and dignified by his image, is for its collective repository not a choice but a duty. Therefore, nothing must be permitted that might endanger the continuation of that presence in the future. Speaking for a moment in my ordinary, nontheological persona: I have tried hard for myself to establish this simple, elementary, and today so important commitment on pure philosophical grounds (persuasive at least, if not compelling), and am by no means sure that I have succeeded. An axiom perhaps to feeling (who would not shudder at the thought of mankind forfeiting its future?), to reason it is a proposition hard to validate, perhaps altogether beyond its scope. Generally, ethics has something to say only about how men should behave to one another, but not that there ought to be men in the first place. Metaphysics must be called in for that—philosophically precarious at best and always dubious in its purported findings. Religion, to the contrary, leaves no doubt about it. What to instinct and emotion is merely repellent—a vanishing of man by our fault—becomes a sacrilege in the theological view.[3]

And so it is with other assaults on the created image, e.g., tampering with the genetic makeup of man. Surely, a theological ethics out of our tradition can here be categorical. I hasten to add that on this point a secular ethics is not helpless either and can speak with considerable authority when it bases itself on evident moral truths. I have found these to converge, though by quite different arguments, with what a theological ethics would have to conclude from *its* grounding verities, namely that in terms of biological endowment for its realization (and culpable stultification) the "image of God" was complete with its creation, as God indicated by resting from his finished work; that therefore a numinous sacrosanctity adheres to its given form and hallows its integrity; that consequently no "genetic engineering" on *man* may go beyond remedial help to alteration by "creative" design.

But here I had better stop playing the theologian's part. Not being a theologian, I have been indulging in a hypothetical and necessarily dilettantic game. For nothing of it do I claim theological validity, not even in the name of Judaism. The Christian theologian's "construing" from *his* sources will anyway look different, certainly more complex. Compared with Christianity, Judaism is quite unsophisticated at its roots; and so my hypothetical task, quite apart from the layman's oversimplifications, was simple compared to what Gustafson has to come up with when carrying out his own construing, for which he has articulated to us the underlying assumptions. To goad him and other theologians into just this is my sole purpose. But I did want to indicate, from the other side of the fence, immodestly perhaps, what *kind* of thing we expect or would like to hear from them. So I close with an entreaty from the rationally confined to the more amply authorized: Use your surplus and give us the real article! The sceptical hedgings we will supply, but first we want the full blast from your strongest guns. For we well know that immanent reason, as it has come to be disciplined and clipped, has not the last word on ultimate questions of our being and at some point must borrow from sources of light beyond itself, or at least consider their witness. Religion is one such source, even for those not within its dogmatic fold.

NOTES

1. His own illustration of "construing the whole theologically" by Jonathan Edwards' *Dissertation Concerning the End for which God Created the World* (p. 191) does not tell me, for God's "infinite fulness" at which the world, having emanated from it, also finally aims, does not readily define ethical norms.

2. I attempted this first in an address to the Central Conference of American Rabbis in 1967, entitled "Contemporary Problems in Ethics from a Jewish Perspective"; now included in my *Philosophical Essays* (Englewood Cliffs, N.J.: Prentice-Hall, 1974), pp. 168-82.

3. Secular ethics, to be sure, can avoid the *metaphysical* issue ("ought there to be men on earth?") by adducing the straightforward *moral* issue of the sufferings and premature deaths of the actual future individuals living at the time of the species' demise, violent or lingering: The prohibition to any generation to cause this for a future one is ethically plain by the common norms of interhuman conduct, which do include the unborn as a class sure to be born in their time. Obviously, the observance of this moral veto alone, from generation to generation, in effect (coincidentally) takes care of the metaphysical issue too, as if it were answered affirmatively without ever having been raised. But that the issue itself, with its own injunction, is nevertheless not otiose can be seen if we imagine a unanimous decision of all humans living at a particular time to stop reproducing and ensure this by universal sterilization: the never-born are not wronged, the living not subjected to suffering; any pain incurred by living and dying childless personally and with no posterity of the species is self-chosen in exchange for some preferred

gain; the latter also exculpates applying the collective decision to the children of the moment though they could not participate in it, i.e., relieving them prophylactically of the curse of their reproductive rights—in their own best interest by the lights of the decision itself. Formal ethical rules seem to be satisfied, the former veto not to apply. Yet we forcibly feel that all such balancing of the sums of temporary happiness and unhappiness, of the observing and overriding of rights, etc., even with a good showing on the credit side, does not touch on the permissibility of putting *this* up for decision at all. Therefore, the metaphysical issue of mankind's "eternal" commitment is not an idle one, even pragmatically. E.g., its affirmative answer would make offspring a collective duty (its measure set by circumstances, and with every allowance for individual abstentions normally comprised in the statistical picture). That group mores and impulse habitually take care of this transcendent duty, sometimes even excessively, does not render the principle trivial. For man stands out from nature and even with this most natural of functions comes under more-than-natural sanctions, positive and negative.

Commentary

Rejoinder to Hans Jonas

James M. Gustafson

MY CHAPTER HAS BEEN correctly perceived by Hans Jonas, and by Richard Beauchamp and Ronald Green in oral criticism, to be more interpretive or descriptive than "positional." One reason for this, though it may not be adequate, is that on a previous occasion in this group I offered a draft of a more "positional" paper and was sharply challenged to make clear its assumptions. My perception, perhaps an inaccurate one, was that it was necessary to interpret to this group *what* theological ethics is about prior to *doing* theological ethics. (Moral philosophers have for decades been telling us *what* ethics is about without being "positional" about morality. Maybe I have learned too well from them.) Perhaps I am too cautious, but theologians have good reasons to be cautious after several centuries of having theology charged with excessive certitude.

In other publications I have been more "positional," and particularly relevant to this symposium, in my Père Marquette lecture, *The Contributions of Theology to Medical Ethics*, cited in note 13. Part of the argument in that lecture is quite in tune with part of Jonas's own hypothetical (they ring, however, with greater authenticity than a purely mental exercise) theological proposals. It is dangerous to promise future work, but I do intend in the next phase of my career to develop a position more fully. I have spent more than a quarter of a century working in a critical analytical way through contemporary and historical Christian ethical literature, to a lesser extent through Jewish materials, and through philosophical and other relevant literature. The paper to which Jonas profoundly and eloquently responds is, indeed, only a short version of what has become to me a very complex agenda—so complex as to create in me persistent anxiety and sometimes despair. Candidly, it is easier for me to preach (an activity I take seriously, intellectually and rhetorically) my position than to defend it on all of its many exposed fronts. That admission may indicate other issues of theological ethics. To whom is the work addressed? What is its proper rhetorical form? How does one engage simultaneously in "language about" *and* "language of"? That admission may also indicate my most authentic "calling." But explanations become excuses, and I turn to some aspects of Jonas's substantial response.

First, with reference to the "transhistorical status of Jesus Christ." To be a Christian theologian is to find some such status to be the case—affectively and intellectually. "Some such" begs hundreds of questions; "just what" has been discussed for almost two thousand years. In *Christ and the Moral Life*, 1968, and some publications subsequent to that I have discussed the issues involved and stated my own view. The absence of more explicit references in this paper, however, stems in part from the conviction which I share with my teacher, H. Richard Niebuhr, that Christ "points beyond himself," that his significance is in what we come to know and articulate about "the Father," that is, about God. I interpret Christ's significance as a source (revelation) of insight into the reality of God more in continuity with the insights of what Christians call the Old Testament than do many theologians. Thus in writing about *theology* and ethics I do not find it necessary always to invoke the name of Christ. The "redemptional significance" of the "Christ event" for me is not so much the event as what it indicates about the Deity. What it indicates about "the Father" is what has "transhistorical" significance.

Second, the dominance of the language of "ultimate power" over the language of "goodness." Jonas's perception is accurate. Surely the Jewish and the Christian claim is that ultimate power and ultimate goodness coinhere, and I affirm that. I can only indicate here, and not give adequate defense, why the language of power dominates. Goodness for whom? Goodness for what? I have been charged with having a "high" God, and with using "chilling" rhetoric in speaking of God, and not without evidence to support the charge. For too many religious persons in the Christian tradition the coinherence of power and goodness has led to the aspiration that what humans perceive to be their "good" is what the ultimate power desires, and on this basis religion has come to have only utility value, in the crassest sense of the term. Not only Job's experience, Jeremiah's experience, the experience of the Jewish people, but also *my* experience cries out against utilitarian religion. If the ultimate power is also goodness, that goodness must not be primarily for my interests or even a generally human perception of what is in the interests of a species recently evolved, but be the good of the "whole." And not the "whole" now, but "for all time." The power of God I confront daily in the limits of human self-sufficiency and (obversely) in the ultimate dependence and interdependence of human life. The goodness of the power is often not perceptible; humans surely err if they believe that their interests (perceptions of their well-being) will be met because the ultimate power is good. I mean "human" not only in individual and social reference, but even in reference to species! To affirm that God is a God "for man" tempts all too many persons to assume that what they desire "for men" is what the goodness of the ultimate power wills. No "special providence" is guaranteed, though one is grateful to the ultimate power for every manifestation of human well-being, "he" being the condition of the possibility of each. We all know the classic issues opened by these remarks—the problem of evil, the problem of omnipotence of divine goodness, eschatology, and so on.

Third, the "practical function" of theology. Jonas, happily, finds that "practical" does not mean mere homiletics, but the practice of life. I hope he agrees that homiletics is a legitimate form of rhetoric in discerning how life ought to be lived. Like "practical," "homiletics" also is a word cheapened by religious persons themselves.

Fifth, "the presence of the Deity in these experiences." I do mean the presence of the Deity *in* the objects of experience and in the events reflected upon. Philosophical-theological explanation of this I cannot undertake here, and am not as skilled in undertaking anywhere as are others. (Ah, the many fronts that have to be defended in theological ethics, the complexity of its agenda!)

Sixth, Jonas suggests that the language of "presence" sounds too passive. Anyone who has deeply imbibed the biblical narratives must concur in Jonas's observation that in the Bible God is seen to be an active participant and not merely a passive presence. The force of this becomes even clearer when the biblically based religious traditions are set in contrast with, for example, the Upanishads. The biblical traditions generally conceive ultimate reality to be a power with a moral will, and will not only in the sense of a "desire," but also in the sense of agency. I think it is quite appropriate to explore the extent to which the analogy of human agency provides an adequate way to indicate principal features of human experience of the Deity. If I infer properly from Jonas's remarks, he suggests that the language of presence, not qualified by the adjective "active" leaves us with the shades of Spinoza, or, in more fervent piety, with mysticism.

But surely much of ethics in the Christian tradition, and perhaps also in Judaism and Islam, has erred on the side of excessive certitude about what this active presence *is* doing or *requires* persons to do. The theologies of active presence provide the possibility of moral fanaticism, for self-righteousness, and for authoritarian moral claims. I have written elsewhere that the practical moral question in theological ethics is "What is God enabling and requiring us to be and to do?" The answer is not arrived at by emotive intuition, or by rationalistic calculation: indeed, given our finitude the answer is always tentative even when sought with overwhelming sophistication. Thus for me one significance of "presence" is to suggest what Christian theologians who inform my work indicate by the dimension of inscrutability in the ways of God. I agree with Jonas that in the biblically grounded traditions an articulation of a divine will or action is required. But every such articulation is conditioned by human finitude. "My ways are higher than your ways," Isaiah has God tell the people; "we see through a glass darkly," the Apostle Paul warns us. We cannot clearly say "what God is doing" in and through recombinant DNA research, though we might get some clues about what humans ought to be doing with the results of such research in light of our perceptions and articulations of what the purposes of the ultimate power are for humanity.

Seventh, I agree with Jonas that a cosmic theology is required to explicate the agenda I have proposed, and clearly it makes a difference whether that is developed in an Aristotelian or a Whiteheadian way. I am not skilled in the art of cosmological speculation, but am persuaded that the language of an active presence which is the condition of possibility of development in nature and history, as well as development in the human understanding of nature and history, requires a cosmology that accounts for what the Whiteheadian cosmology does. Since I am convinced that cosmologies are based on inferences drawn from what is ultimately human experience of "the world," one of their tests is adequacy to our experience (including knowledge) of the world. It is interesting to observe that one reason why Roman Catholic theological ethics is undergoing revision in our time is that certain received "scholastic" forms of the Aristotelian view are judged to be too "static" in the light of contemporary experience and knowledge of "the world." For me, as for Roman Catholics, to argue for greater "openness," however, does not imply that there are no persistent continuities on which to ground "almost absolute" principles and values.

Eighth, I wholly concur in Jonas's exposition of the significance of the biblical affirmation, "God created heaven and earth," and I have expounded my views in *The Contributions of Theology to Medical Ethics* in a way that is similar to his own exposition. I suggested there that when the Psalmist states that man is only a little lower than the angels we ought to see that not as praise for human dominion, but as a charge to moral accountability, based on the evolved capacities of our species, as stewards of creation.

Finally, I am not as sure of Jonas's explication of the *imago Dei* theme in Genesis. I was privileged to hear him expound this orally in his lecture to the Central Conference of American Rabbis, the lecture cited in his response here. He develops it to support the idea that man is an end in himself and thus attacks rigorously all actions which make human beings instruments for nonhumane ends. There are good theological and ethical reasons for this exposition, and it occurs to me that the Jonathan Edwards essay I cited would be one way to support this view. If God's own glory is the proper end of creation, and man is made in God's image, man's own glory is the proper end of man.

"Glory," of course, has unfortunate connotations to some readers. Less offensive would be that God is the end of his creation; man in God's image is also his own end.

I confess that I am not sure how we ought to interpret the *imago Dei* theme. The circularity of any interpretation seems inevitable. Since any conception of God is made by analogy or inference from our perceptions of man and the world, to in turn say that man is created in God's image gives theological authority to those human perceptions. My own preference (and it is no more than that at this time) is to use human agency as the analogy, while properly acknowledging the analogical character of "God language." As the Deity is conceived to be an active purposive presence in nature and history, so is man. I believe this is coherent with what I have said above in favor of a non-Aristotelian view of theological ethics (or at least it requires a significant revision of an Aristotelian view). Or, in relation to Psalm 8, to be a little lower than the angels is to be an accountable agent or steward in the whole of creation.

And therein lies the problem. Can we have Jonas's perceptive exposition of "God created the heavens and the earth" while also holding to his exposition of the *imago Dei* which seems to make man the chief end in creation? I have more abstractly indicated in the Père Marquette Lecture what I believe is implied in "God created the heavens and the earth," namely, that the ultimate power wills the well-being of the *whole* of the creation. This creates the possibility of a moral danger from Jonas's point of view; I acknowledge the danger. There may be occasions when the human is not an end in itself, but must serve the end of the whole. The difference may not be irreconcilable at some levels of general principles; man treated as an end may be judged to be consistent with the well-being of the whole of creation. I, however, have not been persuaded of this. I believe we will in the next decades again be engaged in an ancient inquiry. What is man's place in the universe? What are the ends of man? Will it not be necessary tragically to deny the well-being of some human beings for the sake of the good of the creation (not merely society—as we do deny that in morally justified wars).

I have heard Hans Jonas articulate the tragic character of the morally serious life. I have always resonated with such a view.

Pain, suffering—denial of the rights and goods including life itself to some for the sake of others and the "whole"—these are necessary and inevitable aspects of moral life. What the ultimate power and good enables and requires us to be and to do, though discerned imperfectly, may be costly to at least the apparent goods we judge to be the proper ends of at least some persons.

Jonas closes with a challenge I have heard from others in the Foundations of Ethics group. "Use your surplus. . . . The sceptical hedgings we will supply. . . ." It is too late in the history of theological thought for an academic theologian not to supply his or her own sceptical hedgings. Like Jonas, I believe religion is *a* source of light; if I did not I would be a sociologist or a philosopher, or be satisfied to do "religious studies." Maybe "the full blast from [one's] strongest guns" comes only when one is preaching and not when one is writing a theological paper for nontheological critics.

Doctoring the Disease, Treating the Complaint, Helping the Patient: Some of the Works of Hygeia and Panacea

H. Tristram Engelhardt, Jr.

I. Introduction

MEDICINE HAS HAD A CENTRAL PLACE in the four years of discussions concerning the foundations of ethics and its relations to the sciences that have produced the volumes in this series. The focus has been as much upon the more general theme of the relationship between evaluations and explanations as upon issues of ethics (i.e., evaluations of one particular kind). In the first volume, for example, Marx Wartofsky argued that medicine is a "fundamental form of human knowledge" and a "primary mode of human social practice,"[1] in fact, "a fundamental mode of cognitive praxis."[2] Wartofsky contended that medicine is ineluctably normative; "even in its earliest causal-explanatory mode, medicine is already a normative kind of knowledge, in the sense that it is knowledge for the sake of some good."[3] Considerations of human goods and of medical knowledge are closely intertwined. A similar point was made by Gorovitz and MacIntyre, who argued for the primacy of sciences, such as medicine, which study particulars, and for the need to attend to the goods of the particular entities (e.g., patients) studied.[4] In short, this series began with a reexamination of what it means to know things in medicine and of the role of values in the process of knowing and in the content of the knowledge. What was discovered was an interplay of evaluation and explanation, of theory and practice.

These issues have continued to be explored in subsequent volumes. Eric Cassell, for instance, has traced the role of language in structuring physician-patient relations[5] and in our appreciation of concepts of illness and disease,[6] and Joseph Margolis has indicated why psychoanalysis must recognize man as a culturally emergent entity—especially in accounts of disease and illness.[7] In this essay I will bring many of these themes to a final focus. In so doing I will return to themes I touched upon in my essay in the first volume: states of affairs are termed illnesses for quite divergent reasons (e.g., because of dysfunction, pain, disfigurement, and deformity); states of affairs are recognized as dysfunctional or as conditions of disfigurement, and so on, by reference in part to culturally relative notions of proper human function and proper human form; disease accounts are fashioned in order to account for such illness states. These disease accounts then allow a distinction between *mere* symptoms and the underlying disease, and between symptomatic and etiological treatment (a useful device for distinguishing between the world of medical observations and the world of medical explanations is a stipulative distinction between illnesses and diseases, where the first identifies observable states and the second explanatory models of the latter).[8] Even theoretical disease explanations, disease entities, retain a value-laden character in that they are constructed in order to account for disapproved-of states of affairs—illnesses. In this essay, I will outline the extent to which medicine is defined by patients' complaints. In doing so, I will be agreeing with the more complaint-oriented and grounded nosologies of Sydenham, Sauvages, and Cullen.[9] One might think here, for example, of the illness category of Sauvages, *"dolores vagi, qui nomen a sede fixa non habent"* (pains which do not have a name employed by wandering from a fixed site).[10] I will thus be in disagreement with the notion that the world of illness, the world of the clinician can be deduced from or reduced to the world of the pathoanatomist. I will, in fact, be contending that the reverse is the case—the world of the pathoanatomist, the pathophysiologist, and the pathopsychologist is always dependent upon that of the clinician for its sense and direction. Further, the world of the clinician is defined by people—by their complaints and vexations. One must, in fact, somewhat circularly say that the world of medicine is defined by the medical complaints of people and medical complaints are what medicine could, in principle, address.

This definition loses its circularity when one notes that in the definition there is a difference in accent between the two meanings of medicine. From the side of physicians, nurses, and so on, the focus is on the abilities of the art. From the point of view of patients, the accent is on complaints, upon what the art is there for. Physicians look to the capabilities of their technologies including the possibilities of their art, and patients to what is vexing (of course, the distinction of patient vis-a-vis physician perspectives is artificial, and is made to illustrate two poles of medicine). The availability of medical technology is likely to expand the compass of complaints, and the presence of complaints is likely to expand the legitimate range of medical technology. Thus, complaints evoke the art of medicine, which then influences the understanding and classification of complaints by patients, which then again evokes the art in a different fashion— and the dialectic continues. Where there is a lack of coincidence between these poles of complaints and the art (e.g., because the technologies cannot appreciably help the complaints), vexatious states of dysfunction, pain, or deformity are likely (at least in part) to be considered to be natural and to be accepted, works of the devil to be addressed by prayer, or problems in living to be endured with fortitude.

Also, one may recognize certain states of affairs as open to medical address, but decide not to approach them medically. One could, for example, treat many crimes as neurological dysfunctions by reconditioning prisoners. Yet one may decide not to do so in order to avoid confusing our practices of punishment and of praising and blaming with our practices of treating patients so as to avoid the possibility of the dangerous use (i.e., contrary to the institutions of public liberty) of medical technologies. The lines between what is medical and nonmedical are drawn on the basis of when one acts to control physiological or psychological processes considered as causally determined processes, not directly and immediately under voluntary control, and recognized as the substrata of dysfunctions, pains, or disfigurements. Thus, telling an alcoholic that what he is doing is wrong is not medical treatment if one means to have him mend his evil ways. Nor are programs aimed at teaching individuals how to avoid drinking to the point of sinful overindulgence, economic ruin, or bane to the commonweal, medical programs. However, prescribing Antabuse (disulfram) is a medical act, as is the use of psychoanalysis, or even education as long as they are undertaken in order to avoid or erode psychological and/or physiological dependencies, which are viewed as dysfunctional. Descriptions of the intentions of the intervening individuals are necessary in order to know when an act is medical.[11]

In short, much falls or can fall within the sphere of medicine. After all, in the Hippocratic Oath one calls to witness the goddesses Health and All-Heal. Medicine inspires a search for many senses of full health and the cure of many vexations.[12] As the oath shows, the hopes for medicine have been extensive, even when well-founded expectations could be few. As a result, the term "medicine" gathers together numerous, often quite diverse enterprises. In fact, there is no one such thing as medicine. The term lacks a single referent. Instead, various enterprises are placed under the term. What I shall do here is to sketch some of the major enterprises gathered under the term "medicine" in order to show the interplay between values (and not just ethical values) and the sciences and technologies of medicine. I will do so by examining the role played by patients' complaints in defining medicine. I hope to show, as Wartofsky suggested in the first volume, that medicine "is hopelessly value-bound, centered as it is upon the phenomena of life, death, and human suffering. Its technology and its theory, though they may be construed as achievements of a disinterested scientific understanding, stand in too close a proximity to human weal and woe to permit a distracted divorce from actual medicine practice."[13]

II. Medicine (s)

When one inspects phrases such as "the philosophy of medicine," one is struck not only with the ambiguity of terms like "philosophy," but the ambiguity of "medicine." In part, "medicine" functions as an umbrella term, as "philosophy" does in the degree, Doctor of Philosophy. One must remember here how "philosophy" and "medicine" denote two of the traditional faculties of the European university. With the embrace of surgery as part of medicine, one has not only individuals who hold doctoral degrees in dental medicine and surgery, as well as veterinary medicine, but individuals holding degrees in nursing, occupational therapy, physical therapy, and other allied health-care arts and sciences.

The heterogeneity of enterprises embraced under the term "medicine" is thus imposing. Medicine encompasses endeavors of pharmacological and surgical mitigation of diseases and illnesses; environmental and immunological prevention of diseases: psychological support through counseling; mothering through attention to feeding, bathing, bed care and like forms of nursing; especially disciplined forms of recreation directed to maintaining or restoring fulfillment in human activities; attempts to use pharmacological or surgical interventions to decrease distress or increase well-being and pleasure in life; studies regarding the biological or psychological substrata of all of the above; studies of the application of such basic information toward the above-mentioned goals; special social certifying functions given to physicians; and so on. It is now fashionable to refer to all of these diverse enterprises under the rubric of "health care," the "health-care sciences or arts" or some such variant. In what follows, I will use the term "medicine" to identify this entire gaggle of enterprises. As I will show, there are good reasons for viewing this collage of endeavors as enterprises of therapy, enterprises in the prevention of the need for therapy, studies of the biological and/or psychological bases of the occasions for therapy, or studies of the efficacy of therapy. This way of grouping "medical" endeavors places the weight upon "therapy." Of course, "therapy" is equally wide-ranging in meaning. As did *therapeia* in the Greek, which had a broad meaning, including a waiting on, a service, an attendance, the service of divine worship, as well as a fostering, nurturing, or tending as in sickness, giving medical treatment, and paying court, so also "therapy" in English includes the senses of tending to the sick as well as treating medically with the intent to cure, heal, or give care.[14] This ambiguity in the word "therapy" is of particular importance, for a great proportion of the "therapeutic" activities of physicians involve attending to the worried-well and performing noncurative activities (e.g., prescribing contraceptives). Therapy means much more than curing or healing.

A recognition of this ambiguity and its significance plays a role in practical policy decisions. For example, understanding what one means by therapy is of interest to those wishing to know the rationale for giving health-care insurance coverage to individuals for pregnancies and abortions, areas of medical intervention that are not considered treatment-oriented *in sensu stricto*. Uncertainty regarding where to draw the line for health-care insurance coverage stems in part from the fact that one may give care in a way that is in fact therapeutic, without presuming that it is curative. One can treat symptoms without presupposing that there is an underlying disease. There is no easy way to discover restrictive borders for health care. They are in great measure invented.

Intrusions into controlling nondisease-based distress and displeasure have drawn numerous critiques. For example, Leon Kass has bemoaned the fact that "all kinds of problems now roll through the doctor's door, from sagging anatomies to suicides, from unwanted childlessness to unwanted pregnancies, from marital difficulties to learning difficulties, from genetic counselling to drug addiction, from laziness to crime."[15] It is worth noting that authors such as Kass take this expansive view of medicine to be a rather recent development.[16] "When medicine's powers were fewer, its purpose was clearer. Indeed, since antiquity, medicine has been regarded as the very model of an art, of a rational activity whose powers were all bent towards a clear and identifiable end. Today, though fully armed and eager to serve, the doctor finds that his target is no longer clear to him or to us."[17] The picture is of the physician confused by the lack of conceptual integrity in the demands he or she faces from persons when their complaints do not fall under one notion.

This expansive view of medicine is not new. Rudolph Virchow quotes Descartes (a passage of which Kass makes acknowledgement)[18] as seeing the resolution of most social problems coming from medicine, "Finally let us recall the words of Descartes who said that if it were at all possible to ennoble the human race, the means for this could be found only in medicine. In reality, if medicine is the science of the healthy as well as of the ill being (which is what it ought to be), what other science is better suited to propose laws as the basis of the social structure, in order to make effective these which are inherent in man himself?"[19] Even Aristotle's view of man appears to have been accepting of the manipulation of physiological states as a possible way of diminishing ignorance.[20] One should note as well that many of the controversial expansions of medicine's scope are not of a recent vintage—for example, Thomas Trotter's 1804 treatise on alcoholism as a disease.[21] Thus, when one reads complaints about the medicalization of life[22] or about the distortion of medicine's enterprise through concern with peripheral goals, one should not conclude that these distortions are restricted to the modern era.[23] Instead, one is, for better or worse, encountering a deeply rooted view of medicine.

In any event, expansive views of medicine, such as that implicit in the (in)famous definition of health by the World Health Organization ("health is a state of complete physical, mental and social well-being and not merely the absence of disease or infirmity."),[24] have provoked considerable response. In his critique, for example, Kass has argued for a clarification of medicine's goals and a restriction of its focus, "for without a clear view of its end, medicine is at risk of becoming merely a set of powerful means, and the physician at risk of becoming merely a technician, an engineer of the body, a scalpel for hire, selling his services upon demand."[25] The thrust of Kass's position appears to be that the pure of heart think only one thought. He is seeking to solve moral problems in medicine, not by showing that some usages of medicine are unjustified, but by attempting to show that they are not medical. What follows will in large proportion be a response to Kass's critique of this amplified view of medicine. Medicine is inextricably and usefully (and in the sense properly) complex. Medicine is not, and should not be the pure or simple enterprise that Kass wishes it to be. Moreover, ethical issues in medicine (i.e., justified or unjustified uses of medicine) cannot be solved as problems of definition, but must be faced as ethical issues.

One could, of course, by stipulation narrow the scope of "medicine." For example, one could define or attempt to define medicine as the set of therapeutic endeavors which restores bodily functions by pharmacological or surgical means. However, even leaving aside ambiguities in the terms "pharmacological" or "surgical," there is an ambiguity in "restoring function." This ambiguity is central to the controversy concerning the cultural relativity or independence of concepts of health or disease. Some have argued that what is proffered as a set of complaints for medical explanations and control (i.e., what could, stipulatively, be called illnesses) is determined by the cultural environment and appreciated through socially constructed concepts.[26] Illness is, according to such accounts, socially determined as well as being a social construction. However, in most illnesses biological factors constrain the possible variations among such concepts so that in almost all environments and social contexts, some states will almost always be appreciated (if not indeed always) as illnesses (i.e., there will be a spectrum of transcultural agreement ranging from complaints such as vitiligo to angina). Further, there will be various ways in which one can develop classifications and explanations of the illnesses one discovers (e.g., one can view tuberculosis an an infectious, genetic, or social disease, depending on which causal connections one wishes to highlight).[27] Others, in contrast, wish to view illnesses and diseases in terms of biologically definable senses of function and dysfunction, either by reference to the nature of particular activities or organs, or by reference to an evolutionary sense of natural design.[28]

Were such an essentialist view of disease and dysfunction successful, one could attempt to define medicine as the enterprise of restoring biological functions or preventing such dysfunctions. However, such an account would do violence to the broad scope within which medicine has been viewed and practiced. Medicine has traditionally attempted to mitigate situational worries and distresses, not simply to restore biological functions or to prevent dysfunctions (unless "function" and "dysfunction" are interpreted in a very broad sense, in a sense that individuals such as Kass do not wish to tolerate). Moreover, restrictive or essentialistic interpretations of illness, disease, health, function, and dysfunction do not seem feasible on conceptual grounds. Different senses of illness have varying amounts of cultural dependency (e.g., consider the following questions for the cultural influences they signal: Should homosexuality be considered a disease? Is color blindness a defect given its conferring an ability to spot camouflage and thus increase survival value in particular environments?[29] Is sickle-cell trait a defect given that it increases potential survival in falciparum malaria-infested environments lacking anti-malarial drugs, though the trait possibly could lead to difficulties in environments where there might be a loss of oxygen pressure, as in testing jet planes at high altitudes).[30] The move to restrict medicine to narrow biological goals on conceptual grounds is not likely to succeed, because there are no standard environments in terms of which traits and biological structures have an unambiguous sense of being adapted or maladapted. Also whether particular organs in nonoperational states should be counted as diseased or defective or simply as irrelevant depends upon environmental contexts, goals, and so on (e.g., consider the blindness of bats versus the complex biological changes incident to menopause. Since bats do not reflect on what they might be missing by being blind, blindness to them is not a disease or defect. However, women can consider the consequences of menopause to be a disease state or a state of defect).[31]

Thus, because of the fuzziness of notions of what should count as proper human functions, because of the fuzziness of concepts of health, illness, and disease, because of the considerable cultural dependence of many of those notions (not to mention actual distortions in the psychology of discovery owing to cultural influences),[32] because of the various purposes to which medicine is put, and because of the quite different activities subsumed under "medicine," there is, as suggested above, no single sense of "medicine."

It is, in this regard, worth stressing a point made in my essay in the first volume and elsewhere, namely, that proper human functions and form are context dependent. To be well adapted presupposes a particular environment, and there are no standard human environments in this abstract. Moreover, to be well adapted is to be well adapted to a certain end or ends. But we need not accept as normative for humans some evolutionary "goal," such as maximizing inclusive reproductive fitness. Nor is it clear what the "goals" of evolution are, if evolution can indeed be said to have goals—to maximize the fitness of a species, of an actually interbreeding group, and so on. And even if evolution were to have goals, it is not clear why humans would have to embrace them. We may not agree with evolution—we may decide to have sickle-cell disease count as a disease even if it is the purchase price of better species adaptation. In short, the meaning of "health" and "illness" turn on how we come to view proper human functions, form and freedom from pain.[33]

III. Therapies

In order to indicate the unavoidable range of meanings of "medicine" and how these meanings turn on various complaints or vexations, a list follows (under rubrics of therapy) of different senses of "medicine." It is provided also to suggest the scope of the endeavors in which medicine engages in response to the complaints patients bring and to indicate the goal of or action-oriented nature of medicine—a point made by Wartofsky in the first volume. The classification that follows is oriented around responses with therapy to complaints or possible needs for therapy (activities in anticipation of possible complaints).[34]

A. Therapy

Much of the discussion concerning the status of various modes of therapy turns on whether such therapy is viewed as symptomatic treatment (i.e., simply treating the complaints that the patient brings) or etiologic treatment (i.e., addressed to eradicating the disease entity or causes that occasion the complaints of the patient). That is, with the development of modern disease-entity language, a vocabulary is at hand to contrast those therapies addressed to complaints and those addressed to the causes underlying the complaints. The latter have been seen as the more scientific, less empiric, and therefore the preferable approaches to therapy. Narrower views of therapy also conceive of therapy as being proper only *for* diseases, where diseases (and their symptoms) are authenticated by reference to a canonical nosology. Therapy in fact (historically) has been used more broadly to include activities addressed to resolving complaints that occasion patients seeking health care. One can give therapy for pain and distress attendant to normal processes (e.g., teething, childbirth). One need not be concerned with a disease (in the sense of a recognized pathological condition) in order to give therapy. It is enough that there be biologically or psychologically based distress, pain or dissatisfaction.

Therapy may be distinguished from other activities, such as education and political action, in that acts of therapy are meant to bear upon biological and/or psychological processes not directly under patient control (while learning and political activities are taken to concern more voluntary dimensions of life). The objects of therapy (and of the institutionalized service, medicine) are complaints that are based on (1) inabilities to perform physiological or psychological functions taken to be normal or proper to humans; (2) states of pain; or (3) states of physical deformity, or marked ugliness (e.g., vitiligo, polydachtylia, and others).[35] That is, by understanding therapy in terms of addressing complaints of loss of function, the presence of pain, or the presence of deformity,[36] one is able to include under therapy all the activities that take place in health care, such as giving aspirins, giving penicillin, providing bed pans, feeding the ill in a hospital bed, and so forth. Acts of therapy approach complaints by treating them as (and addressing them as) involuntary, physiological, and/or psychologically based states.

Finally, I shall use therapy and treatment interchangeably. To make that stipulation is to signal as well that my use of the terms "medicine," "disease" and "illness," and so on are in various ways stipulative. They are not simply reports concerning the ways in which those words function in particular natural languages. What is suggested are ways in which those terms must function in order to give a rational account of medicine as an institutionalized service focused on the alleviation of complaints of dysfunction, pain, and deformity, when those complaints are based in biological and/or psychological processes which are beyond immediate voluntary control.

1. Therapy of syndromes

Under this rubric is placed therapy addressing recognized constellations of signs and symptoms, complaints for which there is at least some meager model of explanation. Interventions such as sex-change surgery, mammoplasties, and the provision of estrogen to correct the consequences of menopause will be placed here in order to signal the fact that these states of affairs can, *pace* Kass, be properly viewed as states of dysfunction (i.e., not being able to function with one's original sexual phenotype, being postmenopausal, having sagging breasts, and so on). One is engaged in an activity to change the character of a biological and/or psychological state not under the direct and immediate control of the individual receiving therapy, which state is the basis of the complaints. One is seeking a more adequate biological and/or psychological adaptation to a particular environment.

"Syndrome" in the context of this discussion comes to mean only a recognized constellation of signs and symptoms with at least some meager account of the causal mechanism behind the signs and symptoms, or at least an account in terms of the natural history of the illness. Such therapy is etiologic in this sense if one can say: "What I am doing therapeutically will eliminate the basis of this constellation of complaints." Otherwise, one is only treating symptomatically because one has no reason to believe one is addressing some underlying basis of the symptoms. Treating the fever of a bacterial infection with aspirin is thus symptomatic therapy, giving an antibiotic is etiologic therapy. Helping a patient go through with an unwanted pregnancy is symptomatic therapy, performing an abortion is etiologic therapy. One is, however, in each case oriented by a recognized pattern of complaints concerning which at least a natural history is known.

The same is true of therapies addressed to syndromes, even if the therapies are not curative, but only palliative or supportive. Again, these lines are drawn not to suggest the importance of particular distinctions. On the contrary, they are meant to suggest the expansiveness of medicine and the arbitrariness of restrictive categories.

a. Etiologically directed. The various ways in which therapies are applied and cures achieved can be displayed according to degrees of invasiveness and in terms of the kinds of techniques employed, varying from those more closely associated with contemporary views of medicine in the strict sense (use of penicillin, or a surgical technique), to those less closely so associated (i.e., behavioral therapy, biofeedback), for example:

    i. Pharmacological—e.g., curing syphilis with penicillin.
    ii. Surgical intervention without any anatomical change in the patient. Under this rubric would fall returning a patient to a *status quo ante* some nonvoluntary physiological and/or psychological state of affairs taken to be improper, abnormal or unwanted (i.e., productive of pain in some extended sense), e.g., removal of kidney stones, abortion for an unwanted pregnancy.
    iii. Surgical cure, but with anatomical change in the patient—e.g., appendectomy for an inflamed appendix, or surgical change in sexual phenotype.
    iv. Curative surgical replacement—e.g., corneal transplant, or other forms of surgical reconstruction which are fairly permanent (i.e., in contrast to those organ transplantations and even artifical implants, such as mitral valves, which may not have a longevity equal to that of the patient). Also here, mammoplasties to increase the size of the breast through the use of synthetic implants.
    v. Reconditioning through biofeedback or behavioral modification, and so on—lowering blood pressure to normal by effecting life-style changes in a patient.
    vi. Establishing a normal function by nonsurgically remedying a defect: a possible future example would be by genetic engineering to provide genetic material to an individual unable to synthesize a needed enzyme or hormone.
    vii. Control of a disease entity or defect through replacement:
        a) Pharmacological—e.g., providing insulin for a diabetic, or estrogen replacement for a postmenopausal woman.
        b) Nonpermanent surgical replacement of a body part—e.g., organ transplantation which is not likely to be permanent, such as a heart transplant.
        c) Nonpermanent surgical replacement with an artificial part—e.g., the surgical implantation of an artificial mitral valve.

    viii. Control of the signs and symptoms of a disease state or defect: In such cases the disease entity or process remains, it is simply not allowed to express itself fully.

      a) Pharmacological—e.g., use of antihypertensive agents to control high blood pressure or phenothiazines to control schizophrenia.

      b) Surgical intervention without anatomical change—e.g., removal of a cancer at a primary site, although metastases have spread.

      c) Surgical intervention with consequent anatomical changes—e.g., resecting carcinoma of the large bowel while effecting a colostomy, although there are distant metastases and no prospect of a cure.

b. Symptomatic therapy. Symptomatic therapy as used here involves some fairly nuanced intervention for the purpose of eliminating or mitigating the complaints for which a patient comes for help. Symptomatic relief may be sought whether there is or is not an explanatory account available for the constellation of complaints which one addresses. Again, the interventions can be pharmacologic (e.g., aspirin for the flu, the use of Valium and other minor tranquilizers to control situational stress as a part of a recognized syndrome), surgery without structural change (e.g., sham operation to cure the pain of angina), surgery with consequent structural change (e.g., a hysterectomy performed on the insistence of a patient in response to lower abdominal pains and complaints whose etiology is not known but which is recognized by some empiric surgeon as a syndrome likely to be relieved by the placebo effect of the operation), and through behavioral modification and biofeedback (e.g., curing a phobia through behavioral modification, granting that psychoanalytic explanations hold regarding the underlying causes for phobias being more complex than behavioral theories or treatments recognize). One should note that one can talk of relieving noxious symptoms or states of affairs that are not disease states or considered to be undesirable as such (e.g., teething and normal childbirth); see A2 below.

c. Supportive therapy. Supportive therapy involves activities that are usually parts of social interchanges or of bodily or psychological care for oneself or others, which care is given to individuals who identify themselves as sick (such self-identification or identification by others can be then, but need not be, certified by the diagnosis of an underlying disease state. One would need only a meager account of the constellation of complaints that are presented to the physician as a recognizable syndrome. The vaguely worried-well, thus, are not included here, but individuals such as those described in William Cullen's *Nosology* as suffering from nostalgia simplex would be).[35] Examples of such supportive therapy include talking to patients with specific transient situational disturbances (an activity that consumes a significant amount of the time of primary-care physicians) and giving food and bed care in hospitals, help with eliminative functions, provision of activities that engage patients in occupations and tasks, minor physical exercise, and so forth. In short, a great many of the activities of physicians, nurses, occupational therapists, and physical therapists fall under this rubric as long as some pattern of complaints is recognized and some meager account of those complaints exists.

2. Remedying vague complaints and problems of unrecognized patterns

Mutatis mutandis what has been said about the therapy of syndromes can be said about the curative, palliative, or supportive treatment of complaints that do not form a recognizable disease or syndrome. Thus one can attempt to cure a fever of unknown origin or character, suppress the fever, or make the patient more comfortable. One can also simply "treat" patients who have vague complaints of feeling bad—giving Valium for the vaguely worried-well (though one might decide there are better, that is, more effective, forms of treatment) and a vitamin B-12 shot for the vaguely tired. The line between what lies under this rubric and that of disease entities is hazy and depends simply on how strict one wishes to be in establishing recognized nosological categories. The point of recognizing the line is to indicate that medicine can and should at times pass over the line in order to treat complaints even when they cannot be placed within canonical disease classifications or established syndromes.

**B. Enterprises in the prevention of the
need for therapy**

1. Pharmacological and immunological—e.g., quinine to prevent malaria, smallpox vaccination, and prescribing birth control pills.
2. Surgical—e.g., circumcision to prevent carcinoma of the penis or carcinoma of the cervix.
3. Behavioral—reconditioning individuals to adapt differently to stress in order to avoid tension-related diseases, e.g., hypertension.
4. Environmental—chlorinating water, draining swamps, improving nutrition and housing.

**C. Studies of the biological and/or
psychological bases of the occasions for
therapy**

Here is where one would place the "basic" biomedical sciences from human anatomy to human pathology. Note, such basic sciences are best interpreted as "auxiliary" sciences with respect to medicine. They help achieve the goal of medicine: treating complaints.

**D. Special nontherapeutic applications of
the clinical categories and knowledge**

Here one should place nontherapeutically oriented activities of diagnosis and prognosis, including everything from adventures in therapeutic nihilism to simply filling out insurance and job application forms with statements concerning the health and likely well-being of individuals. Here one probably has a sense of therapy in the broadest sense of "service."

**E. Studies of the efficacy of therapy—e.g.,
pharmacology and clinical studies of
treatment efficacy**

Under this rubric goes clinical research of all kinds.

These rather embracing classifications (i.e., A through E) of various medical enterprises is meant to indicate the heterogeneous nature of the issues gathered under medicine, and medicine's organizing goal—therapy. The classification is purposely provocative in listing abortion as a curative form of medical therapy. Such a way of talking presupposes that complaints of or concerning patients are sufficient grounds for giving therapy as long as those complaints are bona fide (i.e., based on circumstances of biological and/or psychological malfunction, pain, distress, disfigurement, or deformity, not under immediate conscious control). In such circumstances, the response to a complaint is medical (i.e., is predicated upon a regard for the complaints as rooted in a physiologically and/or psychologically-based state of affairs not immediately or directly under voluntary control).[37] The various things that medicine does are gathered under the aegis of medicine (rather than excluding some treatments of biological or psychologically based complaints as illegitimate, as Kass does) because medicine is, as it traditionally has been, complaint-oriented and directed.[38]

IV. In Defense of Dr. Feelgood

The thesis of this paper is that medicine exists to remedy or ameliorate the complaints that patients bring physicians. Such complaints can be distinguished from complaints concerning ignorance or political repression in that they turn on distress about not-directly voluntary malfunction, pain, physical deformity, and ugliness. The point of departure, as the foregoing classification suggests, is patient distress. The preceding discussion is meant to remind the reader of a point that tends to be obscured by the current scientific language and pretensions of medicine—medicine, health care, therapy, and treatment are complaint-oriented and only secondarily to be understood in terms of disease entities and canonical nosologies. This is the case because we come to identify states of affairs as disease states only because we are first confronted with apparently biological and/or psychologically based complaints. We then seek the biological and/or psychological substrates of these complaints in order to give an account of the natural history of the illness at hand, in order to name and distinguish these (if possible patients want names for their afflictions—even the term idiopathic seems soothing), and in order to give treatment. Medicine is not concerned with treating complaints because they are based in disease constructs; rather, medicine erects disease constructs and directs therapy at the underlying causes of illness, because of the complaints that patients have. That is, pathology is distinguished from physiology because some states are found to be accompanied by suffering, pathos. Therefore, whether structures or behaviors are rare or functionless is, as such, irrelevant to medicine. Disease constructs in pathology are irremediably value-freighted, and this freight comes from complaints.[39]

In summary, Leon Kass's intention to remove from medicine acts of "indulgence or gratifications . . . that aim at pleasure or convenience, or at the satisfaction of some other desire . . . but not at health"[40] because they are nonmedical is doomed to failure, for the end of medicine is the relief of various genre of complaints. It must fail not simply because it goes against the historical mission of medicine, but because it fails to recognize the dependence of disease constructs upon illness language, a language of complaints. Moreover, this language of complaints is heterogeneous—there is not a single genre of complaints the relief of which would serve as an end of medicine (Kass, though he speaks of health as the end of medicine, begins by acknowledging that medicine's goals may be multiple.)[41] What strikes home against Kass's position is that neither he, nor any other, has forwarded a single, coherent view of the meaning of health. On the one hand he suggests that: "Health is a natural standard or norm—not a moral norm, not a *value* as opposed to a 'fact,' not an obligation, but a state of being that reveals itself in activity as a standard of bodily excellence or fitness, relative to each species and to some extent to individuals, recognizable if not definable, and to some extent attainable."[41] On the other hand, he hopes: "to make at least plausible the claim that somatic health is a finite and an intelligible norm, which is the true goal of medicine . . ."[43] The reason that health as such is not definable is (if my account of medicine holds) because there are at best healths (to take a phrase from Chester Burns), not health.[44] There are several excellences that concern medicine—the excellence of physical and psychological functions, of freedom from pain, proper physical form. These, however, remain stubbornly best understood by reference to their absences—dysfunction, pain, and deformity. A general sense of health is not forthcoming. Nor will Kass's second and restrictive definition do unless it is meant stipulatively and to be revisionary. Kass is not offering a reconstruction of the meaning of medicine as the institutionalized service that it is. Kass rather wishes to dissuade physicians from a number of acts, not because they are frivolous or immoral (though I suspect he would wish to do so on such grounds as well), but because they fall outside of what he takes to be the pursuit of health and the proper scope of medicine (e.g., removing a normal breast to improve a golf swing or amniocentesis and abortion to prevent the birth of children of an unwanted sex.)[45] Yet an account of health as a single, simple norm which would allow such exclusions as nonmedical is not forthcoming. And if it were, it would have little to do with medicine as it exists—it could have little relationship to the divergent complaints that structure medicine. As a result medical ethical questions remain clearly ethical questions—*improper uses of medicine must be identified on ethical grounds, not through a definition of what is or is not part of the notion of medicine.*

Medicine exists as Kass's Dr. Feelgood practices it—not only treating pneumonia and resecting cancer, but "performing artificial insemination or arranging adoptions, performing vasectomies and abortions for non-medical reasons (i.e., for family planning)."[46] Dr. Feelgood should be restrained from activities such as: "dispensing antibiotics or other medicines simply because the patient wants to take something,"[47] because such care is not a sensible way of treating such complaints—less noxious placebos are available. But in either case the action is medical; *there are, however, differences between good and bad medicine based on proper or improper uses of resources,* and so on. Further, the physician is not made a technician because he or she provides sterilizations on request or gives placebos, any more than the physician is made a technician when he or she treats a patient who says, "I think I'm having a heart attack, will you treat me?" The art of medicine is the art of practicing a skill in a way that effectively treats the complaints of patients. After all, the patient may not need a sterilization (may be shown already to be sterile,

or may wish another form of birth control once sufficient information is forthcoming). Self-diagnosis of a problem does not turn
the physician into a mere technician. Medicine exists as an art of
giving the counsels of finitude, of showing how to achieve as
best one can the various goods that therapy offers (in circumstances under which they can only be achieved imperfectly):
function, freedom from pain, proper human form. Medicine is
not undermined if the patient knows what he or she wants. The
skill of medicine is often displayed in showing the way to goals
patients already have, if only vaguely, understood (a physician
may, however, wish not to pursue some goals out of moral,
financial, or aesthetic reasons; that is, of course, another matter).
Such roles for physicians should cause consternation only if (1)
one thought all well-being or happiness to be of one kind; (2) one
held medicine to be a value-free art and science, or (3) one
wished to avoid some moral decisions in medicine by rendering
them ontological decisions (i.e., by terming some procedures not
truly medical endeavors).

V. Some Conclusions

Medicine as a complex social undertaking has not only roots in
"value-free" science but roots in evaluations as well. Medicine
does not exist simply to describe and explain the world and to
give predictions that can test the explanations—if so, it would be
more easily reducible to such biomedical sciences as physiology
and biochemistry. Because medicine comes into existence
through addressing complaints, it pursues the diminishing of biologically and/or psychologically based distress, pain, and deformity. Because it pursues these goals medicine also plays social
roles in achieving goods external to those of medicine. For
example, medicine sets limits to justified blame and praise by
showing which actions are due to pathological processes, not to
free choice (e.g., "When he said that, he was hypoglycemic—he
is a diabetic"). Medicine also helps toward the achievement of
political and educational goals (e.g., "If we can eliminate the
ascariasis and hookworms in many rural counties of the South,
then the children will not be as anemic, will learn better in the

schools, and will ultimately be better citizens."). This expansive view of medicine is, I believe, implicit in many essays in the earlier volumes in this series. I think here in particular of essays by Marx Wartofsky (e.g., "The Theory of Medicine is for the sake of this practice, and the practice is for the sake of the human weal"),[48] by Lester King,[49] by Eric Cassell,[50] and Marc Lappé.[51] The so-called art and science of medicine is to be understood in terms of the various values that direct its practices, and that give it a place as one social institution among others. It shows itself to be a science and a technology founded on an implicit axiology of human complaints (i.e., on what the disvalues of different dysfunctions, deformities, and so on are). An understanding of the foundations of ethics and how they bear upon the sciences cannot be complete without a recognition of how this axiology grounds the sciences and arts of medicine, and preserves the legitimacy of medical ethical issues as ethical issues.

NOTES

*Numerous individuals have contributed important criticisms concerning prior drafts of this paper, for which I am grateful. These individuals include Tom Beauchamp, Daniel Callahan, Eric Cassell, James Childress, Alasdair MacIntyre, LeRoy Walters, and Marx Wartofsky. Although they have contributed to this paper, they are in no sense responsible for its shortcomings.

1. Marx W. Wartofsky, "The Mind's Eye and the Hand's Brain: Toward an Historical Epistemology of Medicine," in *Science, Ethics and Medicine*, ed. H. Tristram Engelhardt, Jr. and Daniel Callahan (Hastings-on-Hudson, N.Y.: Hastings Center, 1976), p. 167.

2. Ibid., p. 168.

3. Ibid., p. 177.

4. Samuel Gorovitz and Alasdair MacIntyre, "Toward a Theory of Medical Fallibility," in *Science, Ethics and Medicine*, p. 261.

5. Eric Cassell, "Commentary: Moral Questions in a Clinical Setting," in *Science, Ethics and Medicine*, pp. 147–60.

6. Eric Cassell, "Error in Medicine," in *Knowledge, Value and Belief*, ed. H. Tristram Engelhardt, Jr. and Daniel Callahan (Hastings-on-Hudson, N.Y.: Hastings Center, 1977), pp. 295–309.

246   H. TRISTRAM ENGELHARDT, JR.

7. Joseph Margolis, "Reconciling Freud's *Scientific Project* and Psychoanalysis," in *Morals, Science and Sociality*, ed. H. Tristram Engelhardt, Jr. and Daniel Callahan (Hastings-on-Hudson, N.Y.: Hastings Center, 1978), pp. 93–118), "The Concept of Disease," *The Journal of Medicine and Philosophy* 1 (1976), 238–55.

8. H. Tristram Engelhardt, Jr., "Ideology and Etiology," *The Journal of Medicine and Philosophy* 1 (1976), 256–68.

9. Thomas Sydenham, *Observationes Medicae circa Morborum Acutorum Historiam et Curationem* (London: G. Kettilby, 1676). Francois B. de Sauvages, *Nosologia Methodica Sistems Morborum Classes Juxta Sydenhami mentem et Botanicorum ordinem* (Amsterdam: Fratres de Tournes, 1768). William Cullen, *Synopsis Nosologiae Methodicae* (Edinburgh, 1769).

10. Sauvages, ibid., p. 94.

11. A witch doctor using penicillin to treat pneumonia because he believes it to be an act of reverence to the god Squibb is not acting medically. Thus, a Catholic priest may intend to cure a patient by administering Extreme Unction, but that does not make it a medical act except metaphorically, unless the priest is seeking not the grace of God but a placebo effect. Of course, he may be seeking both. The same event can thus be a religious act, a medical act, an educational act, a political act, etc.

12. Some of the consequences of the argument of this paper are that: 1) ethical disputes concerning what is proper medicine cannot be resolved through definitions of what medicine is (i.e., what is proper to the essence of medicine); 2) these are value judgments intrinsic to medicine—to be called deviant, dysfunctional, or deformed involves a form of evaluation, it is always better to be healthy; 3) how patients in a culture view what should count as normal or proper functions, proper absence of pain, and requisite human form direct medicine's labeling of individuals as physiologically or psychologically deviant or healthy (i.e., patient complaints direct medicine); 4) it is possible to say that Nazi physicians engaged in *immoral* experiments were doing *actual* research medicine, which might have had potential *benefits* (i.e., could have proved useful for the alleviation of medical complaints). The world of values and its relationship to the world of medicine is thus complex.

13. Wartofsky, "The Mind's Eye . . . ," p. 188.

14. It is important to note that "therapy" as it is currently used includes not only curing or caring when an individual has a bona fide disease, but also providing care for dysfunctions and pains that we may not take to be based in a disease, e.g., the pain of teething or the pain of menstruation. One can simply treat pain: there can be therapy for menstrual cramps even if it is not associated with a disease.

15. Leon R. Kass, "Regarding the End of Medicine and the Pursuit of Health," *The Public Interest* 40 (1975): p. 11.

16. I have selected Leon Kass's article in that it represents a particularly well developed and articulate presentation of the position he embraces. Though I appear critical of his essay in this article, I must acknowledge my debt to him for his excellent development of one established view of medicine. He has brought the issues into a very helpful focus.

17. Ibid., p. 12.

18. Ibid., p. 15.

19. Rudolf Virchow, "Scientific Method and Therapeutic Stand Points," in *Disease, Life and Man: Selected Essays by Rudolf Virchow*, trans. L. J. Rather (Stanford: Stanford University Press, 1971), p. 66.

20. Joseph Owens, "Aristotelian Ethics, Medicine, and the Changing Nature of Man," in *Philosophical Medical Ethics: Its Nature and Significance*, ed. S. F. Spicker and H. T. Engelhardt, Jr. (Dordrecht: Reidel, 1977), pp. 127–42.

21. Thomas Trotter, *An Essay, Medical, Philosophical, and Chemical, on Drunkenness and Its Effects on the Human Body* (London: Longman, Rees and Orme, 1804).

22. Ivan Illich, *Medical Nemesis: The Expropriation of Health* (New York: Pantheon Books, 1976).

23. Leon Kass, "Regarding the End of Medicine . . . ."

24. "Constitution of the World Health Organization" (Preamble), in *The First Ten Years of the World Health Organization* (Geneva: World Health Organization, 1958), p. 459.

25. Leon Kass, "Regarding the End of Medicine . . . ," p. 12.

26. See notes 7 and 8, as well as Marx W. Wartofsky, "Organs, Organisms and Disease," in *Evaluation and Explanation in the Biomedical Sciences*, ed. H. T. Engelhardt, Jr. and S. F. Spicker (Dordrecht, Holland: D. Reidel, 1975), p. 67–83.

27. H. T. Engelhardt, Jr., "The Concept of Health and Disease," in *Evaluation and Explanation in the Biomedical Sciences*, pp. 125–41.

28. See, for example, Georg Henrik von Wright, *The Varieties of Goodness* (New York: The Humanities Press, 1963), pp. 9, 50–71; and Christopher Boorse, "On the Distinctions Between Disease and Illness," *Philosophy and Public Affairs* 5 (1975): 49–68. The view that one could define the world of the clinician and the patient's world of complaints by reference to underlying functions and dysfunctions or value-free disease states is in great measure a contribution of the pathoanatomical and pathophysiological revolution initiated in medicine by individuals such as Giovanni Morgagni (1682–1771), Xavier Bichat (1771–1802), and Francois Broussais (1772–1838). One might think of the classic

248   H. TRISTRAM ENGELHARDT, JR.

remark by Broussais that "true medical observation is that of the organs and their modifiers . . ." (F. J. V. Broussais, *On Irritation and Insanity*, trans. Thomas Cooper (Columbia, S.C.: S. J. McMorris, 1831), p. ix). In this regard it is interesting to note that Michel Foucault, in his recent book *The Birth of the Clinic* (New York: Pantheon Books, 1973), has in fact, despite the title, described the maiming if not the death of the clinic. That is, he has described how the world of the clinician and of patients' complaints became secondary in importance to the world of the pathoanatomist and pathophysiologist.

29. Richard H. Port, "Population Differences in Red and Green Color Vision Deficiency: A Review, and a Query on Selection Revelation," *Eugenic Quarterly* 9 (1962): 131–46.

30. F. B. Livingstone, "The Distributions of the Abnormal Hemoglobin Genes and Their Significance for Human Evolution," *Evolution*, 18 (1964): 685, and Paul Heller, M. D. "Once More: The Pathogenic Effects of the Sickle Cell Trait," *Journal of the American Medical Association* 225 (1973): 987–88.

31. "Procedures for the Elimination of the Menopause," *Western Journal of Surgery, Obstetrics and Gynecology* 71 (1963): 110–21.

32. H. T. Engelhardt, Jr., "The Disease of Masturbation: Values and the Concept of Disease," *Bulletin of the History of Medicine*, 48 (1974): 234–48.

33. H. T. Engelhardt, Jr., "Is There a Philosophy of Medicine?" *PSA 1976*, vol. II, Symposium, ed. F. Suppe and P. D. Asquith, pp. 94–108.

34. One should note the therapeutic injunction implicit as the bias of all illness and disease language. That is, to recognize that one is ill or diseased implies that one ought, *ceteris paribus*, do something about it. Admitting to being ill or diseased usually invites one to explain if one does not seek treatment. Compare, for example, the following sentences:

I feel ill but don't care.
I'm glad I feel ill.
I feel ill but do not wish to seek treatment.
I wish I felt ill.
I have a disease but don't care.
I'm glad I have a disease.
I have a serious curable disease, but do not wish to seek treatment.
I wish I had a serious disease.
I wish I had a disease so that I could avoid the draft.
I wish I were disabled and could draw the full disability payment
  stipulated in the company's insurance policy.

Only the last two sentences do not invite futher explanations in order not to seem senseless.

35. H. T. Engelhardt, Jr., "Human Well-Being and Medicine: Some Basic Value-Judgments in the Biomedical Sciences," *Science, Ethics and Medicine*, pp. 120–39.

36. William Cullen, *Nosologia Methodica* (Edinburgh: Carfrae, 1820), p. 152.

37. Complaints, then, are sufficient conditions for being medical therapy only if they also meet certain necessary conditions for being medical complaints. Such complaints may still be immoral or ill-advised.

38. Darrell Amundsen, "The Physician's Obligation to Prolong Life—A Medical Duty without Classical Roots," *The Hastings Report* 8 (1978): 23–30.

39. One must note that not all complaints count as medical complaints. Medicine appears to be distinguished as an institution focused on involuntary biologically or psychologically based complaints. It is also true that not all complaints are forwarded by the patient himself. Individuals often forward complaints on behalf of another, that he or she is dysfunctional (e.g., is a paranoid schizophrenic). Furthermore, there is no single conceptual unity to the kinds of complaints forwarded by patients—as indicated, they include complaints regarding dysfunctions, pain, and deformity. And, moreover, the senses of dysfunctions and deformity are context-bound.

40. Leon Kass, "Regarding the End of Medicine . . . ," p. 14.

41. Ibid., p. 12.

42. Ibid., pp. 28–29 (my emphasis).

43. Ibid., p. 29.

44. Chester R. Burns, "Diseases Versus Healths: Some Legacies in the Philosophies of Modern Medical Science," in *Evaluation and Explanation in the Biomedical Sciences*, pp. 29–47.

45. Leon Kass, "Regarding the End of Medicine . . . ," p. 13.

46. Ibid., p. 13.

47. Ibid., p. 13–14.

48. Marx W. Wartofsky, "The Mind's Eye . . . ."

49. Lester S. King, "Values in Medicine," *Science, Ethics and Medicine,* p. 225.

50. Eric J. Cassell, "Error in Medicine," *Knowledge, Value and Belief,* p. 295.

51. Marc Lappé, "The Non-neutrality of Hypothesis Formulation," *Science, Ethics and Medicine,* p. 96.

Commentary

Response to H. Tristram Engelhardt, Jr.

Eric Cassell

EARLY IN HIS EXCELLENT DISCUSSION, Engelhardt establishes firmly (and finally, I hope) that medicine in its practice and its beliefs is inevitably value-laden. How anyone could have thought otherwise is a matter for wonder. But certainly, during my training, I believed in medicine's value-free nature. That is because, like most physicians, I identified medicine with its tools (primarily its science) rather than with its ends. And that is the second point that Engelhardt establishes early on. The end of medicine—what it really does, arises from patients' complaints. These two fundamental understandings, truly accepted in all their ramifications, could provide the basis for profound change in the practice of medicine.

To understand Engelhardt's project we must put it in perspective. The paper comes after several decades in which medicine has been turning away from a description of its functions based solely on definitions of disease. It is turning away not only in practice (and practice has always been wider in scope than definition and theory) but turning away, also, in theory. As witness to this is the increasing crescendo of recent essays and writings dedicated to making distinctions between illness and disease, coming up with new definitions of disease, and all expressing a dissatisfaction with seeing the world of the sick in classic structural disease terms. Another perspective from which to see this

250

essay is that of medicine turning away from a definition of its functions in purely physical terms. For example, my own writings on medicine as a moral profession have been more widely and easily accepted than I would have thought possible at the time of their writing. A more influential example is George Engel's paper on biopsychosocial medicine which appeared a year or so ago in *Science*. And, of course, when something appears in *Science* we know that it has been accepted as conventional wisdom. Only a decade ago, aspects of the environment, the social factors, or indeed the unconscious of the patient while perhaps interesting were often not considered things that had to be taken into account in the actual care of the patient. Now there is a dawning realization that these things are as central to the patient in terms of being sick as are, perhaps, the patient's liver or legs. So that the phrase "treat the patient as a person" has moved from meaning "treat the patient as one would if the patient were a person" to the more current and (I hope) growing belief that it is the person, not the person's disease, that is the central concern of medicine. That, I think, is the important light in which Engelhardt's essay must be seen.

But there is more. Engelhardt also knows better than most that when he casts aside strictly structural disease concerns and concentrates attention on the patient's complaints, he is not turning away from a tradition stretching into antiquity, but is turning away from a tradition that is only a few hundred years old. And in the form that we know it today, a tradition that is only about a hundred and fifty years old. That was the time at which disease categories were developed in the way we use them now and in a way that made them an effective basis for action. And I think action is the key word because medicine is a profession of action—doctors do things for their patients. Before the present disease era, before the last one hundred and fifty years, and certainly before Sydenham, doctors treated the patient's complaints. When the patient was short of breath, for example, the doctor dealt with that symptom as though difficulty in breathing was what was wrong with the patient. And, from the patient's point of view, that *was* what was wrong—he or she could not breathe. In modern times we tend to say that what is wrong with patients who manifest shortness of breath is either congestive heart failure, pulmonary emboli, emphysema, asthma, or a host of other diseases whose symptoms include difficulty in breathing. We speak in these terms because the disease categories laid down in the late nineteenth century provided a useful basis for the systematic and scientific inquiry into disease. Unfortunately, in the era when doctors did treat complaints (such as shortness of breath) as distinct entities, medicine was in chaos. "Shortness of breath," "swelling of the ankles," and fever are common to such a vast array of diseases (that may have little else in common) that, as categories, they do not provide an effective basis for action.

I don't believe that Engelhardt wants us to go back to the chaos. He is pointing the way to an appropriate goal for medicine: the care of the patient's complaints. And he is making it clear that the vexations of the patient which deserve the doctor's concern can arise from sources as diverse as the liver or the landscape, interpersonal relationships or environmental toxins, the sins of the patient or the sins of the fathers. Further, and I could not agree more, he argues that "the world of the pathoanatomist, the pathophysiologist, and the pathopsychologist is always dependent on the clinician for its sense and direction. And further, the world of the clinician is defined by people—by their opinions and vexations."

While I agree with the direction that Engelhardt is going, something vitally important is lacking. A new way of seeing the goals of medicine has to be complemented by a new way of categorizing them. Medicine is not only practiced, it is also taught, researched, communicated, and so forth. All these activities require a language and a system of organization. We know where we don't want medicine to be anymore; many of us have ideas about where we want it to go. But we are short on ideas about how to conceptualize it, how to teach it, and how to do it. That, I think, is where Engelhardt and other philosophers of medicine have to lead us. If medicine is a profession of action, then a philosophy of medicine should be something on which the actions of physicians can be based. The previous philosophical basis for medicine which rested on understandings of disease concepts directed action only insofar as it directed physicians toward the treatment of causes—defined in the narrowest sense.

Engelhardt clearly shows how medicine's theories have moved away from those goals. Doctors, at the present time, do not very frequently treat cause, even at their most effective. With the exception of antimicrobials, most modern advances in treatment, from antidepressants to treatments for gout, are directed at abnormal or even normal physiological processes that are associated with the disease state but are neither its cause nor unique to it. With the broadening of definitions and goals, there should follow also a broadening of our understanding of medical intervention.

I believe that a theory of medical action, however, means something more than that, even though, at this time, I am not prepared to articulate what that might be. My compaint that Engelhardt must go further is, therefore, somewhat unfair. I complain only because it is time for us to move on. It has now been adequately shown that classic disease definitions, etiologic or otherwise, will no longer serve as a sufficient basis for medicine's activities, diagnostic or therapeutic, and it has been shown, past all need ever to demonstrate the point again, that the scope of medicine is wider than the scope of the affliction of a particular organ. What is needed now is some idea of how to get to the future that is more specific than a moral imperative.

I would like to turn to another point. The word "health" occurs many times in Engelhardt's discussion. He uses Leon Kass as a foil against which to promote his own sense of medicine's aims. For Kass, briefly stated, the goal of medicine is the health of the patient. Health, Kass suggests, is "a natural standard or norm—not a moral norm, not a value as opposed to a 'fact,' not an obligation but a state of being which reveals itself in activity as a standard of bodily excellence or fitness. . . ." Engelhardt sees no possibility of defining health, at least not in Kass's Puritan terms. He says, "The reason that health as such is not definable is . . . because there are, at best, healths . . . not health." And goes on to say that "a general sense is not forthcoming." Putting an end to attempts to define health would probably end a major growth industry in the United States, but it is high time that the industry ceased.

I take it that health cannot be defined since it is the value-term of medicine, just as beauty is the value-term in aesthetics, or justice is the value-term in law. As aestheticians of any sophistication do not attempt to define beauty (although they may tell us what they think is beautiful and by what standard they measure it), I suppose those involved in the law do not attempt to define justice—although they might say whether a specific act is just and give us their criteria for making such a statement. These words are more than merely descriptive terms although they have a core of descriptive meaning. As value-terms, a part of their meaning remains undefinable. They are values toward which we aspire or aim. They stand for concepts that are inherently open-ended.

In the same sense, then, the word "health" cannot be defined. For the same reason, *it is a tautology to say that the aim of medicine is health*. I suppose some support for that statement is required. Health is certainly not a fact, in the sense that it is not a datum of experience, something that can be observed. "Health" itself is not an observed or observable fact. The health of a part of the body is not one of the inherent facts of the part—although it depends on the facts (or predicates) of that part. For example, the facts of an arm are the presences of its parts—the muscles, bones, enzymes, and so forth, and their functioning. These are all observable (although a fair amount of technology may be required to observe them). The health of this arm is, however, not observable. To the degree that the arm fulfills the promise of an arm—"duly and efficiently fulfills its function"—as the Oxford English Dictionary says, it is a healthy arm. One might ask whether a baseball pitcher's arm is a healthier arm than a non-baseball pitcher's arm because it can throw farther. To emphasize what Engelhardt said about there being more than one health, the answer is no. The object now being described is not just an arm, but a baseball pitcher's arm. It is healthy if it duly and efficiently fulfills the function of a baseball pitcher's arm. The point is, however, that health is not one of the parts of the arm. The healthy arm has a healthy muscle, but health is not one of the parts of the muscle. The healthy muscle has healthy arteries, but health is not . . . and so on. There is, of course, one teaser about the value-term called health. Even when we talk about the health of a part, we know it to be inseparable from the whole. In other words, the severed arm, although intact from shoulder to fingertips and possessing all the structures of the arm, would never be called healthy. Beautiful, perhaps, but not healthy. That is because health always involves, as the dictionary says, function. It follows from what I have just said that we call someone, or even somebody's body part, healthy *to the degree that* it possesses all the parts, properties, or functions that it requires. Why, then, do we get so muddled when we discuss what we mean by healthy? In the first place, we get muddled by the attempts to define health (as nature abhors a vacuum, medicine—all science—abhors the undefined term). But, as I noted above, although health has a core meaning which can be described, it is in part inherently undefinable. *It is an open-ended concept.*

The reasons why health, as an open-ended concept, defies definition point the way to a deepened appreciation of what "healthy" means and thus, inevitably, to an enhanced medicine.

As the word health is applied, depending on the state of the person's function, what interferes with our knowing about function interferes with our conception of healthy. I do not mean this in the routine way in which doctors say, "we need further research to understand how this (or that) works," meaning that more facts about function are required. Rather, I mean that there are certain basic issues that require solution. Those are problems relating to the complexity of the body, to uncertainty about the facts in general or in particular, and to the nature of subjective information.

Complexity

We are not very good at systematically describing the complexity that is a whole person in operation—or even a whole arm (to say nothing of the brain). We do not have a good language or a good mathematics for simultaneous events in the body occurring over time—which is what function is. To that extent, understanding of health remains stunted. In the same manner contemporary understandings of beauty would be stunted, if artists were still unable to depict dimensionality. Just as artists' work lagged behind human visual capacity before they learned how to show perspective, here also medicine's (science's) systematic ability to describe and understand complex function lags behind native human capacity—which is why common sense and experience often tell us things about life that systematic medicine cannot. And why some scientific conclusions about life as lived seem silly. They are silly next to the richness that common sense appreciates. This is not to make fun of science but to indicate that if "common sense" can do something, then perhaps we can look forward to the development of systematic methods to better approximate that talent.

To solve the problems presented by our inability to systematically understand the function of complex process, indices are constructed that come to stand for the complex functions. These vary from pulmonary function tests to standard tables of height and weight to the pulse rate. All these measures have finite characteristics that define normal and degrees of normal. Indeed, their advantage comes from the limited number of their properties. Thus, applying the term "healthy" or "unhealthy" to their results can be done with considerable certainty and lack of ambiguity because the facts these measures generate are limited in number. In the way they are used, "normal" is generally equated with "health," and "less than normal" is "less than healthy." But these indices are not measures of health. They are measures of—that is, their facts tell us about—function. Since we tend to use the term "health" in relation to function, we tend to use the word "healthy" to apply to their results—thus starting in our own minds a confusion between health as one of the facts and health as a property term. When this last source of facts is used to evaluate the health of the body or its parts they tend to be entered in the following manner: "the patient has a healthy pulse." We speak as though "a healthy pulse" was one of the *facts* to be considered, or one of the facts about the body was that it had "a healthy pulse." But the adjective "healthy" is not part of the facts; it is, instead, a shortcut that is used instead of describing the pulse in detail. Small wonder that the word "health" is often used as though it named a purely factual state of affairs.

Uncertainty

To understand the function of complex things, such as persons or hands, facts are necessary. The number of facts to be known about the functioning hand-in-operation is very large and about the whole body-in-operation, almost infinite and about the whole functioning person, incomprehensible. And yet, knowledge of function (and how to restore function) depends on the facts. When so many facts are present uncertainty is sure to be an issue—for at least two reasons. In any particular instance, are all the facts known that are necessary to understanding? And how accurate is each individual fact? Technology can, and has, increased both the availability and accuracy of the facts but it is obvious that uncertainty will always exist. Further, since the function of a person is always relative to other things—to the environment, to the culture, and so forth—what is considered optimal function is in itself changeable, thus adding further uncertainty. Where uncertainty is present, probability is introduced. Indeed, one of the hallmarks of the profession of medicine is its probabilistic nature. Thus, to understand the function of complex processes—to enhance the conception of health (or at least to act on that conception)—matters of probability must be dealt with. Such probabilistic processes—stochastic processes—are notoriously difficult to handle statistically if they approach any real complexity. Once again, "common sense," or the trained and experienced judgment, seems to be able, sometimes, to deal with such phenomena better than available systematic methods, which suggests that better ways might be developed. That there are limits to "common sense" knowledge of probability is seen in the failure of intuition to deal with small number probabilities with any accuracy. One might expect a native human talent for dealing with uncertainty, since humans, in common with all animals, must act. To act implies choice and choice implies uncertainty. Uncertainty is a cardinal fact of life. For an enlarged and enriched conception of health, uncertainty, like complexity, must be challenged.

The Subjective

Many of the aspects involved in "duly and efficiently fulfills its function" are subjective, which adds to both complexity and uncertainty. Because much of the information needed to appreciate health is subjective increases not only the difficulty of fact gathering, but also makes the process of valuing more difficult. This is because subjectivity exists not only in the patient (the person under observation) but also in the observer. When the observer collects all available facts, then assigns weights to their importance, then makes allowances for uncertainty, he or she is involved in the subjective valuing process about which we know so little. (In part we know so little because we will not meet the subjective valuing process on its own terms, but rather continually try to convert it [measure it] into the objective numerical valuing system that science has created and refined. That simply will not work.) However, the patient's subjective information is frequently dealt with as though everything subjective is contaminated by the valuing process. It seems quite possible to make a distinction between the subjective fact *describing* process and the *valuing* process. Describing what I see or feel—what hurts, when and how—is quite possible apart from what I think or feel about it. Certainly, until the distinction is made and carried out in everyday medical actions, a further source of enrichment of the concept of health will be denied to us.

Conclusion

For the reasons described above, Engelhardt is absolutely correct to discard attempts to define health. He would be equally wrong if he believes that a medicine can be constructed apart from some understanding of (knowing when we are in the presence of) health. That would be similar to a system of laws apart from an understanding of justice, or aesthetics from an understanding of beauty. To repeat: It is a tautology to speak of the aim of medicine as being health. What is wanted is an ever-widening conception of the healthy; an enlargement of our understanding of the well-functioning person. In some ways, that enlarged understanding of function exists already in the minds of patients when they complain to physicians. Their complaints tell us what they think their function ought to be, but is not. What kind of a medicine would we have if it did not devote itself to the support and enlargement of what people believe to be the duly and efficient functioning of themselves as persons?

A widened conception of healthy will require the ability to understand complex function—the function of wholes; better ways of dealing with uncertainty and the probabilistic nature of medicine; and finally, an ability to deal with the subjective in both doctor and patient. These represent a tall order. Engelhardt's essay provides cogent reasons to close the curtain on yesterday's medicine, but it offers no promise that the curtain will not rise anew on a stage of chaos. What is wanted from the philosophers are some solutions to the problems I have described. Karl Jaspers said that what philosophy had to offer medicine was methodology. The need is here.

The Foundations of
Ethics and the
Foundations of Science

Tom L. Beauchamp

I

BECAUSE OUR TOPIC is the foundations of ethics, I begin with a discussion of relevant senses of the term "ethics," a task that merits attention because of the confusing number of different uses found in the various papers in this volume and in previous volumes in this series. When I discuss "senses" of ethics, I do not mean to explore what morality is as distinct from law, etiquette, custom, public policy, and religion. Rather, I mean the possible referents of the term—the different fields of ethics or different ways of inquiring into ethics.

Even at this stage of modern ethics, the distinction between normative and nonnormative fields of ethical inquiry is important and serviceable. It is important because the relationship between the foundations of science and the foundations of ethics could be conceived either as exclusively normative or as exclusively nonnormative, and viewing the relationship in only one of these alternative ways would make a critical difference in one's strategy and argument in the analysis of that relationship. Toward the objective of analyzing this distinction, I would hold that there are at least two nonnormative fields of inquiry. First, there is the scientific study of morality, which is a factual investigation of moral behavior, as reflected in attitudes, codes, beliefs, and so on. Second, there is a discipline still worth distinguishing as metaethics. Metaethicists may often intrude normative biases and presuppositions, but the objective of their work is the nonevaluative analysis of crucial ethical terms, of the logic of moral reasoning, of the nature of justification, and so on. I would also hold that there are two distinguishable fields of normative ethics, though they are less easily distinguished and no doubt overlap. General normative ethics is the attempt to formulate and defend a system of fundamental ethical principles valid for everyone, while applied normative ethics is the attempt to explicate and defend positions on critical moral problems by appeal to such principles of general normative ethics as justice, beneficence, and utility. If there is an exclusively *normative* connection between science and ethics, then these disciplines are related in an action-guiding manner. If the connection is nonnormative only, then science and philosophy merely study the foundations of ethics without any intent to guide action.

II

Let us now ask what task the authors of the papers in this volume envisioned for themselves. The endeavor as they saw it has surprisingly little to do with normative ethics in relationship to the sciences and surprisingly much to do with nonnormative ethics. If constructive normative ethics at its foundations were under discussion, the symposiasts would either be arguing (1) that normative ethics affects the sciences in important respects, or (2) that the sciences do (or at least can) affect the foundations of normative ethics in important ways. I find none of the latter sort of discussion in these papers, or in contemporary ethics for that matter—though I believe this topic to be vital. I also find much less of the former than one might have expected from the designated topic.

However, that there are important *interactions* of various sorts between human values and science seems to me amply argued, and for the most part well, in the papers in this volume. Toulmin and Engelhardt, for example, provide compelling reasons for viewing the foundations of at least some sciences as value-laden. But the very term "value," as used by both Engelhardt and Toulmin, hides an intriguing question of axiology: What do the values they mention have to do with ethics, let alone with the foundations of ethics? When Engelhardt speaks of the "relationship between medicine and values" and the "action-oriented nature of medicine," he correctly represents the theme of his paper. But what has this theme to do with the foundations of *ethics*? The values he discusses fall in the class of *nonmoral* values— i.e., values that are general goals of human striving and not specifically ethical in the way, for example, doing justice or fulfilling a moral obligation are ethical goals and distinctly moral values. Moreover, many values discussed in these papers are not even what Rawls has referred to as primary goods—those goods such as rights and wealth that all rational persons want, whatever else they may want. We might wonder, then, in what sense the values that are mentioned rest at the *foundations* of either ethics or evaluation in general.

Toulmin, by contrast to Engelhardt, specifically discusses ethics and even the foundations of ethics—though not in those passages where he is discussing value-ladenness. In these passages, like Engelhardt, Toulmin speaks of the "value-free" and "value-laden" character of the "basic concepts of the sciences." He thus confuses me by talking subsequently, without augmented argument, about contacts with "moral philosophy." Again, I see a value connection, but not a specifically moral connection.

Presumably it can be replied to the objections I have offered either that they are trivially semantic or that when Engelhardt speaks of medicine as "hopelessly value-bound, centered as it is upon the phenomena of life, death, and human suffering" (quoting from Wartofsky), it is obvious that such values are moral. While I would grant that there are ethical problems that arise from medical practice and from research involving human and animal subjects, this premise does not provide grounds for the conclusion that medicine, biology, or any form of scientific research is evaluative in *methodology* any more than similar reasoning would show that journalism, cartography, or the training of airline pilots is evaluative because moral objectives and problems are present in these fields. Rather, such reasoning shows only that the treatment of human beings in medical practice and research, as everywhere else in the controlled search for knowledge, is subject to moral restraints and is motivated by attempts to realize general human goods.

III

To turn now to the nonnormative study of ethics, I find in the papers in this volume a surprisingly slanted focus of attention on nonnormative issues. This orientation is surprising, because such nonnormative analysis *studies* ethics without affecting, interpreting, or making a contribution to the *foundations* of normative ethics. At best, nonnormative studies reveal a relationship between the discoveries of science (or metaethics) and our understanding of moral behavior and language. We are perhaps not surprised to find this direction in Alexander's primarily scientific paper, where there is not only a discussion of the biological basis of ethics but also discussions of both ethics and science as "social enterprises." But it is surely surprising to find so much space devoted to this endeavor in the philosophical papers by Toulmin, Engelhardt, and MacIntyre. In much of what they write, they seem to function more as sociologists of morals than moral philosophers. Thus, Toulmin writes often about considerations, historical and sociological, of "the professional organization of scientific work"; Engelhardt discusses why medicine exists and how "we come to identify states of affairs as disease states" throughout his paper; and MacIntyre focuses on how moral philosophy is but a reflection of our cultural condition.

I do not intend to fall prey to MacIntyre's condemnation of artificial "intellectual boundaries" in the professions. But I do wish to emphasize that there is little in the way of a discussion of the causal or rational relationships between the foundations of ethics and the sciences. That is, there is little discussion of the single most difficult and unresolved issue: If science is inquiry into general causal laws and explanation, and ethics is inquiry into noncausal justification and general action-guiding reasons, how can there be an interconnection *at their foundations*?

I am not denying that there is considerable positive discussion in these papers of what Loren Graham characterizes as "the interaction of science and ethics." Toulmin convincingly argues (though not for the first time) that "the professional organization of scientific work can no longer be concerned *solely* with considerations of intellectual merit—as contrasted with ethical acceptability. . . . " This thesis argues at most that various actions performed by scientists—particularly those directly involving human subjects—are subject to ethical judgment. Institutional review boards charged to scrutinize research protocols notoriously are ethics committees. Their work is no more scientific or medical, however, than is the work of the Senate Ethics Committee senatorial. Indeed, Toulmin's claim that professionals must be concerned with more than the intellectual merit of their work is true of all actions performed by persons in all roles whatsoever, insofar as those actions might impinge harmfully on others. Thus, Toulmin's is hardly a distinctive or compelling thesis—no more informative or challenging than maintaining that corporations have moral responsibilities to their employees, and encounter increased moral responsibilities when working conditions negatively affect the health and welfare of workers. This is not an informative or controversial claim about the relationship between the foundations of business and the foundations of ethics—even if it has been doubted or ignored in some historical periods that corporations have such moral responsibilities to their employees.

IV

The distinction between explanation and justification might also be employed to advance the arguments I have offered. The papers in this volume are infrequently concerned with justification in ethics (or with how science might aid in the justification of moral arguments), because they are almost wholly concerned with various forms of explanation (scientific, metaethical, and so on). Gustafson's theological effort is a prime instance. His entire account of foundational principles is descriptive—a causal explanation or perhaps an elucidation of a tradition. Despite his discerning analysis of the assumptions shared by theologians, his paper is not an attempt to show either how theology can help justify moral claims or how science plays a role in contributing to ethics and theology. Gustafson does hold out the prospect that knowledge of a divine purpose would affect ethics by providing a theological foundation and that religious symbolism can create a moral way of life (as in his useful Exodus example). However, he offers no argument for this prospect and tends to undermine it through his discussions of the relativity of theological knowledge, of faith as radically different from science, and of the ways in which theological convictions are affected by changes in scientific knowledge (the one possible point of contact between the foundations of science and the foundations of ethics in his paper). The new effect of his analysis seems to be that there *may be* a connection between theology and ethics (though no justificatory claims are made), but that there probably is no connection between science and theology save for the way changing scientific accounts can modify religious convictions.

One task set for authors in this series is that of starting to *reconnect* the sciences with the foundations of ethics. Though mentioned by several symposiasts, I am puzzled as to how the "frayed links," in Toulmin's words, are to be mended. Toulmin himself suggests a "philosophical reexamination of 'Humanity's Place in Nature'." Apart from the proclamation that "function" and "adaptation" should play a prominent role in this reexamination, I have only an embryonic picture of the general outlines of this program. The same must be said about MacIntyre's grand scheme. In his case, my understanding is even muddier as to how we are to "transcend the immediate crisis" to a "vision of the whole" so that philosophy is no longer a "mirror-image of its age." Forgetting my considerable sympathy for the contrary view of philosophy as a tool for analyzing "the concept of x" and "our commonsense beliefs," I do not understand what MacIntyre proposes to substitute. Nor do I see how any such replacement or reconnection could have anything to do with the "traditions" that MacIntyre seems so much to appreciate. And, finally, I suspect that if such a replacement were found, MacIntyre would not be happy with it.

Relatedly, I do not understand how a program of "my station and its duties," as mentioned by Toulmin and MacIntyre, can be worked out from an examination of role-structures in the sciences. The idea is to halt moral dilemmas arising from conflicts of obligation by using structured professional roles as models of what ought to be done and of who is to be held responsible. Medical ethics, business ethics, journalistic ethics, and so on would then stand as instructive models for philosophical ethics. The virtues of role conduct could also serve to instruct philosophical accounts of virtue ethics. Indeed, in the MacIntyre-Toulmin program, virtue ethics presumably could come to replace or underlie an ethics rooted in a theory of obligations and thus could prevent the moral dilemmas spawned by obligation ethics. This ideal seems to me to hold out a false hope. There will inevitably be conflicts among role-obligations and conflicts among virtuous acts as well. Thus we will have made no advance on the problem of dilemmas-through-conflict by the adoption of the MacIntyre-Toulmin vision.

V

I now want to turn to the more constructive task of exploring points of connection between ethics and the social sciences—a set of disciplines almost everywhere ignored in the papers in this volume. In particular, positive connections might be established through an alliance of normative ethics and research in such fields as social psychology, political science, economics, and political economy. I have some doubt that work in these fields will substantially alter the *foundations* of ethics in the sense of altering fundamental moral principles. But they might be called upon to help resolve moral issues that have proved intractable or at least resistant to solution by moral argument alone.

Consider two examples. Moral disputes often turn on the predicted consequences of actions, where the structure of the debate is the following: One contending party argues that a positive outcome is the likely result of an action or rule, while another party argues that a negative outcome is likely. Whether or not one embraces a consequentialist ethic, many moral problems can turn on the accuracy of such predictions. One social scientific method that promises to help resolve such problems of predictability is cost/benefit analysis. It offers the hope of an objective arrayal of possible outcomes of actions set within a framework that allows the comparison and weighing of positive and negative outcomes. If thoroughly carried out, cost/benefit studies can prove to be the single most important factor in a decision procedure. Such current ethical disputes as those about the levels of toxic substances to be permitted in the environment, about the allocation of scarce resources, and about the social control of technology may in the end find keys to their solution through the use of thoroughly arrayed cost/benefit studies. This conclusion is rather obviously suited to the program of utilitarian ethics, but the argument could be appreciated and found acceptable within any deontological framework that permits appeals to consequential reasoning.

As a second example, we might consider a number of well-known problems about informed consent to biomedical and behavioral therapy and to research involving human subjects. Prevailing standards of informed consent have recently come under the critical scrutiny of ethical and jurisprudential thinkers, and—judging by the recent actions of courts—these standards are currently under revision and virtually certain to be amplified in upcoming years. The major problem (or set of problems) has been to provide adequate standards for the disclosure of information. A number of general and specific standards have been proposed, some requiring only brief disclosures. In all cases, those who have proposed these standards have done so without benefit of empirical information regarding the information-processing capacities of patients and subjects under the conditions in which their consent is normally proffered. Those proposing standards for consent to surgery, for example, have failed to distinguish between the radically different conditions under which patients may be asked to give their consent; and the actual abilities of patients to process, retain, and utilize such information in reaching their decisions has not been studied in their arguments. Yet, the standards they propose largely (though not exclusively) find their roots in critical assumptions about the information-processing capacities of patients and subjects. If the actual capacities were known—and techniques of modern psychology can provide reasonably accurate data on such matters—important issues about the adequacy of proposed standards might vanish. I would, in fact, argue the stronger thesis that data drawn from the social sciences is more likely in upcoming years to influence moral problems of consent than is moral philosophy.

VI

I conclude with an argument against the view that there could be a *common* basis or set of ultimate premises on which the foundations of normative ethics and the foundations of science rest. The foundations of normative ethics—whatever the precise character of these foundations—will be prescriptive (or at least nondescriptive), for ethics is an action-guiding discipline that provides reasons for human actions and that attempts justifications of moral claims (which are ultimate justifications at the level of the foundations of morals). Science, by contrast, is not action-guiding in its methodological principles (except, of course, in its use of inductive principles), and deals with the causes of events and human behaviors and with causal explanations of phenomena (which one hopes are ultimate explanations at the level of foundations). The statements in these two domains thus display an unbridgeable logical difference; one is based ultimately on nondescriptive sentences and the other on descriptive sentences. It is, therefore, logically impossible that the foundations of ethics find their ultimate roots (premises) in the foundations of science, or vice-versa.

Those familiar with modern ethical theory will recognize that this argument is merely a corollary of one use of the fact/value distinction. Some uses of this distinction have come under attack in recent years, but I see no reason to think that, in the context of recent moral theory and the discussions in this volume, arguments of the sort I have used favoring a sharp fact/value contrast have been brought into question. Indeed, when we are addressing questions of the *foundational premises* of ethics and science, the distinction as I have drawn it finds its most plausible application. Accordingly, I doubt that there exists any nontrivial connection between science and normative ethics at the level of foundational premises.

Should We Return to Foundations?

Ronald M. Green

IN AN INTRODUCTORY ESSAY to an earlier volume in this series, H. Tristram Engelhardt, Jr. offered a sage bit of advice. Those engaging in an intellectual quest as bold as this, remarked Engelhardt, should learn when to ask questions and what questions to ask.[1] No brief commentary on this series or even on this single volume can hope to detail the rich variety of substantive issues that have been explored. But a commentator can consider whether Engelhardt's advice has been taken. Have the right questions been asked? And have they been asked in the appropriate context?

As important as it is, answering this question about questions is difficult, because the broad title of this inquiry, "The Foundations of Ethics and Its Relationship to Science," involves a really quite diverse set of issues or problems. For example, the phrase *foundations of ethics* by itself admits of several different interpretations. It can mean: Where do our moral judgments and principles come from? What is their basis or explanation? We can term this the *explanatory* sense of the question about the foundations of ethics, and it can be further subdivided into requests for either a scientific or historical account of the origins of ethics. Thus, in searching for the foundations of ethics in this sense, we can be asking for a scientific explanation of how human beings have developed the capacity to make moral judgments, or we can

269

be asking about the specific historical and cultural factors that underlie our present moral standards.

Quite different from this explanatory sense of the question is its *justificatory* significance. One who asks about the foundations of ethics in this way does not want to know why we happen to hold our values, but whether we ought to. What are the principles or values that should guide our conduct and why should they do so? Do these principles have a rational basis, a justification? This, of course, is the sense of this question explored by Kant in his own study of the foundations of ethics and it is the sense that has most interested philosophers since him. In fact, it is an axiom of modern moral philosophy that this question of rational justification is at least logically independent of the question of explanation and that the two questions are confused only at the risk of committing a fallacy.

To make matters more complex, it appears that this question of justification itself has two different senses. It can mean: Why should there be morality? What is the general justification of the practice of morality? Or, it can mean: Why should *I* be moral? Why should I do *my* part in supporting what is a generally rational practice? These two types of questions—what might be called the questions of the *general* and the *personal* justification of morality—have often been thought to be identical, and it is one of the more heated disputes in current moral philosophy as to whether these questions really should ultimately be separated.[2] But at the same time, there is substantial agreement that at least in a superficial way these two questions ought to be kept distinct, since it is not clear that any general justification of the practice of morality indicates why each of us should always be moral.

We can see, therefore, that the phrase "Foundations of Ethics" allows a variety of interpretations. Fortunately, the other term within the broad title of this series, "science," appears less ambiguous, but the question of the relationship of the foundations of ethics to science is itself open to several interpretations. It can mean: How do the methods or information of the sciences assist us in the 1) explanation or 2) justification of moral principles or morality (in both the general and personal senses of justification)? or it can mean: How do the methods or principles of ethics bear on the conduct or inquiries of science?

Naturally, all of these different questions are interrelated. A valid scientific or historical explanation of our moral judgments has some bearing on the various questions of justification. Scientific information is vital with respect to the formulation of specific moral rules. And clarity with respect to the justification of our values underlies any exploration of the impact of ethics on science. But it is also true that keeping our questions precise and asking the appropriate question at the appropriate time are essential for clarity in any intellectual venture. We are returned, then, to Engelhardt's advice and its evaluative implications. Specifically, as we look at the contributions to this and earlier volumes in the series, we must ask: Which of these questions have been addressed? Have the most important received their fair share of attention? And have the differences between these questions been properly respected? To summarize my remarks in advance, I shall argue that, despite a great amount of useful insight generated by this discussion, there has been a repeated tendency to confuse important questions, and a major reason for this is because the key question for this whole inquiry has not always received the attention it deserved.

The key question I refer to is that of the general justification of morality—the identification and rational defense of the most basic principle or principles of morality. This question is central, I contend, because virtually all the other questions I have mentioned must be less precisely stated until this one is addressed, and, because until this one is dealt with, some of these other questions probably cannot be answered at all. For example, how can one answer the question "Why should I be moral?" until one has a clear idea of what being moral involves? And how can one *explain* our morality in either scientific or historical terms until one has an adequate account of what one is explaining.

In quite different ways, the essays in this volume by Richard Alexander and Alasdair MacIntyre help illustrate this point and show the limits of an approach which bypasses the central question of ethics. Alexander's aim is to provide an account of all past normative standards by relating these to our inclusive-fitness-maximizing behavior, specifically to our (nonconscious) efforts to promote our reproductive advantage or that of our close relatives.[3] In a criticism of Alexander, Paul Ramsey notes the oddity of such an evolutionary view. We can readily understand how rational self-consciousness might have evolved if it served the primary function of gene proliferation, says Ramsey. "But how or why rational consciousness evolved to *suppress* that primary function into the secondary functions of human cultural enterprises remains a great mystery, even or especially in evolutionary terms."[4] Where morality is concerned, this question becomes even sharper. How can a process designed to ensure reproductive success for the individual or family lead to a practice, morality, which can require an individual to sacrifice his reproductive opportunity or even his life in the name of the total community? I have no doubt that Alexander can probably forge an answer to this question. It seems to be true that in its present form his inclusive explanation of behavior comprises every other form of explanation until, if Ramsey is correct, it ends in contradiction by swallowing itself. But my point here is not to renew the criticism of Alexander's method. It is rather to suggest that because he begins his explanation without an explicit or clear conception of morality, it becomes far easier for him to pass over the real difficulties morality may pose for the present stage of evolutionary theory. Despite Alexander (or sociobiologists like Edward Wilson), nepotism and nepotistic altruism are *not* morality, and though they may eventually be related to morality, any useful effort to explain the biological basis of morality must at least begin with an understanding of what morality involves.

MacIntyre's historical account of the present state of moral philosophy betrays a similar inattention to this central question of ethics. It is McIntyre's view that contemporary moral debates are "unsettlable and interminable" and that our moral intuitions, principles, and even our basic moral theories are essentially in conflict. He attributes this condition to the fact that ethics today is a "ghost discipline" trying to make sense of conflicting fragments of discarded philosophical systems of the past. Hence our confusion has an historical explanation: like the Hawaiians of a century ago we are in the position of cherishing taboos whose original logic or purpose we have forgotten long ago.[5]

MacIntyre's discussion is filled with difficulties, some of which have been indicated by Gerald Dworkin in his excellent commentary.[6] For example, MacIntyre appears to assume that dispute between moral philosophers necessarily indicates ultimate and unresolvable disagreement at the foundations of the discipline of moral philosophy (though I assume he would not hold sharp disagreement between, say, Soviet and American geneticists as indicative of the absence of foundations for the discipline). He also does not consider the way in which some moral philosophers have precisely tried to offer a methodology capable of resolving moral dispute and bringing some order to our most basic moral intuitions. Rawls's use of a rational decision procedure to ground moral principles and his ingenious effort to harmonize some of our traditionally conflicting precepts of economic justice (for example, precepts of need and productivity) go unmentioned in MacIntyre's account. Finally, as Dworkin observes, MacIntyre appears to confuse the question of general justification (Why should there be morality?) with the question of personal justification (Why should I be moral?), and extends the very real difficulty of answering the second question to the less difficult task of answering the first.

My aim here is not to multiply criticisms of MacIntyre's provocative essay, but rather to use these criticisms to support the point I made earlier that an understanding of morality and its basic concepts must be preliminary to any exploration of it. In fact, MacIntyre's discussion offers a curious illustration of this truth: behind MacIntyre's historical account and motivating it, I think, is his prior and philosophically informed conviction that moral philosophy today really has no adequate conceptual foundations. Now, MacIntyre may be right in this claim, but his contention, to be shown correct, would require conceptual justification in its own right.

If Alexander's or MacIntyre's essays were unique, the difficulty I am signaling here would be less important. But, in fact, when we regard other contributions to this and earlier volumes in this series, this inattention to the question of moral justification becomes representative. Of course, there are exceptions. Michael Scriven's insightful opening essay, "The Science of Ethics,"[7] and Dworkin's commentary on MacIntyre in this volume directly address the question of foundations, and their treatment of these is attentive to major issues in ethical theory. But set against these are a number of essays that either proceed as though oblivious to the need for a rational justification of values and to recent work in ethical theory or which openly challenge some of the key methods and assumptions of this theory. The proposal for an evolutionary ethic advanced by Bernard Towers and Alexander's work in some of its moods exemplify the former tendency, and the essays by David Burrell and Stanley Hauerwas, Thomas Nagel and MacIntyre are examples of the latter.[8]

If what I am saying is correct, this raises a curious question: How in an examination of the foundations of ethics can we explain this relative inattention to the key question involved in the foundations of ethics? In fact, a variety of explanations suggest themselves. Perhaps the most obvious explanation is that critics like MacIntyre are right: that ethics has no sound conceptual basis; that Thomas Nagel's perception of "radical disagreement" about this basis is accurate; and that the past "disarray" of the discipline, rightly indicated by Engelhardt and Callahan at the beginning of this series, continues even today.[9] I will be pardoned if I reply rather bluntly that I believe this estimate to be incorrect. In fact, recent work by a number of moral philosophers has identified a substantial area of agreement on the fundamental procedures of moral justification. For example, whatever their specific disagreements (and I do not deny there are many), writers like Baier, Rawls, Richards, Gert, Warnock, Singer, Brandt, and Gewirth are agreed that moral principles are properly derived by a method that involves rational choice under conditions of impartiality.[10] On this shared account, moral principles are generated by a single procedure according to which a rational individual is asked to pursue his advantage while deprived of knowledge that is likely to particularize his judgment. By virtue of this procedure, moral principles evidence their characteristics of universality, publicity, and their supremacy over merely private volitions. As for the procedure itself, it is variously justified in terms of some very basic moral axioms—Rawls and Scriven perhaps exemplify this tendency—or more properly and more basically, I think, its rationale is traced to the very conditions of rational justification itself.

In addition to this broad consensus on the conceptual foundations of ethics, there is also some agreement that this understanding is not just newly discovered, but was already suggested, although with some confusions, in the writings of Kant.[11] Indeed, along with this agreement there is the perception that Kant's insistent connection of morality and rationality is substantially correct, though in need of clarification. I mention this to indicate that current moral philosophy has not only managed to illuminate its foundations and narrow the range of responsible disagreement concerning them, but like any valid science, it is built upon a tradition of disciplined reflection.

If this account of the state of contemporary moral philosophy is correct, it suggests that the reason for our inattention here to philosophical work on the foundations of ethics is not because such work has been unfruitful, but because its conclusions have not been properly reported or assimilated to this interdisciplinary discussion. It may be that the ethicists and philosophers among us share some of the responsibility for this, but I suspect that, more fundamentally, we may be perceiving here a very special difficulty of interdisciplinarity where ethics and science are concerned. As the essay by Stephen Toulmin and the commentary by Loren Graham make clear, ethics and science have long been on an unequal footing. Ethics has been considered as the domain of "sentiment" and subjective preference whereas science has had the authority of "demonstrable fact," clarity and productivity.[12] Nor has genuine interdisciplinarity (which as Eric Cassell reminds us, requires a respect for one another's disciplinary competence)[13] been fostered by the pervasive assumption that where ethics is concerned one person's view is as good as another's. In this relative inattention to disciplined work on the foundations of ethics, therefore, and in the excessive attention paid to less representative critical voices within philosophy and ethics, we may be seeing a subtle manifestation of this continued prejudice against ethics as a discipline in its own right.

Another explanation for our relative inattention to the basic question of moral justification has the effect of qualifying a perhaps too strong claim I made earlier. In point of fact, not every question concerning the relationship between the foundations of ethics and science requires a fully developed concept of morality or its justification. Perhaps because ethics and rationality are so intimately connected, all of us, as rational persons, possess an ability to make fairly accurate moral judgments (which is not to say we all find it necessary to be moral). This means that for many purposes we possess sound intuitive notions of the basic concepts or principles of ethics.

Certainly, many of the most important contributions to this ongoing interdisciplinary discussion have successfully utilized general intuitive conceptions of this sort. Writers like John Ladd or Marc Lappé, for example, are able to affirm the ultimate accountability of science to morality without specifying precisely what is meant by morality, and our very sense of the supremacy of moral reasons supports their contentions (though along with a critic like Edmund Pellegrino we also know that there are good *moral* reasons for according science a strong measure of autonomy).[14] Nor, for that matter, do we have to engage in a systematic scrutiny of the relationship between our theoretical and practical reason, as Kant did, to appreciate Wartofsky's, Toulmin's or Engelhardt's point that there is a practical and moral impulse at the basis of our scientific and medical endeavors.[15] And we do not need the moral philosopher to tell us that information delivered by the sciences concerning nature and our place within it is vitally important to the formulation of specific moral rules or responses to new situations of moral decision. We know intuitively that the decision procedure for ethics is essentially formal and requires for its application a sensitive appreciation of general laws and concrete factual information.

The fact that all these interrelations between science and ethics have been recognized and productively explored over the past four years, therefore, qualifies my claim that an understanding of the conceptual foundations of ethics—the justification of morality—is really central to an interdisciplinary discussion of this sort. Nevertheless, having made this claim I am unwilling to relinquish it, and in my brief final remarks I want to indicate some areas where more attention to the foundations of ethics would have served our conversation. Having already indicated some instances where I believe a lack of attention has led us astray, I want now, in a more positive way, to indicate some instances where greater clarity about the foundations of ethics might have actually assisted the development of some provocative insights or methods emerging in the course of this interdisciplinary inquiry.

Returning, first, to Richard Alexander's essays I want to make clear that moral philosophy has nothing to fear and much to learn from evolutionary biology. Biological studies of altruistic behavior may even be a useful introduction to our understanding of the emergence of morality. But to go beyond this beginning, biologists must themselves understand that morality amounts to even more than simple altruism: it is a sophisticated cognitive skill that involves a capacity for rational choice and imaginative self-transcendence (impartiality). As such, it is closely connected with—indeed it may be nothing more than the practical expression of—our general rational ability itself. If this is so, proper attention to morality may require Alexander and others to pay even more attention to the role of group selection in the evolutionary process or to the kinds of multifactorial explanations that Kenneth Schaffner has called for.[16]

I might add here that relative clarity about the conceptual foundations of ethics might also be productive for a variety of other scientific disciplines concerned with the study of human nature. The work of Lawrence Kohlberg—despite his own lamentable excursions into a form of hard-core scientism—shows that a dialogue with moral philosophy can be fruitful for the discipline of psychology. And a field like anthropology would seem equally to stand to gain by the moral philosopher's exploration of our human rational justificatory procedure.[17] The relative productivity of recent moral philosophy, in other words, adds depth to the repeated observation in the course of these discussions that human evaluations may be very relevant even from a strictly scientific point of view.

On another level, greater clarity with respect to the conceptual foundations of ethics may further illuminate a contention running through various essays here but never sufficiently brought to prominence: the contention that science and ethics both form part of a similar rational endeavor, so that our intellect really is unified in its basic methods of cognizing and responding to the world.[18] In this respect, Toulmin's comment that the model of scientific objectivity might have been useful to ethics earlier in this century has a touch of irony about it.[19] In fact, the fundamental objectivity found at the heart of the moral reasoning process suggests the possibility that in longer historical perspective, science itself may be methodologically indebted to ethics, so that both domains of inquiry are really branches of our shared rational capacity. If so, we have here a matter for continuing philosophical, historical, and scientific inquiry.

This matter of the shared cognitive terrain of ethics and science leads me to a final area where greater clarity about the foundations of ethics—and the questions appropriate to those foundations—might have helped advance our interdisciplinary discussion. I refer specifically to Gunther Stent's intriguing observation that both science and ethics seem to culminate in a series of fundamental paradoxes. When pursued to "the bottom of the night," says Stent, the postulates of reason in both domains appear to reveal fundamental "internal inconsistencies."[20] If Stent's documentation for this claim on the side of science, including his reference to basic work in nuclear physics, is impressive, his argumentation with respect to morality is less so. Indeed, Ramsey's criticism indicates that Stent may have overdrawn the specific moral problems he identified.[21]

Despite this, I would suggest that Stent is actually on firmer ground than he realizes, for within recent ethical theory our developing understanding of the procedure of moral justification has exposed a very serious problem or paradox at the core of our whole justificatory process. Specifically, the recognition that all moral justification relies on the use of impartial reason has raised the perplexing question of how one justifies the adoption of moral impartiality to individual rational agents. Involved here is the question "Why should I be moral?" and in connection with this there is a developing recognition that in this special instance our usual procedure of justification by impartial reason breaks down. This is because all appeals to act impartially must, in circular fashion, rely upon the very concept of impartiality which is at issue.[22] Thus, impartial reason seems to be inherently incapable of rational justification, and even as ethics has become clearer about the foundations of morality, it has become less capable of grounding individual moral obligation.

In a recent treatment of this issue, I have argued that careful attention to this problem of ethics may lead contemporary moral philosophy—as it led Kant—to found its concepts on the kinds of suprarational beliefs furnished by religion.[23] I note that several contributors to this series—MacIntyre, Ramsey, and Bemporad in an earlier volume and Gustafson in this one—have found it imperative to dwell, at least in a very general way, on the relation of religion to moral justification.[24] Keeping in mind the fact that religion speaks to only one special problem in the foundations of ethics, the problem of personal justification, these discussions become central to our larger topic.

Whether or not rational moral activity necessarily leads to suprarational "faith" commitments of some sort, it is important to observe that this discussion within moral philosophy supports Stent's contention. No less than in science, pursuit of the ultimate postulates of our thought "to the bottom of the night" eventuates in inconsistency and paradox that may take us out of the familiar domain of reason altogether. In fact, if I am correct, this result is predictable since science and ethics are two expressions of the same rational capacity.

I realize that this final point can be mentioned here only in an elliptical way. I raise it, however, to indicate how fruitful direct attention to the conceptual foundations of ethics—and to each of the separate questions that bear on these foundations—might be for an ongoing dialogue between science and ethics. The fact that even without this direct attention our discussions here have produced so much fresh thinking about the relation of science to ethics makes continuing consideration of this topic, with ethical theory fully an equal partner, even more important for the future.

NOTES

1. "Knowledge, Value and Belief," in *Knowledge, Value and Belief*, ed. H. Tristram Engelhardt, Jr. and Daniel Callahan (Hastings-on-Hudson, N.Y.: Hastings Center, 1977), p. 23.

2. Discussions of the question: Why should I be moral? abound within the contemporary literature of rational ethical theory, with substantial disagreement over whether the question is separable from the general justification of morality. Some of the more important contributions to the debate include Kurt Baier, *The Moral Point of View* (Ithaca, N.Y.: Cornell University Press, 1958), chap. 12; Bernard Gert, *The Moral Rules* (New York: Harper & Row, 1971), chap. 10; G. J. Warnock, *The Object of Morality* (London: Methuen & Co., 1971),

chap. 9; Marcus Singer, *Generalization in Ethics* (New York: Alfred A. Knopf, 1961), pp. 319–27; Paul Taylor, *Principles of Ethics* (Belmont, California: Dickenson Publishing Co., 1975), chap. 9; Kai Nielsen, "Why Should I Be Moral?" *Methodos*, 25(1963): 275–306; and Marvin Glass, "Why Should I Be Moral?" *Canadian Journal of Philosophy* vol. 2, December 1973, pp. 191–95.

3. Richard D. Alexander, "Evolution, Social Behavior, and Ethics," this volume pp. 127, 131f. See also his essay "Natural Selection and Societal Laws," in *Morals, Science and Sociality*, ed. H. Tristram Engelhardt, Jr. and Daniel Callahan (Hastings-on-Hudson, N.Y.: Hasting Center), pp. 249–90.

4. Paul Ramsey, "Stent's Moral Paradoxes: To Be Resolved or Deepened?", this volume, p. 111.

5. Alasdair MacIntyre, "Why Is the Search for the Foundations of Ethics so Frustrating?", this volume, pp. 20, 21, 25ff.

6. Gerald Dworkin, "Ethics, Foundations and Science," this volume, pp. 38. In addition to its perceptive criticisms of MacIntyre's essay, Dworkin's discussion has the virtue of attempting to determine what we might mean by "the foundations of ethics." See especially pp. 39–43.

7. In *Science, Ethics and Medicine*, ed. H. Tristram Engelhardt, Jr. and Daniel Callahan (Hastings-on-Hudson, N.Y.: Hastings Center, 1976), pp. 15–43.

8. Bernard Towers, "Toward an Evolutionary Ethic"; David Burrell and Stanley Hauerwas, "From System to Story: An Alternative Pattern for Rationality in Ethics"; and Thomas Nagel, "Commentary: The Fragmentation of Value," in *Knowledge, Value and Belief*, pp. 111–52, 207–24, 279–94.

9. Nagel, p. 293; Engelhardt and Callahan, "Preface," in *Science, Ethics and Medicine*, p. ix.

10. Kurt Baier, *The Moral Point of View*; John Rawls, *A Theory of Justice* (Cambridge, Mass.: Harvard University Press, 1971); Bernard Gert, *The Moral Rules*, David Richards, *A Theory of Reasons for Actions* (Oxford: Clarendon Press, 1971); G. J. Warnock, *The Object of Morality*; Marcus Singer, *Generalization in Ethics*; Richard Brandt, "The Concept of Rationality in Ethical and Political Theory," in *Human Nature in Politics: Nomos XVII*, ed. J. Roland Pennock and John W. Chapman (New York: New York University Press, 1977), pp. 265–79; Alan Gewirth, *Reason and Morality* (Chicago: University of Chicago Press, 1978).

11. Rawls, *A Theory of Justice*, Section 40; Paul Taylor, *Principles of Ethics*, chap. 5; Singer, *Generalization in Ethics*, chaps. 8 and 9;

Thomas E. Hill, "The Kingdom of Ends," *Proceedings of the Third International Kant-Congress*, L. W. Beck, ed. (Dordrecht: D. Reidel, 1972), pp. 310ff.

12. Stephen Toulmin, "How Can We Reconnect the Sciences with the Foundations of Ethics?" and the Commentary by Loren Graham, this volume, p. 56.

13. Eric Cassell, "How Does Interdisciplinary Work Get Done?" in *Knowledge, Value and Belief*, p. 358.

14. John Ladd, "Are Science and Ethics Compatible?"; Marc Lappé, "The Non-neutrality of Hypothesis Formulation"; and commentaries by E. D. Pellegrino in *Science, Ethics and Medicine*, pp. 49–119.

15. Marx W. Wartofsky, "The Mind's Eye and the Hand's Brain: Toward an Historical Epistemology of Medicine"; Toulmin, "The Moral Psychology of Science," in *Morals, Science and Sociality*, pp. 48–67; and Engelhardt, "Doctoring the Disease, Treating the Complaint, Helping the Patient: Some of the Works of Hygeia and Panacea," this volume, p. 225.

16. Kenneth I. Schaffner, "Sociobiology and Evolving Legal Systems: Comments on Richard A. Alexander's 'Natural Selection and Societal Laws' " in *Morals, Science and Sociality*, p. 7.

17. For an early but suggestive effort to apply a Kantian ethic to anthropological study see A. Macbeath, *Experiments in Living* (London: Macmillan and Co., 1952).

18. The similarity between the methods of science and rational ethical theory, for example, is noted by Burrell and Hauerwas, though they reject such a scientific model of ethics themselves. See "From System to Story . . . ," pp. 112f.

19. Toulmin, "How can we Reconnect the Sciences . . . ," pp. 46f.

20. Stent, "Science and Morality as Complementary Aspects of Reason," pp. 78–80.

21. Ramsey, "Stent's Moral Paradoxes."

22. This problem was perhaps first recognized by Kai Nielsen in his article "Why Should I be Moral?"

23. See my *Religious Reason: The Rational and Moral Basis of Religious Belief* (New York: Oxford University Press, 1978).

24. MacIntyre, "Can Medicine Dispense with a Theological Perspective on Human Nature?" Ramsey, "Commentary: Kant's Moral Theology or a Religious Ethics?" in *Knowledge, Value and Belief*, pp. 25–74; James Gustafson, "Theology and Ethics: An Interpretation of the Agenda," and the Commentary by Hans Jonas, this volume, pp. 181–217. Ramsey's discussion of the paradox of justice and compassion in his commentary on Stent in this volume, pp. 112f., represents another

facet of this basic problem of justification: the self which cannot always justify being impartial invariably finds itself also unable to acquit itself of the ensuing condemnatory judgment issued by impartial reason. For a discussion of this, see my *Religious Reason*, chap. 4.

Index